AF605859

Variable Properties in Language

Selected Titles in the Georgetown University Round Table on Languages and Linguistics Series

Useful Assessment and Evaluation in Language Education
JOHN MCE. DAVIS, JOHN M. NORRIS, MARGARET E. MALONE, TODD H. MCKAY, AND YOUNG-A SON, EDITORS

Diversity and Super-Diversity: Sociocultural Linguistic Perspectives
ANNA DE FINA, DIDEM IKIZOGLU, AND JEREMY WEGNER, EDITORS

The Usage-based Study of Language Learning and Multilingualism
LOURDES ORTEGA, ANDREA E. TYLER, HAE IN PARK, AND MARIKO UNO, EDITORS

Languages in Africa: Multilingualism, Language Policy, and Education
ELIZABETH C. ZSIGA, ONE TLALE BOYER, AND RUTH KRAMER, EDITORS

Measured Language: Quantitative Studies of Acquisition, Assessment, and Variation
JEFFREY CONNOR-LINTON AND LUKE WANDER AMOROSO, EDITORS

Variable Properties in Language

Their Nature and Acquisition

David W. Lightfoot and Jonathan Havenhill, Editors

Georgetown University Press
Washington, DC

Library of Congress Cataloging-in-Publication Data

Names: Georgetown University Round Table on Languages and Linguistics (2017 : Washington, D.C.), author. | Lightfoot, David, 1945- editor. | Havenhill, Jonathan, editor.
Title: Variable properties in language : their nature and acquisition / David W. Lightfoot and Jonathan Havenhill, editors.
Description: Washington, DC : Georgetown University Press, 2019. | Series: Georgetown University Round Table on Languages and Linguistics series | Includes bibliographical references and index.
Identifiers: LCCN 2018030728 (print) | LCCN 2018033845 (ebook) | ISBN 9781626166646 (pbk. : alk. paper) | ISBN 9781626166639 (hardcover : alk. paper) | ISBN 9781626166653 (ebook)
Subjects: LCSH: Language and languages--Variation--Congresses.
Classification: LCC P120.V37 (ebook) | LCC P120.V37 G46 2017 (print) | DDC 417/.7--dc23
LC record available at https://lccn.loc.gov/2018030728

♾ This book is printed on acid-free paper meeting the requirements of the American National Standard for Permanence in Paper for Printed Library Materials.

20 19 9 8 7 6 5 4 3 2 First printing

Printed in the United States of America

Cover design by Debra Naylor. Cover image by Shutterstock.com.

Contents

Illustrations

Figures

Tables

Preface

THE GEORGETOWN UNIVERSITY ROUND Table on Languages and Linguistics was created in 1949 by James E. Alatis (1926–2015) and has taken place every year since then, without interruption. Each GURT is devoted to a different theme every year and is organized by different individuals and by different teams of faculty and students, so it is very much the product of a diverse department of linguistics and a major focus for that department.

GURT 2017 was devoted to the theme of *Variable Properties: Their Nature and Acquisition.* It recognized the fact that the field had been successful in identifying general, invariant principles underlying all languages but that we have been much less successful in understanding *variable* properties. Linguists have studied variable properties in silos, sociolinguists producing quite different accounts from generative syntacticians, historical linguists quite different frameworks from discourse analysts. The goal of GURT 2017 was to bring people together from across our field and across many countries, focusing on variable properties and seeking a general biological understanding of variation in language.

This volume contains papers selected from those presented at the meeting, deals with a wide range of different types of variation and seeks to avoid an over-theorization that has bedeviled earlier analyses of variable properties, particularly parametric analyses. We hope that readers will enjoy a novel approach to variation and help to bring improvements to our understanding in future work.

Chapter 1

Re-thinking Variable Properties in Language: An Introduction

DAVID W. LIGHTFOOT AND JONATHAN HAVENHILL
Georgetown University

Invariant Principles, Their Successes

The Biolinguistic Program reflects the work of many people from many countries analyzing many very different grammars, discovering a huge range of interesting, abstract properties. A "grammar" is what we used to call the formal, generative system that characterizes a person's mature language faculty, which is represented in an individual's mind/brain; this is now often referred to as an internal, individual or "I-language." Grammars, I-languages, are subject to general, restrictive principles that appear to be common to the species and have been discovered over several decades.

Rich, invariant principles have emerged, often in response to arguments from the poverty of the stimulus; such principles, defined universally, bridge the gap between information conveyed by a child's typically very limited experience and the rich information that characterizes mature grammars. Other methods have been used, but invariant principles, it was postulated, are available to children through their biology, attributes of their genetic material. The principles explain how simple experiences can trigger rich structures in the biological grammars of some form of Japanese or of Javanese. Understanding the successful invariant principles and the thinking behind them illuminates how we might gain new approaches to variable properties, where linguists have been conspicuously less successful.

Over the past two decades, under the Minimalist Program, linguists have sought to simplify the principles, "minimizing" the information they embody. Part of the motivation is the legacy of William of Occam's simplicity in theorizing, always seeking simpler and more beautiful analyses, and part is to provide a plausible biological account whereby we might attribute the evolution of the language faculty in the species to a single mutation. Invariant computational operations of Project and (internal and external) Merge build hierarchical structures from the bottom up, which combine heads and complements, phrasal categories and adjuncts; this applies for all languages. A repeatable operation assembles two syntactic elements *a* and *b* into a unit, which may, in turn, be merged with another element to form another phrase, and so on. That universal, invariant property raises the prospect that the option of Merge was the mutation that made language and thought possible for *Homo sapiens*. Berwick and Chomsky (2016) showed why such a view might be productive and elicited a judicious and informed review from paleoanthropologist Ian Tattersall (2016).

Thinking in terms of hierarchical structures resulting from Minimalist computational operations has also informed remarkable neuroscientific work linking brain activity to the structural units underlying language and thought in novel ways. Ding et al. (2016) showed that when people listen to connected speech, cortical activity of different timescales tracks the time course of abstract structures at different hierarchical levels, such as words, phrases, and sentences. Results indicate that "a hierarchy of neural processing timescales underlies grammar-based internal construction of hierarchical linguistic structure"; David Poeppel and colleagues have found neural activity that reflects directly the abstract structures that linguists have postulated for the infrastructure of language, needed to account for the way that expressions are understood and used. See also Nelson et al. (2017). We always knew that the brain would have to have a mechanism for encoding the abstract structures of different levels, and now we know what the mechanism is, a huge achievement.

Minimalist ideas about hierarchical structures being formed by multiple applications of Merge not only help us think differently about the evolution of the language faculty and of thought in the species and stimulate new neuroscientific work, but they have also facilitated new approaches to the acquisition of language by children. The hierarchical structures formed by multiple applications of Merge constitute the means by which people, including very young children, begin to analyze and "parse" what they hear—the key component of the acquisition process. We may now be at the point where we can dispense with independent parsing principles or procedures, and, given the way in which hierarchical structures are built, we might argue that assigning structures to expressions is simply a matter of using the binary branching structures that Universal Grammar (UG) makes available and the structures that children discover/invent as they parse the ambient external language they hear (E-language); under this view, parsing is not a function of nonlinguistic conditions on structures permitted in "working memory" and so forth. There is an interplay between E-language, which is parsed, and I-languages, which result from parsing.

Work has shown repeatedly that children rely on the tools provided by their biology and learn much from very little experience. Research has examined language acquisition by children exposed only to unusually restricted data, much of the work focusing on the acquisition of signed systems. A striking fact is that 90 percent of deaf children are born to hearing parents, who are normally not experienced in using signed systems and often learn a primitive kind of pidgin to permit rudimentary communication. In such contexts, children surpass their models readily and dramatically and develop effectively normal mature capacities, despite the limitations of their parents' signing (Newport 1998; Hudson Kam and Newport 2005; Singleton and Newport 2004).

This is not surprising in light of studies of Creoles more generally (Aboh 2017), and of new languages beyond Creoles, which show that children exposed to very limited experiences go well beyond their models in quickly developing the first instances of rich, new I-languages (Lightfoot 2005, 2006). Not much is needed for a rich capacity to emerge, as demonstrated by many contributors to Piattelli-Palmarini and Berwick (2013) and now by Belletti (2017). Belletti offers a new kind of poverty-of-stimulus argument, showing that children sometimes overextend certain constructions, using them much more freely than their adult models, hence creatively.

Extraordinary events have cast new light on these matters: the birth of new languages in Nicaragua and in the Bedouin community in Israel. In Nicaragua the Somoza dictatorship treated the deaf as subhuman and barred them from congregating. Consequently, deaf children were raised mostly at home, had no exposure to fluent signers or to a language community, were isolated from each other, and had access only to home-signs and gestures. The Sandinistas took over the government in 1979 and provided a school where the deaf could mingle, soon to have four hundred deaf children enrolled. Initially the goal was to have them learn spoken Spanish through lip reading and finger spelling, but this was not successful. Instead, the schoolyard, streets, and school buses provided good vehicles for communication and the students combined gestures and home-signs to create first a pidgin-like system, then a kind of productive Creole, and eventually their own language, Nicaraguan Sign Language. The creation of a new language community took place over only a few decades. This may be the first time that linguists have witnessed the birth of a new language *ex nihilo* and they were able to analyze it and its development in detail. Kegl, Senghas, and Coppola (1998) provide a good general account and Senghas, Kita, and Özyürek (2004) examine one striking development, whereby certain signs proved to be not acquirable by children and were eliminated from the emerging language.

Sandler, Meir, Padden, and Aronoff (2005) discuss the birth of another sign language among the Bedouin community, which has arisen in ways similar to Nicaraguan Sign Language and was discovered at about the same time. These two discoveries have provided natural laboratories to study the capacity of children exposed to unusually limited linguistic experience to go far beyond their models and to attain more or less normal mature I-languages.

If successful language acquisition may be triggered by exposure only to very restricted data, then perhaps children learn only from simple expressions. They only need to hear simple expressions, because there is nothing new to be learned from complex ones. This is "degree-0 learnability," which hypothesizes that children need access only to unembedded material (Lightfoot 1989). Such a restriction would explain why many languages manifest computational operations in simple, unembedded clauses, which do not appear in embedded clauses (e.g., English subject-inversion sentences like *Has Kim visited Washington?* but not comparable embedded clauses **I wonder whether has Kim visited Washington*), but no language manifests the reverse, operations that appear only in embedded clauses and not in matrix clauses. One explanation for this striking asymmetry is that children do not learn from embedded domains. Therefore, much that children hear has no consequences for the developing I-language; nothing complex triggers any aspect of I-languages.

Parameters, Their Problems

Postulating hierarchical linguistic structures formed by a simple Merge operation has yielded new understanding of the invariant properties of language and has generated an immensely fruitful research program, bringing explanatory depth to a wide range of phenomena, indeed discovering a huge range of properties (den Dikken 2012). However, a hallmark of human language, alongside its invariant properties, is its VARIATION. The environmentally induced variation that one finds in language is biologically unusual, not what one sees in other species or in other areas of human cognition, and requires a biologically coherent treatment. Children attain significantly different internal languages, depending on whether they are raised in contexts using some form of Swedish or a kind of Vietnamese. English-speakers in seventeenth-century London typically acquired different grammars from those acquired three generations earlier. Furthermore, people speak differently depending on their class background, their geography, their interlocutors, their mood, their alcohol consumption, and other factors.

For a good biological understanding, variation in grammars, I-languages, needs to take its place among other types of variation. This is an area where we have made much less progress than with invariant properties, and it is now clear that there needs to be new thinking. Chomsky (1981) initiated the Principles-and-Parameters approach, seeking to find a Universal Grammar with both invariant principles and a set of formal parameters that children were thought to set on exposure to Primary Linguistic Data. For four decades, linguists have been postulating parameters, ideally binary parameters (either structure *a* or structure *b*), but no real, general theory has emerged and genuinely binary parameters are scarce. Minimalists set on reducing the complexities of the invariant principles that had emerged by the mid-1990s have not devoted equivalent efforts to minimizing the complexities of UG parameters nor to giving an account of how parameter settings might be acquired by young children.

Linguists study variation in silos: syntacticians studying parameters have little to do with sociolinguists studying variable rules, and proponents of variable rules do not interact much with Optimality theorists studying constraint reranking. Indeed, Minimalists have devoted little attention to variation and acquisition (the two go together: variable properties must be acquired by children during development, whereas invariant properties may be provided in advance by UG and not need to be acquired); UG parameters (macro- and micro-) grossly violate Minimalist aspirations to minimize information at UG. Indeed, Chomsky (2001) invoked a Uniformity hypothesis, abstracting away from variation: "In the absence of compelling evidence to the contrary, assume languages to be uniform, *with variety restricted to easily detected properties of utterances*" (our emphasis, DWL-JH). Hornstein's (2009) effort to transform the Minimalist Program to a Minimalist Theory has essentially no discussion of variation or acquisition, apart from a four-page discussion of the history of parameters (164–68). Boeckx (2015) went further and sought to eliminate lexically determined features on the remarkable grounds that "they are obstacles in any interdisciplinary investigation concerning the nature of language," as if linguists should deal only with analytical machinery invoked by biologists.

Difficulties with parameters are aggravated by the absence of an adequate account of which Primary Linguistic Data set which parameters. It is often supposed that children evaluate candidate grammars by checking their generative capacity against a global corpus of data experienced, converging on the grammar that best generates all the data stored in the memory bank. But that entails elaborate calculations by children and huge feasibility problems (Lightfoot 2006, section 4.1).

Even considering a small number of parameters, the problems become clear. If parameters are independent of each other, forty binary parameters entail over a trillion possible grammars, each generating an infinite number of structures. Parameters, of course, are not always independent of each other, and therefore the number of grammars to be evaluated might be somewhat smaller. On the other hand, Longobardi et al. (2013) postulate fifty-six binary parameters just for the analysis of noun phrases in Indo-European languages, which would suggest much larger numbers. On any account, the relevant numbers are astronomical.

There are other conceptual problems with viewing children as evaluating the generative capacity of numerous grammars, calculating how best to match the input experienced and setting binary parameters accordingly (see also Boeckx 2014; Lightfoot 2006; Newmeyer 2017). Certainly, given the abstractness of grammars, it will not do to suppose that triggers for elements of I-languages are sentences that those elements serve to generate. It may be opportune to consider other approaches.

We have proposed that rather than evaluating the generative capacity of grammars and setting formal parameters, children are born to parse, endowed with the tools provided by a restrictive and Minimalist Universal Grammar and no specific parsing principles (Lightfoot 2017). They parse what they hear and use the structures necessary to do so, thereby discovering or inventing them, in principle one by one. Those structures are part of the child's emerging I-language and, in aggregate, they constitute the mature I-language. Such an approach enables us to understand how children develop their internal system and how those systems may change from one generation to another, as revealed by work on historical change in syntactic systems. After all, *all* syntactic variation must originate in change (Lightfoot 2018).

An Alternative

In short, a common approach is to think of I-languages as consisting of invariant properties and a set of formal parameter settings; children evaluate numerous grammars against a corpus of data experienced and flick on/off switches on binary parameters, rating the generative capacity of I-languages in the fashion of Clark (1992). A better alternative might be to think of internal languages as consisting of invariant properties over a certain domain *plus* supplementary structures that are not invariant but required in order to parse what children hear, consistent with the invariant properties. Put differently, children parse the external language they hear, assigning to expressions structures provided by Merge, and discover/invent specific I-language elements required for certain aspects of the parse. To do so, they make use of what UG makes available, notably the bottom-up procedures of Project and Merge. The aggregation of those parsed elements constitutes the complete I-language. When external language shifts, children may parse differently and thus attain a new I-language, as revealed in work on syntactic change. Children discover variable properties of their I-languages through parsing with the available hierarchical structures; there is no evaluation of I-languages and no binary parameters provided by UG, and no special parsing principles.

There is no merit in postulating a formal parameter, part of UG, that a head may precede or follow its complement, {head, complement}, as opposed to saying that a child may parse expressions as [$_{V}$sing $_{DP}$[three songs]], [$_{N}$books $_{PP}$[about cities in California]]. The parameter solves no poverty-of-stimulus problem and does not reduce the information needed for a child to converge on the right structure. It is not helpful to say that languages like Dutch have a parameter set to yield verb-second structures like $_{DP}$[drie studenten] $_{CP}$[$_{C}$bezoeken $_{VP}$Utrecht] "three students visit Utrecht," as opposed to saying that children parse such structures and consequently have I-languages that generate such structures. It would be equally unhelpful to say that English I-languages have a parameter set to allow complex DPs like *the man from Utrecht's daughter with long hair* as opposed to saying that children parse such expressions with *'s* analyzed as a Determiner clitic licensing the complex DP *the man from Utrecht*, $_{DP}$[the man from Utrecht] $_{Det}$'s $_{NP}$[daughter with long hair]. Rather, UG is open to such structures to be postulated when children are exposed to relevant ambient language that requires or "expresses" such structures. Such parameters stated at UG have no useful role to play here.

This approach allows good understanding of why English has adopted so many structural innovations not shared by its closest historical relatives and apparently quite idiosyncratic and unprincipled. Two examples are presented very briefly; for details see Lightfoot (2017).

First, in the early sixteenth century a change was completed whereby, after the loss of very rich verbal morphology, a set of preterite-present verbs came to be categorized as Inflection elements with a very different syntax from verbs, unlike in any other European language; this change has been studied by many diachronic syntacticians and is now well understood. After the widespread loss of inflectional morphology in Middle English, only two verbal inflections survived, the third person singular marker in *-eth* or *-s* and the second person in *-st*. The preterite-present verbs never had the third person marker, and that absence was just one of many facts, but, after the great simplification of morphology, it came to make those verbs categorically distinct, unlike any others. The evidence is that they were assigned to a distinct, nonverb category of Inflection, which entailed a different syntax and the simultaneous obsolescence of formerly robust forms like *He has could see stars*, *She wanted to can see stars*, *She will can see stars*, and so on.

Second, with the loss of case morphology on nouns, which therefore no longer occurs in the ambient E-language, a set of forty or so psych-verbs underwent a kind of reversal of meaning and a new syntax, *like* changing from "please" to "enjoy," *repent* changing from "cause sorrow" to "feel sorrow," and a Theme subject changing to a Patient with both verbs. With the loss of morphology, no longer occurring in the ambient external language, children came to parse expressions differently, assigning different structures: *Gode ne licode na heora geleafleast* "to-God did not like their faithlessness" was no longer parsed with *Gode* as a dative case, *heora geleafleast* as a nominative subject, and *like* meaning "please" or "cause pleasure." Instead, children acquired new I-languages that entail the new structures and new semantics of these psych-verbs, *God* as a nominative, *faithlessness* as a Theme, and *like* with a new meaning, "enjoy" or "experience pleasure." It is hard to see how an explanation could be provided if children are evaluating multiple grammars and setting formal parameters, and it is equally hard to see what binary structural parameters might be implicated.

This is a brief account, but it is time for an alternative to parameter setting as an approach to variable properties that matches our success with invariant principles. We suggest that, rather than being parameterized, UG is open; see Lightfoot (2017) for much more. Given what they experience in their ambient external language, children may or may not invent nominal case endings or verbal suffixes in their I-languages; that is determined by the interplay between E-language and I-languages, and UG does not specify particular parameters.

Under this approach we do not over-theorize variation by trying to specify particular options in a very rich UG. Rather, UG is open to demands that emerge from parsing E-language, which are accommodated by the categories, structures, and operations made available by UG. Variation is inherent to the language faculty by virtue of its openness. This approach recalls the 1970s distinction between core and peripheral properties, whereby UG provides skeletal structures that are enhanced by the results of parsing.

It remains to be seen whether this yields a productive approach to variation beyond what we have viewed in the past as syntactic parameters. The 2017 Georgetown University Round Table focused on the nature and acquisition of variable properties in all domains of language, and this volume includes several papers presented there. Hopefully they will facilitate new approaches to variation, leading to an understanding of why human language, unlike other aspects of cognition, encompasses so much variation.

The Volume

This chapter begins the volume by noting the success of generative work in identifying invariant principles and the relative failure of comparable work on "parameters" designed to capture variable properties. We argue for an alternative approach to variable properties, whereby children parse the external language they hear (E-language) and postulate specific I-language elements required for certain aspects of the parse, making use of what UG makes available, notably through the bottom-up procedures of Merge and Project. The aggregation of those elements constitutes the complete I-language. When E-language shifts, children may parse differently and thus attain a new I-language, as revealed in work on syntactic change. Children discover variable properties of their I-languages through parsing; there is no evaluation of I-languages and no binary parameters, but UG is open. In this way we can understand the emergence of the profuse idiosyncratic properties of modern English in ways that parameters do not help.

One of the big new ideas at the GURT 2017 meeting was B. Elan Dresher's exploration of Roman Jakobson's 1941 *Kindersprache*, widely considered to be a groundbreaking work, but one that has nevertheless been much criticized for its hypothesis that phonological development proceeds in a fixed order; subsequent investigation has found considerably more variation than Jakobson had supposed. Controversy over this issue has obscured Jakobson's more basic insight that learners gradually acquire the contrastive features of their language in a hierarchical order, whereby a small number of initial broad contrasts are elaborated until the full set of contrasts of the adult language has been acquired. Dresher proposes that it is the concept of a contrastive feature hierarchy that is universal, not the features themselves or their ordering. He adopts the Contrastivist Hypothesis, which holds that only contrastive features can be computed by the phonology. The connection between contrast and activity implies that learners are guided both by phonological activity and by surface phonetics in acquiring the feature hierarchy for their language. He argues that these principles suffice to account for many of the ways that phonological systems resemble each other. He shows how contrastive feature hierarchies contribute to accounts of the synchrony, diachrony, and acquisition of phonology, allowing for considerable variation, but governed by a uniform universal template.

Elizabeth Cowper and Daniel Currie Hall adopt Dresher's contrastive hierarchies for morphosyntactic features and show that those hierarchies offer insights into syntactic variation and diachronic change. They illustrate with English number features, contrasting with Mandarin, and English tense/aspect features, contrasting with Romance and earlier stages of English.

Using naturalistic data collected during an allophonic restructuring in Philadelphia, Betsy Sneller argues that allophonic systems may act as a competing variable in the speech of speakers who were raised during a period of phonological change, suggesting that abstract phonological rules may be the target of phonological competition.

Daniel Milway offers an account of how a variable semantic property (resultative secondary predication) could be acquired from a surface phenomenon (compounding). He does so by applying Chomsky's label theory to previous empirical work by Kratzer and Snyder on adjectival resultatives.

Norbert Corver asks what is the grammatical nature of adverbial *-s* (e.g., *sideways*) and what underlies cross-linguistic and cross-constructional variation in the appearance of this *-s*. He proposes that *-s* is an affixal realization of no/ao and variation relates to properties of the selected root (√). Data come from Dutch (varieties) and English.

Marjorie Pak notes that many English speakers have an alternation between [ði] and [ðə] in the definite article that bears a striking resemblance to the familiar *a* ~ *an* and *ðə* ~ *ði* alternations before consonant/vowel initial words. She presents an acquisition model for *a* ~ *an* and *ðə* ~ *ði* that accounts for a previously unnoticed asymmetry in the (inter- and intraspeaker) variability of both alternations.

Marit Westergaard and Terje Lohndal use data from a spoken corpus and discuss the loss of verb second (V2) word order in the Norwegian heritage language spoken in the United States. They show that the context for V2 (non-subject-initial declaratives) is severely reduced, and that there is a clear correlation with non-V2 word order.

Correlations between word order and word structure are widespread in natural languages, and manifest early in language development. Heidi Getz offers a learning-based, input-driven theory of how these correlations are acquired and why they are so prevalent cross-linguistically, supported by quantitative studies of spontaneous speech and miniature language experiments.

Alicia Avellana, Lucía Brandani, Hannah Forsythe, and Cristina Schmitt examine the acquisition of agreement and direct object realization by children exposed to two varieties of Spanish in Buenos Aires, Argentina: Rioplatense and Paraguayan Spanish. Comparisons between parental input and children's production show that children use all the forms but do not make use of the same featural composition.

Gregory Guy presents evidence from variable processes in English, Spanish, and Portuguese demonstrating several aspects of mental representations. Morphological structure and exceptional allomorphy are revealed when variable processes affect word classes differently. Morphological acquisition is observable in child language variation. Homophonous morphemes can be distinguished by differential variable behavior.

Marlyse Baptista challenges the notion that variation in Creole languages is due to a continuum punctuated by a basilect and an acrolect. Instead, she proposes that variation within a single variety and across varieties is reflective of competing I-languages and feature recombinations both synchronically and diachronically.

Gillian Sankoff begins her investigation of the relationship between language change across the life span and language change in history by considering the temporal incommensurability of the two processes. Conditioned by biology, language change across the life span is temporally constrained, involving the differential plasticity of individuals at different life stages. It is also conditioned by the different social environments in which people are immersed as they grow, mature, and age. The temporal progress of language change may range anywhere from decades to centuries. Labov's model of transmission relates language change to the life course via the concept of incrementation in intergenerational acquisition: changes in progress are incremented across successive cohorts of those acquiring the language. Sankoff's longitudinal research on Montreal French illustrates the mutual influence of the social and the biological and may help to explain why some changes have a very long tail.

In this era of "big data," it's increasingly tempting to base linguistic and sociolinguistic studies on large corpora, often internet data, and to focus on big-picture patterns of language and dialect variation and change. However, Natalie Schilling demonstrates how the in-depth, in-person sociolinguistic study of small communities can augment large-scale studies of the geographic and social patterning of dialect variation and change. Drawing on her work on Smith Island, Schilling shows that underlying the distinctive patterns of variation and change found in small communities are factors, such as close-knit social networks allowing for the cross-generational transmission of subtle intracommunity patterns of variation, endocentric orientations emphasizing intracommunity social distinctions; she shows how small dialects illustrate locally grounded community identity in an ever-globalizing world.

Lisa Green considers overt third singular marking on verbs, which is often claimed to be absent from the I-languages of adult African American English (AAE) speakers, although native speakers may produce third person singular verbal morphology in limited contexts. Past tense marking, although produced variably, is part of the AAE I-language. It is sometimes claimed that in early stages, children use bare forms of verbs to mark events without reference to tense, agreement, or aspect. In later stages, children also use bare forms of verbs or zero morphological marking in variation with overt morphological marking to indicate tense (and aspect): *She* ***go*** *to the chicken and* ***picks*** *up eggs*; *The cat* ***spilled*** *the milk and the dog* ***make*** *a mess on the floor*. Green investigates past and nonpast contexts in data from three- to six-year-old AAE-speaking children in Louisiana and Mississippi to test the claim that not all examples of nonovert or zero morphological marking (e.g., *She* ***grab*** *the bowl and open the bag of flour.* "She grabs the bowl and opens the bag of flour" or "She grabbed the bowl and opened the bag of flour") are equal. The data reveal patterns in zero marking associated with third person singular *-s* and past tense morphology that are related to the difference in their connections to AAE I-languages. Furthermore, the data also reveal that although developing AAE resembles adult AAE in zero morphological marking, such marking in some stages in child speech may be an indication of developmental properties and not equivalent to zero marking in adult AAE.

Some Reflections

Most of the discussion at GURT concerned either properties that vary across languages or properties that vary within the (primary linguistic) data that an individual learner is exposed to. The first deals with variation mostly considered by generative grammarians; the second is the focus of much work in sociolinguistic, Labovian traditions. It was heartening to hear engagement across these silos, and perhaps there will be some coming together as people see interactions between the two paradigms: after all, variation within external language (E-language) triggers different individual, internal languages (I-languages). Indeed, Yang's work considers variation within a language but from a theoretical learnability perspective.

Another theme was the role of statistics with respect to I-languages: statistics can complement theories of language, not replace them, if we see statistical variation within a language as something to be explained, not the explanation. Again Yang's work uses statistics as an aid to acquiring I-languages; statistics *reflect* properties of I-languages. And Getz shows that the age of learning categorical rules may restrict their nature. One can hope that different types of variation may be understood in a shared perspective and silos may become more porous.

It is interesting to reflect on how thinking has changed about the invariant principles of UG and the variable parameter settings since the early days of the Principles-and-Parameters approach of the early 1980s (Chomsky 1981). In those early days the general goal was to find principles and parameters of UG that could solve the poverty-of-stimulus problems that were identified. Since researchers have sought to get "beyond explanatory adequacy," the strategy has been to reduce UG to a minimum. This does not mean that we should retreat from solving poverty-of-stimulus problems (Boeckx 2015; see Lightfoot 2017 for discussion); it does mean that we need richer notions of learning beyond simply invoking properties of UG.

Two examples where this has happened: First, Getz has shown that we can get better understandings of some well-known poverty-of-stimulus solutions with a richer understanding of the learning involved and how it may come from parsing ambient language. Second, Dresher, Cowper, and Hall's contrastive theory does not assume innate features, unlike in earlier generative phonology. They can give up innate features because they postulate something else innate: contrastive hierarchies and the concept of features.

We hope that GURT will help get the field to a better, more unified understanding of variable properties and their acquisition, recognizing that understanding their acquisition will yield a better understanding of their nature.

References

Aboh, Enoch O., ed. 2017. "Complexity in Human Languages: A Multifaceted Approach." Special issue, *Language Sciences* 60.

Belletti, Adriana. 2017. "Internal Grammar and Children's Grammatical Creativity against Poor Inputs." *Frontiers in Psychology: Language Sciences* 8. doi:10.3389/fpsyg.2017.02074.

Berwick, Robert C., and Noam Chomsky. 2016. *Why Only Us: Language and Evolution.* Cambridge, MA: MIT Press.

Boeckx, Cedric. 2014. "What Principles and Parameters Got Wrong." In *Linguistic Variation in the Minimalist Framework*, edited by M. Carme Picallo. Oxford: Oxford Scholarship Online. doi:10.1093/acprof:oso/9780198702894.001.0001.

Boeckx, Cedric. 2015. *Elementary Syntactic Structures.* Cambridge: Cambridge University Press.

Chomsky, Noam. 1981. "Principles and Parameters in Syntactic Theory." In *Explanation in Linguistics: The Logical Problem of Language Acquisition*, edited by Norbert Hornstein and David W. Lightfoot, 32–75. London: Longman.

Chomsky, Noam. 2001. "Derivation by Phase." In *Ken Hale: A Life in Language*, edited by Michael Kenstowicz, 1–52. Cambridge, MA: MIT Press.

Clark, Robin. 1992. "The Selection of Syntactic Knowledge." *Language Acquisition* 2 (2): 83–149.

den Dikken, Marcel. 2012. *The Cambridge Handbook of Generative Grammar.* Cambridge: Cambridge University Press.

Ding, Nai, Lucia Melloni, Hang Zhang, Xing Tian, and David Poeppel. 2016. "Cortical Tracking of Hierarchical Linguistic Structures in Connected Speech." *Nature Neuroscience* 19:158–64.

Hornstein, Norbert. 2009. *A Theory of Syntax.* Cambridge: Cambridge University Press.

Hudson Kam, Carla L., and Elissa L. Newport. 2005. "Regularizing Unpredictable Variation: The Roles of Adult and Child Learners in Language Formation and Change." *Language Learning and Development* 1 (2): 151–95.

Kegl, Judith, Ann Senghas, and Marie Coppola. 1998. "Creation through Contact: Sign Language Emergence and Sign Language Change in Nicaragua." In *Language Creation and Change: Creolization, Diachrony and Development*, edited by Michel DeGraff, 179–237. Cambridge, MA: MIT Press.

Lightfoot, David W. 1989. "The Child's Trigger Experience: Degree-0 Learnability." *Behavioral & Brain Sciences* 12 (2): 321–34.

Lightfoot, David W. 2005. "Learning from Creoles." *Lingua* 115:197–99.

Lightfoot, David W. 2006. *How New Languages Emerge.* Cambridge: Cambridge University Press.

Lightfoot, David W. 2017. "Discovering New Variable Properties without Parameters." In *Parameters*, edited by Simin Karimi and Massimo Piattelli-Palmarini, special issue, *Linguistic Analysis* 41 (3–4): 409–44.

Lightfoot, David W. 2018. "Nothing in Syntax Makes Sense Except in the Light of Change." In *Language, Syntax, and the Natural Sciences*, edited by Angel Gallego and Roger Martin, 224–40. Cambridge: Cambridge University Press.

Longobardi, Giuseppe, Cristina Guardiano, Giuseppina Silvestri, Alessio Boattini, and Andrea Ceolin. 2013. "Toward a Syntactic Phylogeny of Modern Indo-European Languages." *Journal of Historical Linguistics* 3 (1): 122–52.

Nelson, Matthew J., Imen El Karoui, Kristof Giber, Xiaofang Yang, Laurent Cohen, Hilda Koopman, Sydney S. Cash, Lionel Naccache, John T. Hale, Christophe Pallier, and Stanislas Dehaene. 2017. "Neurophysiological Dynamics of Phrase-Structure Building During Sentence Processing." *Proceedings of the National Academy of Sciences* 114 (18): E3669–E3678. doi:10.1073/pnas.1701590114.

Newmeyer, Frederick J. 2017. "Where, If Anywhere, Are Parameters? A Critical Historical Overview of Parametric Theory." In *On Looking into Words (and Beyond)*, edited by Claire Bowern, Lawrence Horn, and Raffaella Zanuttini, 547–69. Berlin: Language Science Press. doi:10.5281/zenodo.495465.

Newport, Elissa L. 1998. "Reduced Input in the Acquisition of Signed Languages: Contributions to the Study of Creolization." In *Language Creation and Change: Creolization, Diachrony and Development*, edited by Michel DeGraff, 161–78. Cambridge, MA: MIT Press.

Piattelli-Palmarini, Massimo, and Robert C. Berwick, eds. 2013. *Rich Languages from Poor Inputs*. Oxford: Oxford University Press.

Sandler, Wendy, Init Meir, Carol Padden, and Mark Aronoff. 2005. "The Emergence of Grammar: Systematic Structure in a New Language." *Proceedings of the National Academy of Sciences* 102 (7): 2661–65.

Senghas, Ann, Sotaro Kita, and Asli Özyürek. 2004. "Children Creating Core Properties of Language: Evidence from an Emerging Sign Language in Nicaragua." *Science* 305:1779–82.

Singleton, Jenny L., and Elissa L. Newport. 2004. "When Learners Surpass Their Models: The Acquisition of American Sign Language from Impoverished Input." *Cognitive Psychology* 49:370–407.

Tattersall, Ian. 2016. "At the Birth of Language." Review of *Why Only Us: Language and Evolution*, by Robert C. Berwick and Noam Chomsky. *New York Review of Books*, August 18.

Chapter 2

Contrastive Feature Hierarchies in Phonology: Variation and Universality

B. ELAN DRESHER
University of Toronto

AS A WAY OF addressing the Georgetown University Round Table on Languages and Linguistics (GURT) 2017 conference theme, "Variable Properties: Their Nature and Acquisition," I would like to ask the question: what is variable and what is fixed in phonology? In particular, I want to focus on phonological representations, and on the nature of features: are features innate and universal, or are they "emergent" and language particular? The assumption that features are innate does not seem to leave enough room for the variability that we find; but the assumption that they are emergent could leave us with *too* much variation, with no account of why phonologies resemble each other as much as they do.

Modifying a line of thought that can be traced back to Roman Jakobson, I propose that it is the concept of a *contrastive feature hierarchy* that is universal, not the features themselves or their ordering. I further adopt the Contrastivist Hypothesis, which holds that only contrastive features can be computed by the phonology. This hypothesis makes a connection between contrast and phonological activity that has implications for phonological theory as well as for language acquisition: it follows from this theory that learners are guided by phonological activity as well as by phonetics in acquiring the feature hierarchy for their language. I will argue that these principles suffice to account for many of the ways that phonological systems resemble each other. I will show how contrastive feature hierarchies contribute to accounts of synchronic and diachronic phonology, allowing for considerable variation, but governed by a uniform universal template.

I will begin by reviewing the groundbreaking contributions of Jakobson (1941). Building on Jakobson's ideas about the emergence of phonological oppositions, I will then present a theory of phonological contrast. Next, I briefly rehearse the arguments against innate phonological features, and propose some prerequisites for a theory of emergent features. Finally, an example from Inuit vowel systems illustrates how contrastive feature hierarchies contribute to explanatory accounts of phonological patterning.

Jakobson's *Kindersprache*: A Reconsideration

Roman Jakobson's *Kindersprache, Aphasie und allgemeine Lautgesetze* (Jakobson 1941), translated into English as *Child Language, Aphasia, and Phonological Universals* (Jakobson 1968), is important for its theory of phonological acquisition, as well as for how it connects acquisition to phonological theory more generally. Of the many influential ideas advanced in this book, the one that has attracted much discussion and criticism is the claim that acquisition proceeds in a fixed order. Jakobson does indeed emphasize this idea throughout the book. For example, he writes (Jakobson 1968, 20–28), "The fact that a fixed order must be inherent in language acquisition, and in phonological acquisition in particular, has repeatedly been noticed by observers. . . . Again and again a number of constant features in the succession of acquired phonemes are observed."

In passages such as this, Jakobson appears to be claiming that the fixed order of emergence refers to *phonemes*; for example, he writes that the acquisition of vowels is launched with a wide (low) vowel, *a*, and that the first consonant is generally a labial stop, *p* (hence, the first syllable is expected to be *pa*). In other places, however, he refers to the emergence of *oppositions*—that is, *contrasts*—not individual phonemes. Thus, he proposes that the first vocalic opposition opposes the wide vowel, *a*, to a more narrow (high) vowel, *i*.

If the key notion, however, is contrasts, then the predictions about the order of emergence of individual sounds become much more obscure. This is because a contrast between a wider and a narrower vowel can be phonetically realized in a variety of ways: the phonemic labels "/a/" and "/i/" can each represent a broad range of phonetic vowels. Also, the boundary between two such phonemes can vary considerably from language to language. Hence, the apocryphal tale recounted by Hyman (2008), in which Jakobson asserts in a lecture that in all languages the child's first word is *pa*. An audience member objects that *his* child's first utterance was *tʃɪk*. Jakobson replies, "Phonetic [tʃɪk], yes, but phonologically /pa/!" This may be a joke, but there is truth to the notion that an emphasis on contrasts can overshadow the individual sounds that participate in a contrast.

This makes it harder than one might suppose to test Jakobson's predictions about a fixed order of acquisition (Ingram 1988). Nevertheless, it appears that child phonology shows more variation, even within a single language, than Jakobson 1941 allows (Menn and Vihman 2011; Bohn 2017). But the claim that acquisition of phonology proceeds in a fixed order is not the only idea put forward in *Kindersprache*. More consequential, in my view, is the notion that contrasts are crucial and that they develop in a *hierarchical order*.

In particular, Jakobson proposes that learners begin with broad contrasts that are split by stages into progressively finer ones. He observes (1968, 65), "This system is by its very nature closely related to those stratified phenomena which modern psychology uncovers in the different areas of the realm of the mind. Development proceeds 'from an undifferentiated original condition to a greater and greater differentiation and separation'" (citing E. Jaensch, *Zeitschr. f. Psychol.* 1928).

With this basic idea in mind, consider again the acquisition of vowel systems set out in Jakobson 1941 and its sequel, Jakobson and Halle 1956. At the first stage, there is only a single vowel. As there are no contrasts, we can simply designate it /V/ (Example 2.1a). Jakobson and Halle write that this lone vowel is the maximally open vowel [a], the "optimal vowel." But we do not need to be that specific: we can understand this to be a default value, or a typical but not obligatory instantiation. For contrastive purposes, any phonetic vowel will fit; for example, [ɪ^{k}]!

(1) Early stages of vowel acquisition (Jakobson 1941; Jakobson and Halle 1956)

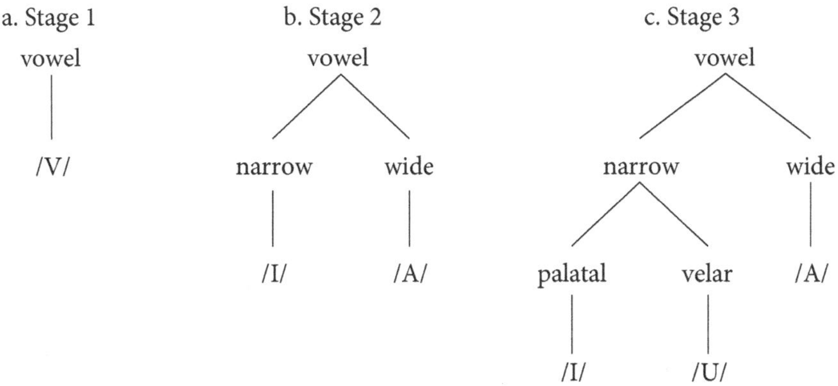

In the next stage (Example 2.1b), it is proposed that the single vowel splits into a narrow vowel, which is typically [i], and a wide vowel, typically [a]. I will continue to understand these values as defaults; I use capital letters to represent vowels that fit the contrastive labels that characterize them. Subsequently (Example 2.1c), the narrow vowel splits into a palatal (front) vowel and a velar (back or round) vowel, typically [u]. Jakobson (1968, 49) observes that this stage corresponds to the common three-vowel system /i, a, u/.

Of course, systems designated as /i, a, u/ vary considerably in their phonetic realizations. Dresher and Rice (2015) survey some three-vowel systems that are included in the online phonological database called PHOIBLE Online (Moran, McCloy, and Wright 2014). It lists twelve Pama-Nyungan (Australia) three-vowel languages. Of these, eight are given as having the vowels /i, a, u/. The other four are listed as having different inventories: /i, ɑ, u/, /ɪ, a, ʊ/, /ɪ, ɐ, ʊ/, and /i, a, ə/. We found that there are no principled criteria for distinguishing between these systems: distinctions between /i/ ~ /ɪ/, /a/ ~ /ɑ/ ~ /ɐ/, and /u/ ~ /ʊ/ ~ /ə/ do not necessarily indicate significant differences between the languages. Conversely, the inventories designated /i, a, u/ exhibit considerable variation in the phonetic ranges covered by their three vowels.

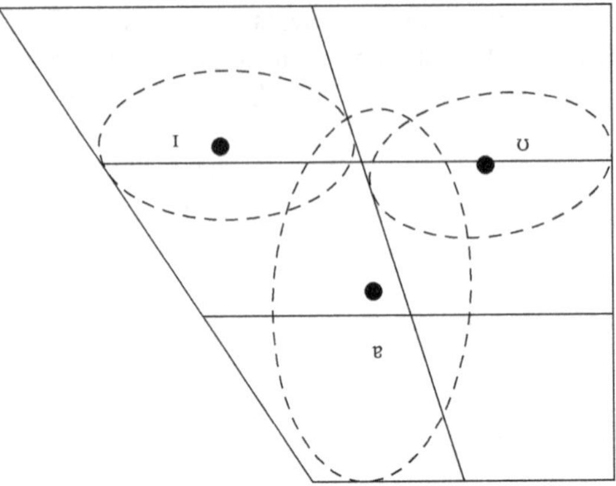

Figure 2.1: Pitjantjatjara vowel ranges (Tabain and Butcher 2014, 194)

Compare, for example, the vowel systems of two dialects of the Western Desert Language of central Australia: Pitjantjatjara (Figure 2.1, from Tabain and Butcher 2014) and Antakarinya (Figure 2.2, based on Douglas 1955). The distributions of the vowels in the two languages are different, particularly that of the low vowel. They suggest that the languages may have different contrastive features, derived from different contrastive splits.

The phonetic distribution of the vowels in Antakarinya is consistent with Jakobson and Halle's Stage 3 in Example 2.1c, in having a basic split between the low vowel and the other two. Updating the terminology, we can represent the contrasts as in Example 2.2a; I assume, for purposes of this example, that the features [high] and [round] are the positive (marked) features, and their negative poles are defaults (on markedness see below).[1]

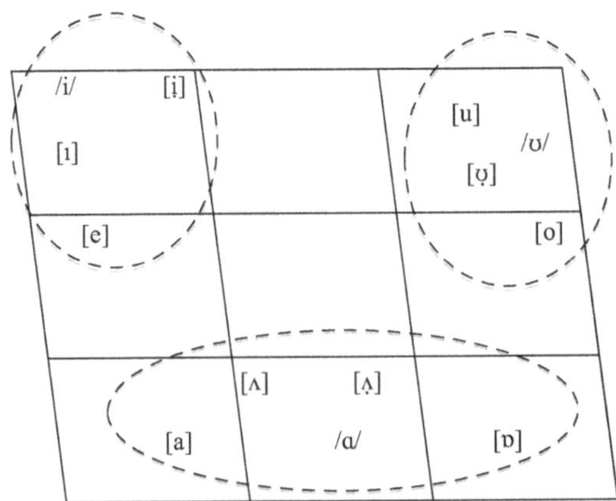

Figure 2.2: Antakarinya vowel ranges (based on Douglas 1955, 221)

(2) Other types of contrasts in three-vowel systems

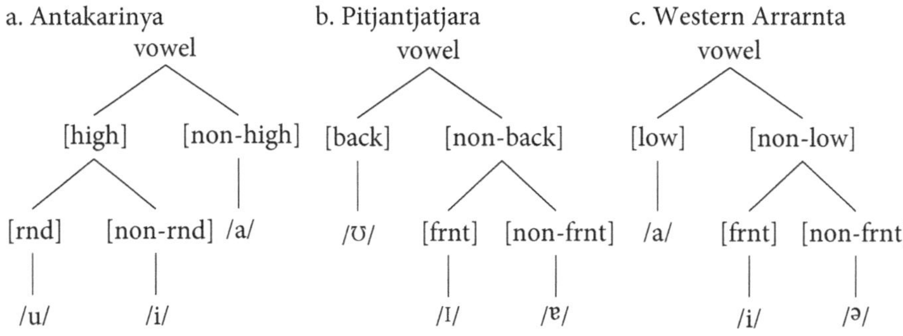

In Pitjantjatjara, however, it appears that /ɐ/ is not restricted to the low part of the vowel space, but ranges fairly high in the center of the space, whereas /ɪ/ and /ʊ/ have more restrictive ranges. These phonetic distributions might suggest a set of vertical contrasts, shown in Example 2.2b, whereby /ʊ/ is characterized by a feature such as [back] and /ɪ/ is characterized by [front]; this leaves /ɐ/ as [non-back] and [non-front].[2]

The vowel ranges of another Pama-Nyungan language, Western Arrarnta (Anderson 2000, 36–40), are shown in Figure 2.3. Here, /a/ is restricted to a very small space; we infer it is [low]. /i/ "varies in quality from [ɛ] to [i]." We can assign it [front]. According to Anderson, /ə/ is "extremely variable" in height and backness, with unrounded and rounded allophones (so it could be written /u/, if we want to stick to /i, a, u/). It also appears to be the epenthetic vowel. This distribution is consistent with /ə/ being [non-low] and [non-front]; in Jakobson's terms, narrow and velar, that is, /U/ in (1c). Unlike /U/ in the other languages, however, this one appears to have only default feature values, as in Example 2.2c.

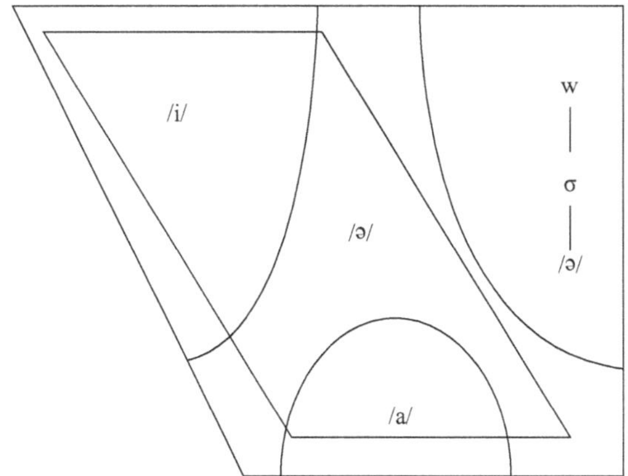

Figure 2.3: Western Arrarnta vowel ranges (Anderson 2000, 37)

We conclude, then, that the characterization of many three-vowel systems as /i, a, u/ may conceal the fact that they are very diverse. Similarly, the first stages of phonological acquisition may not be as unvarying as proposed by Jakobson (1941) and Jakobson and Halle (1956). Conversely, if Jakobson's basic idea about the development of contrasts is correct, then all three-vowel systems *are* similar in being characterized by two features, even if these features are not the same in each case, or even universal.

After the first two stages, Jakobson and Halle allow variation in the order of acquisition of vowel contrasts. The wide branch of Example 2.1c can be expanded to parallel the narrow one. Or the narrow vowels can develop a rounding contrast in one or both branches. Continuing in this fashion, we will arrive at a complete inventory of the phonemes of a language, with each phoneme assigned a set of contrastive properties that distinguish it from every other one.

In a number of publications, I have tried to reconstruct a history of "branching trees" in phonology (Dresher 2009, 2015b, 2016, 2018). Early, though inexplicit, examples can be found in the work of Jakobson (1931) and Trubetzkoy (1939) in the 1930s, and continuing with Jakobson 1941 and Jakobson and Lotz 1949; then more explicitly in Jakobson, Fant, and Halle 1952; Cherry, Halle, and Jakobson 1953; Jakobson and Halle 1956; and Halle 1959. This approach was imported into early versions of the theory of generative phonology; it is featured prominently in the first generative phonology textbook (Harms 1968). Nevertheless, for reasons discussed by Dresher (2016, 70), branching trees were omitted from Chomsky and Halle's *The Sound Pattern of English* (1968), and disappeared from mainstream phonological theory for the rest of the century.

In child language studies, however, branching trees continued to be used, for they are a natural way to describe developing phonological inventories (Pye, Ingram, and List 1987; Ingram 1988, 1989; Levelt 1989; Dinnsen et al. 1990; Dinnsen 1992, 1996; see Dresher 1998a for a review). Fikkert (1994) presents observed acquisition sequences in the development of Dutch onsets that follow this general scheme, shown schematically in Example 2.3.

(3) Development of Dutch onset consonants (Fikkert 1994)

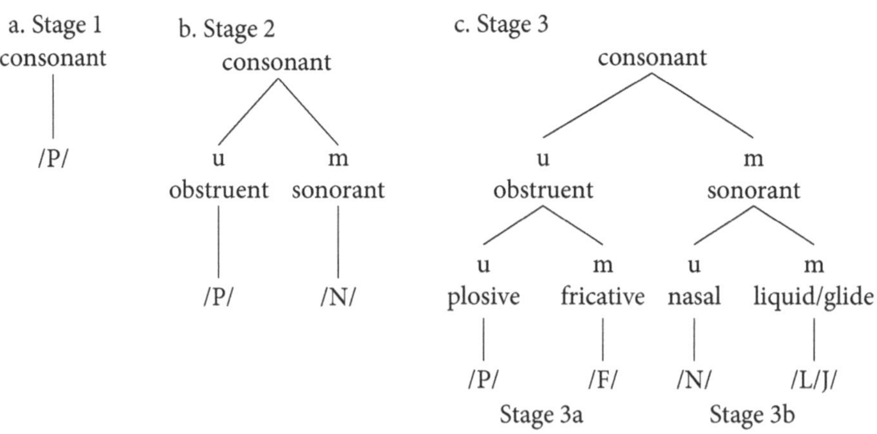

At Stage 1 (Example 2.3a), there are no contrasts; the value of the consonant defaults to the least marked onset, namely an obstruent plosive. The first contrast (Stage 2) is between obstruent and sonorant (Example 2.3b). The former remains the unmarked option (*u*); the marked (*m*) sonorant defaults to nasal. After this stage, children differ (Example 2.3c). Some expand the obstruent branch first, bringing in marked (*m*) fricatives in contrast with plosives (Stage 3a). Others (Stage 3b) expand the sonorant branch, introducing marked sonorants (either liquids or glides). And so on from there.

As a general theory of phonological representations, branching trees were revived, under other names, by Clements (2001, 2003, 2009) and independently at the University of Toronto, where they are called contrastive feature hierarchies (Dresher, Piggott, and Rice 1994; Dyck 1995; Zhang 1996; Dresher 1998b; Dresher and Rice 2007; Hall 2007; Dresher 2009). It is the latter approach I will be presenting here. It has gone under various names: Modified Contrastive Specification (MCS), Toronto School phonology, contrast and enhancement theory, or contrastive hierarchy theory. I will present the theory as I understand it.[3]

A Theory of Phonological Contrast

The first major building block of our theory is that contrasts are computed *hierarchically by ordered features* that can be expressed as a branching tree. Branching trees are generated by what I call the Successive Division Algorithm (Dresher 1998b, 2003, 2009), given informally in (4).

(4) The Successive Division Algorithm
Assign contrastive features by successively dividing the inventory until every phoneme has been distinguished.

Since feature hierarchies can vary from language to language, it is crucial to have criteria for selecting and ordering the features. Phonetics is clearly important, as we have seen in the discussion of three-vowel systems in (2), in that the selected features must be consistent with the phonetic properties of the phonemes. For example, a contrast between /i/ and /a/ would most likely involve a height feature like [low] or [high], though other choices are possible (e.g., [front] or [advanced/retracted tongue root]).

It should be noted that the contrastive specification of a phoneme can sometimes deviate from its surface phonetics. Proto-Eskimo, the ancestor of present-day Inuit dialects, has been reconstructed with four vowels: */a, i, u, ɨ/ (see Compton and Dresher 2011 for references and further discussion). In modern dialects the fourth vowel */ɨ/ has merged with /i/. In some dialects the merger is complete, and there is no synchronic trace of an original distinction between */i/ and */ɨ/; in these dialects, there are only three underlying vowels, /i, a, u/.

Some dialects, however, still show evidence of an underlying distinction between /i/ and a fourth vowel. In Barrow North Alaskan Iñupiaq, for example, some instances of *i*, called “strong *i*,” cause palatalization of a following consonant (5b), but instances of “weak *i*” do not (5c). In this case, /i/ and the fourth vowel (designated /ɨ/) need to be distinguished by a contrastive feature, even though their surface realizations are identical (see below).

(5) Barrow palatalization after strong *i* in noun stems (Kaplan 1981, 81–82)

	Vowel	Analysis	Gloss	Stem	"and a N"	"N OBL.PL"	"like a N"
a.	*u*	/u/	"house"	iɣlu̲	iɣlu-lu	iɣlu-nik	iɣlu-tun
b.	Strong *i*	/i/	"wound"	iki̲	iki-ʎu	iki-ɲik	iki-sun
c.	Weak *i*	/ɨ/	"place"	ini̲	ini-lu	ini-nik	ini-tun

As this example shows, the way a sound *patterns* can override its phonetics (Sapir 1925). Thus, we consider as most fundamental that features should be selected and ordered so as to reflect the phonological activity in a language, where activity is defined as in (6) (adapted from Clements 2001, 77):

(6) Phonological activity
A feature can be said to be *active* if it plays a role in the phonological computation; that is, if it is required for the expression of phonological regularities in a language, including both static phonotactic patterns and patterns of alternation.

The second major tenet has been formulated by Hall (2007) as the Contrastivist Hypothesis (7):

(7) The Contrastivist Hypothesis
The phonological component of a language L operates only on those features which are necessary to distinguish the phonemes of L from one another.

That is, *only* contrastive features can be phonologically active. If this hypothesis is correct, then (8) follows as a corollary:

(8) Corollary to the Contrastivist Hypothesis
If a feature is phonologically active, then it must be contrastive.

One further assumption is that features are binary, and that every feature has a marked and unmarked value. I assume that markedness is language particular (Rice 2003, 2007) and accounts for asymmetries between the two values of a feature, where these exist. I will designate the marked value of a feature F as [F], and the unmarked value as [non-F]. I will refer to the two values together as [±F].

Unless a vowel is further specified by other contrastive features (originating in another vowel or in the consonants), it is made more specific only in a postphonological component. Stevens, Keyser, and Kawasaki (1986) propose that feature contrasts can be *enhanced* by other features with similar acoustic effects.[4] Thus, /u/ in Example 2.2a can enhance its [round] feature by adding [back], and /ʊ/ in Example 2.2b can enhance [back] by adding [round]. These enhancements are not universal, however, as shown by the realizations of /ə/ in Example 2.2c.[5]

Why Do Phonological Features Emerge?

There is a growing consensus that phonological features are not innate, but rather emerge in the course of acquisition. Most of the contributions to a volume titled

Where Do Phonological Features Come From? (Clements and Ridouane 2011) take an emergentist position; none argue for innate features. Mielke (2008) and Samuels (2011) summarize the arguments against innate features. From a biolinguistic perspective, phonological features are too specific, and exclude sign languages (Sandler 1993; van der Hulst 1993). Empirically, no one set of features have been discovered that "do all tricks," as Hyman (2011) writes with respect to tone features, but the remark applies more generally. Finally, since at least some features have to be acquired based on evidence of language-specific phonological activity, a prespecified list of features becomes less useful in learning than had once been thought.

But if features are not innate, what compels them to emerge at all? It is not enough to assert that features *may* emerge, or that they are a useful way to capture phonological generalizations. Assuming that phonological representations are composed of distinctive features, we need to explain why features *inevitably* emerge, and why they have the properties that they do. In particular, we have to explain why some learners do not simply posit segment-level representations. Further, are there limits to how broad or narrow features are, or how many features can be associated with a given phonological inventory?

Contrastive hierarchy theory provides an answer to these questions: learners must arrive at a set of hierarchically ordered features that distinguish among all the phonemes of their language. This requirement imposes strong constraints on the number of features that can be posited, and on what feature systems can look like. We have already seen that a three-vowel system allows for exactly two contrastive features. The features may vary, as well as their ordering, and either the marked (Example 2.2a) or unmarked (Example 2.2b, c) branches of the first feature may be expanded; but this is the extent of variation that is permitted.

In general, the number of features required by an inventory of n elements falls in the following ranges: the minimum number of features is the smallest integer greater than or equal to $\log_2 n$; and the maximum number of features is equal to $n - 1$. Some sample values of feature minima and maxima for inventories of different sizes are shown in Table 2.1. By putting limits on the number and organization of feature systems, the contrastive hierarchy together with the Contrastivist Hypothesis account for why phonological systems resemble each other in terms of representations, without requiring individual features to be innate.

Table 2.1: Minimum and maximum number of features for various-sized phoneme inventories

Phonemes	$\log_2 n$	min	max	Phonemes	$\log_2 n$	min	max
2	1	1	1	11	3.46	4	10
3	1.58	2	2	16	4	4	15
4	2	2	3	22	4.46	5	21
5	2.32	3	4	29	4.86	5	28
8	3	3	7	36	5.17	6	35

Concluding Example: Inuit Vowel Systems

To illustrate some of the principles discussed, consider again the Inuit dialects with three and four vowels. Dialects with four underlying vowels, such as Barrow Iñupiaq, can support three contrastive features, as in Example 2.9a; the presence of [front] is what enables /i/ to cause palatalization.

(9) Contrastive feature hierarchies in Inuit dialects

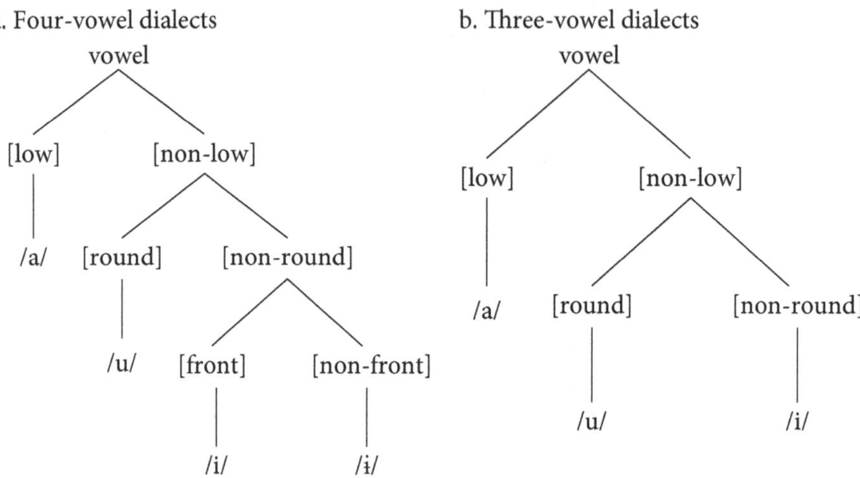

In three-vowel dialects, however, where Proto-Eskimo */ɨ/ has completely merged with */i/, there is room for only two contrastive vowel features (Example 2.9b). Compton and Dresher (2011) argue that there is evidence that [±low] and [±round] are active, hence contrastive features, leaving /i/ with no marked feature that can trigger palatalization. The prediction that /i/ does not cause palatalization in three-vowel Inuit dialects is strikingly borne out: whereas there are four-vowel dialects with and without palatalization, no three-vowel dialects have palatalization. Contrastive hierarchy theory accounts for this conspicuous gap in the typology of Inuit dialects, demonstrating the close connection between contrast and phonological activity.

Notes

This chapter is a slightly revised version of portions of a talk presented at GURT 2017. I would like to thank participants and audience members for their comments and questions. For discussion, ideas, and analyses, I would like to thank Graziela Bohn, Elizabeth Cowper, Daniel Currie Hall, Paula Fikkert, Ross Godfrey, Christopher Harvey, Ross Krekoski, Will Oxford, Keren Rice, Christopher Spahr, and Zhang Xi.

1 These feature assignments are made for the sake of concreteness, but they are underdetermined by the diagram. It is also possible that [low] is marked rather than [high], and [front] or [back] rather than [round]. Further study of these languages might reveal more phonological or phonetic facts to support or modify the assignments in (2).

2 Again, there are other possibilities which are subject to disambiguation by further investigation.
3 For a more complete summary of contrastive hierarchy theory, see Dresher (2015a).
4 See also Keyser and Stevens (2006) and the references therein.
5 See Dyck (1995) and Hall (2011) for further discussion and examples.

References

Anderson, Victoria Balboa. 2000. "Giving Weight to Phonetic Principles: The Case of Place of Articulation in Western Arrernte." PhD diss., University of California, Los Angeles.

Bohn, Graziela. 2017. "How to Get There from Here: Building Hierarchies in Brazilian Portuguese." Presented at Georgetown University Round Table, March 2017.

Cherry, E. Colin, Morris Halle, and Roman Jakobson. 1953. "Toward the Logical Description of Languages in Their Phonemic Aspect." *Language* 29 (1): 34–46.

Chomsky, Noam, and Morris Halle. 1968. *The Sound Pattern of English*. New York: Harper & Row.

Clements, G. N. 2001. "Representational Economy in Constraint-Based Phonology." In *Distinctive Feature Theory*, edited by T. Alan Hall, 71–146. Berlin: Mouton de Gruyter.

Clements, G. N. 2003. "Feature Economy in Sound Systems." *Phonology* 20 (3): 287–333.

Clements, G. N. 2009. "The Role of Features in Speech Sound Inventories." In *Contemporary Views on Architecture and Representations in Phonological Theory*, edited by Eric Raimy and Charles E. Cairns, 19–68. Cambridge, MA: MIT Press.

Clements, G. N., and Rachid Ridouane, eds. 2011. *Where Do Phonological Features Come From? Cognitive, Physical and Developmental Bases of Distinctive Speech Categories*. Amsterdam: Benjamins.

Compton, Richard, and B. Elan Dresher. 2011. "Palatalization and 'Strong *i*' across Inuit Dialects." *Canadian Journal of Linguistics/Revue canadienne de linguistique* 56 (2): 203–28.

Dinnsen, Daniel A. 1992. "Variation in Developing and Fully Developed Phonetic Inventories." In *Phonological Development: Models, Research, Implications*, edited by Charles A. Ferguson, Lisa Menn, and Carol Stoel-Gammon, 191–210. Timonium, MD: York Press.

Dinnsen, Daniel A. 1996. "Context-Sensitive Underspecification and the Acquisition of Phonemic Contrasts." *Journal of Child Language* 23 (1): 57–79.

Dinnsen, Daniel A., Steven B. Chin, Mary Elbert, and Thomas W. Powell. 1990. "Some Constraints on Functionally Disordered Phonologies: Phonetic Inventories and Phonotactics." *Journal of Speech and Hearing Research* 33 (1): 28–37.

Douglas, Wilfrid H. 1955. "Phonology of the Australian Aboriginal Language Spoken at Ooldea, South Australia, 1951–1952." *Oceania* 25 (3): 216–29.

Dresher, B. Elan. 1998a. "Child Phonology, Learnability, and Phonological Theory." In *Handbook of Language Acquisition*, edited by Tej Bhatia and William C. Ritchie, 299–346. New York: Academic Press.

Dresher, B. Elan. 1998b. "On Contrast and Redundancy." Presented at the Annual Meeting of the Canadian Linguistic Association, University of Ottawa, Ontario.

Dresher, B. Elan. 2003. "Contrast and Asymmetries in Inventories." In *Asymmetry in Grammar*. Vol. 2, *Morphology, Phonology, Acquisition*, edited by Anna-Maria di Sciullo, 239–57. Amsterdam: Benjamins.

Dresher, B. Elan. 2009. *The Contrastive Hierarchy in Phonology*. Cambridge: Cambridge University Press.

Dresher, B. Elan. 2015a. "Contrastive Hierarchy Theory: An Overview." 2 parts. Presented February 2015 at the University of Connecticut, Storrs, and September 2015 at the University of Massachusetts, Amherst. http://homes.chass.utoronto.ca/~dresher/talks/Combined_UConn-UMass_slides-PART1.pdf, and http://homes.chass.utoronto.ca/~dresher/talks/Combined_UConn-UMass_slides-PART2.pdf.

Dresher, B. Elan. 2015b. "The Motivation for Contrastive Feature Hierarchies in Phonology." *Linguistic Variation* 15 (1): 1–40.

Dresher, B. Elan. 2016. "Contrast in Phonology 1867–1967: History and Development." *Annual Review of Linguistics* 2: 253–73.

Dresher, B. Elan. 2018. "Contrastive Feature Hierarchies in Old English Diachronic Phonology." *Transactions of the Philological Society* 116 (1): 1–29.

Dresher, B. Elan, Glyne L. Piggott, and Keren Rice. 1994. "Contrast in Phonology: Overview." *Toronto Working Papers in Linguistics* 13 (1): iii–xvii.

Dresher, B. Elan, and Keren Rice. 2007. "Markedness and the Contrastive Hierarchy in Phonology." Accessed September 23, 2017, http://homes.chass.utoronto.ca/~contrast/.

Dresher, B. Elan, and Keren Rice. 2015. "Phonological Typology with Contrastive Hierarchies." Presented March 2015 at the MOLT Phonology Atelier, University of Toronto, Ontario.

Dyck, Carrie. 1995. "Constraining the Phonology–Phonetics Interface, with Exemplification from Spanish and Italian Dialects." PhD diss., University of Toronto, Ontario.

Fikkert, Paula. 1994. *On the Acquisition of Prosodic Structure (HIL Dissertations 6)*. Dordrecht, Netherlands: ICG Printing.

Hall, Daniel Currie. 2007. "The Role and Representation of Contrast in Phonological Theory." PhD diss., University of Toronto, Ontario.

Hall, Daniel Currie. 2011. "Phonological Contrast and Its Phonetic Enhancement: Dispersedness without Dispersion." *Phonology* 28 (1): 1–54.

Halle, Morris. (1959) 1971. *The Sound Pattern of Russian: A Linguistic and Acoustical Investigation*. The Hague: Mouton.

Harms, Robert T. 1968. *Introduction to Phonological Theory*. Englewood Cliffs, NJ: Prentice-Hall.

Hyman, Larry M. 2008. "Universals in Phonology." *Linguistic Review* 25 (1–2): 83–137.

Hyman, Larry M. 2011. "Do Tones Have Features?" In *Tones and Features*, edited by John A. Goldsmith, Elizabeth Hume, and W. Leo Wetzels, 50–80. Berlin: Mouton de Gruyter.

Ingram, David. 1988. "Jakobson Revisited: Some Evidence from the Acquisition of Polish Phonology." *Lingua* 75 (1): 55–82.

Ingram, David. 1989. *First Language Acquisition: Method, Description and Explanation*. Cambridge: Cambridge University Press.

Jakobson, Roman. (1931) 1962. "Phonemic Notes on Standard Slovak." In *Selected Writings I. Phonological Studies*, 221–30. The Hague: Mouton.

Jakobson, Roman. 1941. *Kindersprache, Aphasie, und allgemeine Lautgesetze*. Uppsala: Uppsala Universitets Årsskrift.

Jakobson, Roman. 1968. *Child Language, Aphasia, and Phonological Universals*. Translated by A. R. Keiler. The Hague: Mouton.

Jakobson, Roman, C. Gunnar M. Fant, and Morris Halle. (1952) 1976. *Preliminaries to Speech Analysis*. MIT Acoustics Laboratory, Technical Report No. 13. Reprint, Cambridge, MA: MIT Press.

Jakobson, Roman, and Morris Halle. 1956. *Fundamentals of Language*. The Hague: Mouton.

Jakobson, Roman, and John Lotz. 1949. "Notes on the French Phonemic Pattern." *Word* 5 (2): 151–58.

Kaplan, Lawrence D. 1981. *Phonological Issues in North Alaskan Inupiaq*. Fairbanks: Alaska Native Language Center.

Keyser, Samuel Jay, and Kenneth N. Stevens. 2006. "Enhancement and Overlap in the Speech Chain." *Language* 82 (1): 33–63.

Levelt, Clara C. 1989. "An Essay on Child Phonology." Master's thesis, Leiden University.

Menn, Lise, and Marilyn Vihman. 2011. "Features in Child Phonology: Inherent, Emergent, or Artefacts of Analysis?" In *Where Do Phonological Features Come From? Cognitive, Physical and Developmental Bases of Distinctive Speech Categories*, edited by G. N. Clements and Rachid Ridouane, 261–301. Amsterdam: Benjamins.

Mielke, Jeff. 2008. *The Emergence of Distinctive Features*. Oxford: Oxford University Press.

Moran, Steven, Daniel McCloy, and Richard Wright, eds. 2014. "PHOIBLE Online." Leipzig: Max Planck Institute for Evolutionary Anthropology. http://phoible.org.

Pye, Clifton, David Ingram, and Helen List. 1987. "A Comparison of Initial Consonant Acquisition in English and Quiché." In Vol. 6 of *Children's Language*, edited by Keith E. Nelson and Ann Van Kleeck, 175–90. Hillsdale, NJ: Lawrence Erlbaum.

Rice, Keren. 2003. "Featural Markedness in Phonology: Variation." In *The Second Glot International State-of-the-Article Book: The Latest in Linguistics*, edited by Lisa Cheng and Rint Sybesma, 387–427. Berlin: Mouton de Gruyter.

Rice, Keren. 2007. "Markedness in Phonology." In *The Cambridge Handbook of Phonology*, edited by Paul de Lacy, 79–97. Cambridge: Cambridge University Press.

Samuels, Bridget D. 2011. *Phonological Architecture: A Biolinguistic Perspective.* Oxford: Oxford University Press.
Sandler, Wendy. 1993. "Sign Language and Modularity." *Lingua* 89 (4): 315–51.
Sapir, Edward. 1925. "Sound Patterns in Language." *Language* 1 (2): 37–51.
Stevens, Kenneth N., Samuel Jay Keyser, and Haruko Kawasaki. 1986. "Toward a Phonetic and Phonological Theory of Redundant Features." In *Symposium on Invariance and Variability of Speech Processes,* edited by Joseph S. Perkell and Dennis H. Klatt, 432–69. Hillsdale, NJ: Lawrence Erlbaum.
Tabain, Marija, and Andrew Butcher. 2014. "Pitjantjatjara." *Journal of the International Phonetic Association* 44 (2): 189–200.
Trubetzkoy, N. S. 1939. *Grundzüge der Phonologie.* Göttingen: Vandenhoek and Ruprecht.
van der Hulst, Harry. 1993. "Units in the Analysis of Signs." *Phonology* 10 (2): 209–41.
Zhang, Xi. 1996. "Vowel Systems of the Manchu-Tungus Languages of China." PhD diss., University of Toronto, Ontario.

Chapter 3

Scope Variation in Contrastive Hierarchies of Morphosyntactic Features

ELIZABETH COWPER
University of Toronto
DANIEL CURRIE HALL
Saint Mary's University

MORPHOSYNTACTIC FEATURES EXHIBIT HIERARCHICAL dependencies, in which the presence of one feature implies that of another. Following Bonet (1991) and Harley (1994), among others, these dependencies have often been represented using feature geometries like those used in autosegmental phonology (e.g., Clements and Hume 1995). However, the explanatory value of morphosyntactic feature geometries has been questioned (Harbour 2011, 2016; Harbour and Elsholtz 2012). We propose that another kind of hierarchical structure, also borrowed from phonology, serves as a useful model for morphosyntax: the contrastive hierarchy (Dresher 2009, 2015, 2016, this volume). Treating morphosyntactic hierarchies as contrastive hierarchies, we argue, can explain feature dependencies and their cross-linguistic variability as products of a general mechanism for acquiring contrasts from language-particular input (Cowper and Hall 2014). For the specific case of grammatical person, we further show that adopting the contrastive hierarchy approach makes it possible to capture Harbour's (2016) typological generalizations while reducing the formal complexity of the features involved: the necessary features can be represented as familiar first-order predicates rather than as functions that add or subtract entities from a semilattice. Dresher's (2009) procedure for building contrastive hierarchies also implies a possible learning path; adopting this approach may thus make interesting predictions about the acquisition of morphosyntactic contrasts.

Feature Geometries and Their Faults

Morphosyntactic feature geometries can express dependency relations and provide a useful visualization of what feature combinations are possible. For example, (1) shows the geometry proposed by Harley and Ritter (2002, 486) for φ-features (person, number, and gender). Underlining indicates default values; for example, Speaker is the default interpretation of a PARTICIPANT node with no marked dependent features.

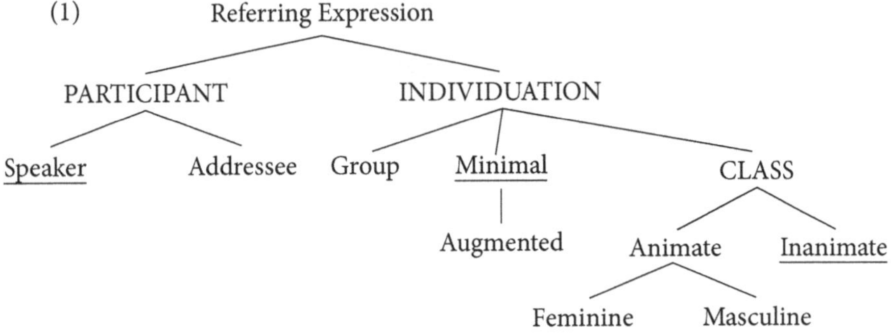

In this tree, the dependency of Feminine and Masculine on Animate encodes the fact that only animate nominals exhibit gender contrasts; likewise, Speaker and Addressee, which refer to specific discourse participants, each entail the presence of the more general PARTICIPANT. In addition to restricting the possible combinations of features through entailments of this sort, the geometry also provides a visual representation of specificity, which is relevant for Vocabulary Insertion in Distributed Morphology (Halle and Marantz 1993): a Vocabulary item that spells out a subordinate feature in the tree is more specific than one that spells out any feature or node that dominates it, and will thus take precedence over it in the competition for insertion.

However, the motivation for feature geometries in morphosyntax is not as robust as in phonology. Feature geometries in phonology are supported by processes of spreading or delinking that operate on nonterminal nodes in the dependency structure. For example, homorganic nasal assimilation in various languages can be analyzed as spreading of the Place node to the nasal from an immediately following consonant (Clements and Hume 1995, 270–71), taking with it all features dominated by Place (potentially Labial, Coronal, Dorsal, [±anterior], etc.) but leaving the manner and voicing of the nasal unaffected. No such support is found in syntax for morphosyntactic feature geometries: their subtrees do not move independently as syntactic constituents, nor can syntactic agreement reasonably be represented as spreading, sensitive to adjacency on a tier, as is phonological assimilation. Likewise, Béjar's (2003, 77, 81) proposal for feature deletion in complex agreement systems simply deletes all marked features, rather than delinking proper subtrees of the geometry.

The motivation for geometric dependencies in morphosyntax has also been challenged, notably by Harbour (2011, 2016) and Harbour and Elsholtz (2012). Some are derivable from semantic entailment, and thus redundant. For example, in

Cowper's (2005b, 446) geometry for grammatical number features, shown in (2), the dependency of >2 (which distinguishes plural from dual) on >1 (which distinguishes dual and plural from singular) is mathematically inherent in the denotations of the features themselves:

(2) Number feature geometry from Cowper (2005b, 446)

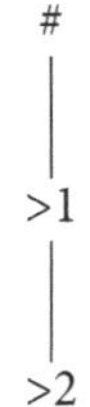

Béjar (2003, 44) also explicitly takes feature-geometric trees to represent entailments. In such cases, the geometry merely represents a logical necessity; it may be a convenient tool for visualizing dependencies, but contributes nothing substantive of its own. Other feature-geometric dependencies, Harbour and Elsholtz (2012) argue, are pure stipulations, encoding unexplained observations. For example, consider the position of Finite in (3):

(3) Tense/mood/aspect feature geometry from Cowper (2005a, 14)

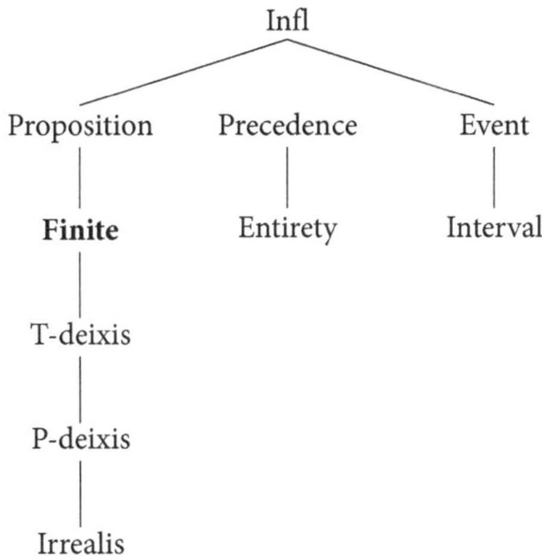

Finite is a purely syntactic feature with no semantic content, representing the presence of subject case and φ-feature agreement. Its dependence on Proposition in (3) expresses, but does nothing to explain, the generalization that all finite clauses denote propositions (but not all propositional clauses are finite). Whereas the dependencies in (2) are redundant, derivable from the semantic content of the features themselves, the position of Finite in (3) is a stipulation. In neither instance does the feature geometry contribute directly to explaining the patterns it encodes.

Finally, the particular feature-geometric approach to person proposed by Harley and Ritter (2002) raises an empirical problem. In languages without a clusivity distinction, Speaker is the default interpretation of a bare PARTICIPANT node (Harley and Ritter 2002, 486); that is, it is not a marked feature of first-person pronouns. However, languages with a clusivity distinction use both Speaker and Hearer as marked dependents of PARTICIPANT. Exclusive first-person forms are specified with Speaker, second-person forms with Hearer, and inclusive forms with both Speaker and Hearer. Harley and Ritter (2002, 490) propose that "the learner can deduce that Speaker is not underspecified in her language from the presence of this inclusive/exclusive contrast." The problem with this approach is that such languages make no use of a bare PARTICIPANT node, contra Harley and Ritter's (2002, 509) expectation "that if a language has a pronoun with a complex geometry, the simpler geometries that form the subconstituents of the complex geometry are also available in that language." But if a bare PARTICIPANT node were available in languages with four-way person systems, we would (wrongly) expect to find pronouns referring to an undifferentiated participant both in these languages and in those that make only a participant/nonparticipant contrast, but not in languages with a three-way system (where a bare PARTICIPANT node is interpreted as specifically first person).

The Contrastive-Hierarchy Approach

Instead of feature geometries, then, we propose that morphosyntactic features are organized into contrastive hierarchies of the sort used in phonology by Dresher (2009) and others cited therein. Unlike a feature geometry, a contrastive hierarchy is not a subsegmental constituent structure; rather, it expresses the relative contrastive scope of features in the inventory as a whole.

Contrastive Hierarchies in Phonology

In phonology, contrastive hierarchies have been used as a mechanism for generating underspecified representations for segments: each phoneme is assigned enough features to distinguish it from the other phonemes with which it contrasts, but redundant features are omitted. Dresher (2009, 16) provides an explicit procedure for constructing a contrastive hierarchy by using features to divide a phonological inventory until each phoneme has a unique representation; this is the Successive Division Algorithm (SDA), shown in (4):

(4) Successive Division Algorithm (SDA; Dresher 2009, 16)

a. Begin with *no* feature specifications: assume all sounds are allophones of a single undifferentiated phoneme.
b. If the set is found to consist of more than one contrasting member, select a feature and divide the set into as many subsets as the feature allows for.
c. Repeat step (b) in each subset: keep dividing up the inventory into sets, applying successive features in turn, until every set has only one member.

The SDA is neutral as to whether features are selected from a universal set (Jakobson, Fant, and Halle 1952 and much subsequent work), or induced by learners from the primary linguistic data (e.g., Mielke 2008). Even if the set of features is universal, though, their hierarchical ordering can vary from one language to another, so that languages with phonetically similar inventories may use different sets of feature specifications. For example, consider languages with three high vowels /i y u/, like Finnish or French. If the features [±back] and [±round] are used to differentiate these phonemes, the SDA allows two different sets of feature specifications. Whichever feature is used first will be assigned to all three vowels, dividing them into one subset of two and one singleton. The second feature will divide the subset of two, but will not be assigned to the third vowel, because that vowel has already been distinguished from the others by the first feature. The two resulting hierarchies are shown in (5) (adapted from Burstynsky 1968, 11):

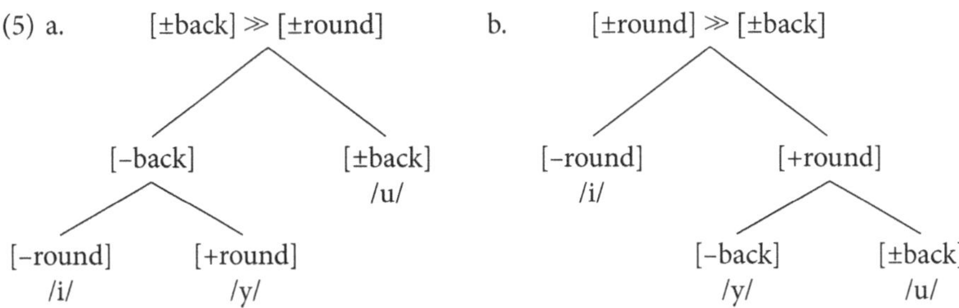

As Burstynsky argues, the phonological behavior of these vowels in Quebec French indicates that the language uses the hierarchy in (5a): the high front vowels /i/ and /y/ pattern together as a natural class in triggering assibilation of dental stops. In Finnish, however, (5b) appears to be the correct ordering: while the round vowels /y/ and /u/ participate in place harmony, /i/ is transparent to it, behaving as though it is unspecified for [±back] (Hall 2017; see also Mackenzie 2011, §3 for another example of cross-linguistic variation in feature scope).

The SDA guarantees that no more features will be used than are required to differentiate the contrasting elements in the inventory. It thus limits the features that can be assigned to any given inventory, while still allowing for cross-linguistic variation within those limits. Contrastive hierarchies also offer insight into phonetic enhancement and the typology of phonemic inventories (Hall 2011), patterns of reduction (Spahr 2014), and diachronic change (Dresher, Harvey, and Oxford 2014).

Contrastive Hierarchies in Morphosyntax

We propose that the dependency relations among interpretable morphosyntactic features reflect contrastive hierarchies, not feature-geometric structures. The central insight of a contrastive hierarchy is that the applicability and the interpretation of a feature depend on the domain in which it is contrastive, as defined by the features above it in the hierarchy. Both feature geometries and contrastive hierarchies provide a way to describe scope relations among features. However, the expressive possibilities made available by feature geometry differ from those that can be expressed by a contrastive hierarchy. In a feature geometry with privative features, only marked features can have dependents. Suppose that a feature F has two dependents, G and H. If H is a dependent of G, giving a nonbranching geometry like the one in (2), then there are three possible representations, listed in (6a). If H and G are sisters in the dependency structure, both dependent on F but neither of the two on the other, then there are four possible representations, listed in (6b). There is no way, without specifying [–G] explicitly, to restrict the domain of [H] to only those instances of F that do not bear [G] (i.e., to rule out the combination FGH in (6b)).

(6) a. {F, FG, FGH} b. {F, FG, FH, FGH}

With a contrastive hierarchy, the assignment of features divides the inventory, rather than structuring the representation, and a given feature takes scope only over the subinventory that it divides. This means that there are three possible contrastive hierarchies in which a set defined by the feature [F] is divided first by [G] and then by [H]. In all three cases, [G] divides the inventory of [F]-bearing elements into those bearing [G] and those lacking [G]. This gives two subinventories, specified [F] and [FG]. [H] can then divide either one or both of these subinventories. If [H] divides only the [FG] set, the result is the same as in (6a). If [H] divides both subinventories, the result is the same as (6b). The third possibility, though, is that [H] divides the [F] set but not the [FG] set; this yields three subinventories {F, FG, FH} in which [G] and [H] do not co-occur.

If features are privative, as assumed in most feature-geometric approaches, then contrastive hierarchies allow more different dependency structures than feature geometries do. The difference in expressive power between the two approaches is less obvious with binary features, but we show in the following section that in the specific case of person features, contrastive hierarchies allow an account of the typological patterns using simpler features than those proposed by Harbour (2016), while retaining the key advantages of his approach. The question of whether features in general are binary, privative, or a mix of the two is a separate issue (on which see Cowper and Hall 2014); in all cases, contrastive hierarchies offer a principled, nonstipulative way of representing dependencies, and their expressive power can reduce the burden on the definitions of the features themselves.

The Representation and Typology of Person

As just stated, the notion of contrastive scope is not tied to any particular conception of what a feature is. Contrastive hierarchies can be combined with features with various formal properties. However, in at least one case, the contrastive-hierarchy approach makes it possible to use a less powerful kind of feature.

Harbour's Person Features

Harbour (2016) presents a comprehensive theory of grammatical person that accounts for the attested typological range of systems of contrast, but requires features to be formalized as operators that add or subtract elements of semilattices, rather than as first-order predicates. The features operate on a universal person ontology comprising a unique speaker *i*, a unique hearer *u*, and arbitrarily many others *o*. From an extensive typological survey, Harbour observes that only five of the fifteen logically possible sets of person contrasts ("partitions") are attested. These are shown in (7); in Harbour's notation, a subscript *o* indicates the addition of zero or more others (third persons):

(7)	a	"Monopartition"	no contrasts	$\{i_o, iu_o, u_o, o_o\}$
	b	Author bipartition	first vs. non-first	$\{i_o, iu_o\} / \{u_o, o_o\}$
	c	Participant bipartition	non-third vs. third	$\{i_o, iu_o, u_o\} / o_o$
	d	Standard tripartition	first vs. second vs. third	$\{i_o, iu_o\} / u_o / o_o$
	e	Quadripartition	excl. vs. incl. vs. second vs. third	$i_o / iu_o / u_o / o_o$

Other logically possible sets of contrasts are unattested; for example, no language is known to make only an addressee bipartition (second vs. nonsecond). Such a partition may arise as a syncretism in a particular morphological paradigm, but only in a language with a richer overall system of person contrasts (tripartition or quadripartition).

The fact that the most richly articulated system has quadripartition suggests that there are no more than two binary features available for marking person contrasts. The existence of author and participant bipartitions suggests that these features are [±author] and [±participant], and the absence of addressee bipartitions suggests that [±hearer] is not available, at least not as the only feature in a system. The challenge, then, is to explain how tripartition and quadripartition, each of which requires two features, can exist as distinct types of systems without positing features that would also generate unattested partitions.

Like others, notably Halle (1997), Harbour posits that Universal Grammar provides two binary person features, [±author] and [±participant]. Harbour's crucial innovation is that his features, rather than denoting first-order predicates such as "includes the speaker" or "includes a discourse participant," are functions that operate on (semi)lattices to add or subtract individuals. The effects of his features are as follows:

- [+author] adds the speaker *i* to a lattice.
- [−author] subtracts the speaker *i* from a lattice.
- [+participant] disjointly adds all discourse participants {*i*, *iu*, *u*} to a lattice.
- [−participant] subtracts all participants {*i*, *iu*, *u*} from a lattice.

As in other accounts, monopartition systems use no person features, and each of the two attested bipartitions uses one feature. The importance of Harbour's formal implementation of the features as operations emerges in his account of tripartition and quadripartition. Each of these two systems uses both features, but in opposite orders. Applying [±author] before [±participant] derives the standard tripartition as in (8).

(8) [±author] before [±participant] (Harbour 2016, 99)

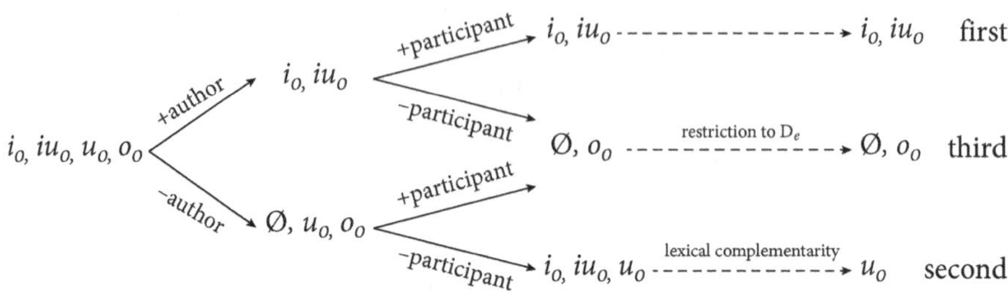

Applying [±participant] before [±author] derives quadripartition as in (9).

(9) [±participant] before [±author] (Harbour 2016, 99)

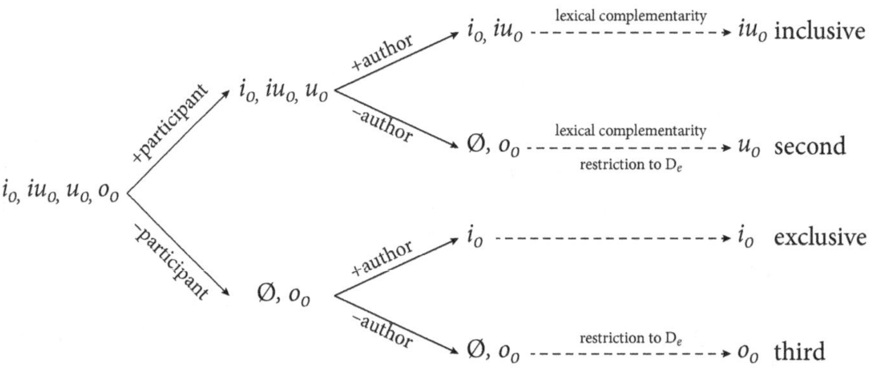

In addition to the redefinition of the features themselves as operations that can apply in a particular order, Harbour requires two interpretive principles that apply to their output. The first, restriction to the domain of entities (D_e), excludes the empty set Ø from the output. In both (8) and (9), the sequences of features that generate third person yield semilattices that include the empty set as well as all nonempty sets of nonparticipants; restriction to D_e ensures that only nonempty third persons are included.

The second principle, lexical complementarity, eliminates overlap between subsets in accordance with the Elsewhere Principle. In (8), for example, because the output of [−author, +participant], $\{i_o, iu_o, u_o\}$, is a superset of the output of [+author, +participant], $\{i_o, iu_o\}$, lexical complementarity restricts [−author, +participant] to u_o (its only member that is not also in [+author, +participant]). Likewise, the sequence [+participant, +author] in (9) yields $\{i_o, iu_o\}$, which would be a general first person rather than a first person inclusive; its interpretation is restricted to the inclusive (iu_o) because [−participant, +author] yields i_o. Lexical complementarity is similar to, but must apply independently from, other instances of the subset principle. For example, the fact that a form like English *you* in a tripartition system is interpreted as not including the speaker cannot be merely a scalar implicature, nor can it be derived from competition between Vocabulary items in Distributed Morphology.

Harbour's approach generates exactly the attested range of systems of grammatical person contrasts, but it is formally complex. The features themselves must be defined as operations rather than as predicates, and their output must be subject to further rules. Additionally, in the derivation of tripartition in (8), third person has two possible representations: [−author, −participant] or [+author, −participant]. Harbour (2016, 92–93) posits a parameter to allow tripartition languages to use one or the other, but not both.

The diagrams in (8) and (9) are not contrastive hierarchies like those generated by the SDA using traditional first-order predicate features. Notably, they are not trees, as (8) contains two routes from $\{i_o, iu_o, u_o, o_o\}$ to third person. However, the sequencing of operations in Harbour's approach is broadly analogous to the role of contrastive scope in the SDA: the first feature defines the formal objects to which the second applies, which in turn determine the interpretive consequences of the second feature. We propose that the key insights of Harbour's approach can be retained with formally simpler features if the ordering of features is recast as scope-taking in a contrastive hierarchy.

Simplifying the Person Features

In general, interpretable morphosyntactic features, like their phonological counterparts, have been understood as first-order predicates, denoting a property [F] that a given lexical item either has (represented by [+F] in a binary system, or by [F] if the feature is privative) or lacks (represented as [−F] or the absence of privative [F]). When a lexical item is specified with more than one such feature, the two compose intersectively. In the absence of the scope differences made possible by the contrastive hierarchy, this means that the order of application of features should make no difference to the result. However, the adoption of the contrastive-hierarchy approach can create a situation in which order makes a difference.

We assume Harbour's (2016) ontology of persons, repeated in (10), where *i* is the unique author, *u* the unique addressee, and *o*, *o′*, *o″*, and so on an arbitrary number of others.

(10) $\pi = \{i, u, o, o', o'', \ldots\}$

The inventory to be divided is the set of possible combinations of persons; in other words, the power set of π.[1]

Like Harbour, we posit two binary features, [±author] and [±participant]. However, we propose that they denote first-order predicates as in (11).

(11) a. [+author] = "includes the speaker"
b. [−author] = "does not include the speaker"
c. [+participant] = "includes a(t least one) discourse participant"
d. [−participant] = "does not include a discourse participant"

The person system of a given language may use one, both, or neither of the two features. If a language uses both, then one of the features will take scope over the other. Cross-linguistically, either order is possible. This gives five possible situations, the first three of which are listed in (12).

(12) a. The language uses no person features. No person-based distinctions are found in the grammar. This is monopartition, as in (7a).

b. The language uses only [±author]. First persons (both inclusive and exclusive) are distinguished from all others. There is no clusivity contrast, and second persons do not contrast with third persons. This yields the author bipartition (7b), dividing [−author] persons (u_o, o_o) from [+author] persons (i_o, iu_o).

c. The language uses only [±participant]. First and second persons are together distinguished from third persons. There is no clusivity contrast, and no contrast between first and second persons. This is the participant bipartition in (7c), which separates [+participant] persons (i_o, u_o, iu_o) from [−participant] persons (o_o).

If the language uses both features, then their relative scope determines how the inventory is partitioned. If [±participant] takes wider scope, then an initial division is made between [+participant] first and second persons, on the one hand, and [−participant] third persons on the other. Then, [±author] makes a second division among the [+participant] members, separating those that include *i* from those that do not. This gives the standard tripartition (7d), with contrasting first, second, and third persons but no clusivity distinction, as shown in (13).

(13) Tripartition: [±participant] takes scope over [±author]

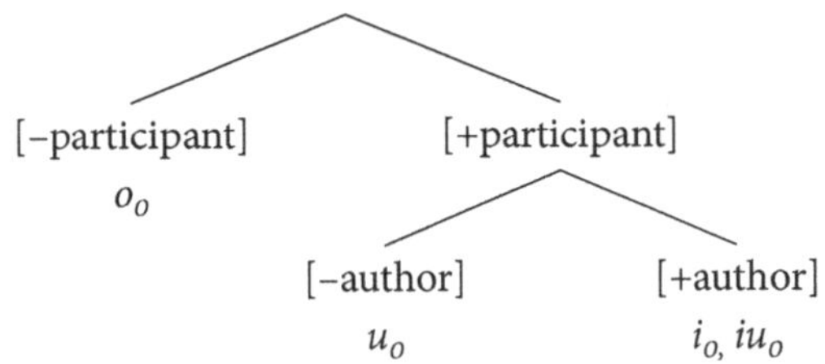

The final possibility has [±author] taking wider scope, making the first division between all first persons (inclusive or exclusive) on the one hand, and second and third persons on the other. Then [±participant] divides each of the subinventories. The division of the [−author] subinventory is straightforward: all elements including *u* are [+participant], and all those that lack *u* are [−participant]. The division of the [+author] subinventory is slightly less obvious, since at first blush, all of its members are [+participant] as defined in (11c). We propose that in this instance, the interpretation of [±participant] is automatically narrowed to "{includes, does not include} a participant other than speaker." Essentially, the effect is to reinterpret [±participant] as referring only to the addressee. This is the only possible interpretation that allows it to be contrastive over an inventory where the inclusion of the speaker has already been marked. Note that this same narrowing, while not strictly necessary, does no harm if it applies to the division of the [−author] subinventory by [±participant].

Dividing the [+author] subinventory with the more narrowly defined [±participant] gives the clusivity distinction, deriving (7e) as in (14).

(14) Quadripartition: [±author] takes scope over [±participant]

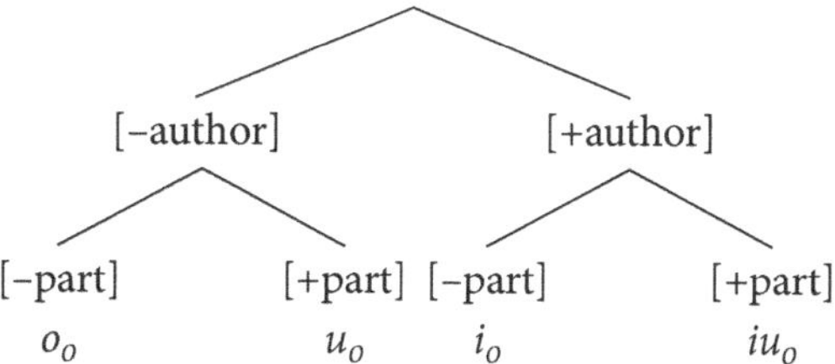

One might argue that this approach smuggles the feature [±hearer] into the set of possible person systems, making the account vulnerable to Harbour's (2016, §8.2) objections. He persuasively argues against approaches that involve parametric choice either between the use of [±participant] and [±hearer] or between allowing and excluding the combination of values that would distinguish inclusive from exclusive first persons (e.g., Halle 1997). While such systems maximally distinguish the same four possible persons as do Harbour's features and the ones proposed here, the logical combinations of the three binary features predict more than the five attested partitions. Specifically, they do not explain why [±hearer] is never used alone, distinguishing second persons from an undifferentiated category including first and third persons. In addition, they do not explain why, if one combination of features can be "parametrically deactivated," others cannot.

We avoid these objections by linking the parametric variation in the semantics of [±participant] to its contrastive scope. A given feature's interpretation is consistently contingent on the domain in which it marks a contrast. This is analogous to the phonetic interpretation of phonological features. For example, consider a vowel inventory specified first with [±high], and then within each resulting subinventory for [±back]. The articulatory and acoustic difference between [−back] /i/ and [+back] /u/ in the [+high] subinventory is likely to be appreciably greater than that between [−back] /e/ and [+back] /o/ in the [−high] subinventory; the shape of the oral cavity dictates that the phonetic distance between [−back] and [+back] narrows as the height of the tongue decreases. Similarly, Clements (1991) represents degrees of vowel height by successive hierarchical application of a single feature [±open].[2] A vowel marked [+open] at the highest division in the hierarchy is low relative to the phonetic space as a whole. Specifying [+open] within the [−open] branch picks out the lowest vowels within the non-low category, namely mid vowels. While [±open] consistently indicates a single dimension of phonetic contrast, the difference along that dimension is wider or narrower according to the feature's place in the hierarchy. Although the meaning of [±participant] is not gradient as vowel features are, its interpretation similarly depends on its position in the contrastive hierarchy.

The proposed features thus give exactly the attested set of person systems, with no need to invoke lexical complementarity: each combination of features straightforwardly denotes the appropriate set of possible referents, not a proper superset. The interpretive narrowing of [±participant] in (14), which gives essentially [±hearer], derives from its position in the contrastive hierarchy. No analogous narrowing of [±author] is possible to allow full cross-classification in (13), because the interpretation "speaker other than a discourse participant" is nonsensical; this ordering of the features produces only the standard tripartition. We conclude that with a contrastive hierarchy, it is possible to account for exactly the attested person partitions with first-order features and no more additional machinery than Harbour (2016) requires.

Acquisition

In addition to ensuring that representations include only contrastive features, the SDA suggests a learning path: as children acquire contrasts, they build the representations that encode them (Dresher 2014, §4). Ideally, we might expect the order of acquisition to correspond to hierarchical scope: features that are higher in the tree would be acquired first.

However, actual acquisition paths will likely turn out to be more complicated. Some proposed phonological contrastive hierarchies do not map readily to acquisition sequences, and suggest that learners may need to do some backtracking. For example, Hall (2007) proposes a hierarchy for Czech consonants in which the first two features divide the inventory into sonorants, obstruents, and the trilled fricative /r̝/; /r̝/ is typically the *last* consonant Czech children accurately produce, though this could plausibly be attributed to its articulatory complexity rather than to its phonological encoding.

In the most straightforward mapping from contrastive scope to order of acquisition, our person feature hierarchies make the following predictions. In a tripartition language, where [±participant] takes wider scope, children will first distinguish participants from third persons. Early learners may fail to distinguish the representations of first and second person, and thus seem to confuse first- and second-person forms. In a quadripartition language, with [±author] above [±participant], children will begin by distinguishing first persons from second and third; early learners may conflate second person with third, and inclusive with exclusive.

To what extent are these predictions borne out? It is difficult to say, partly because of an abundance of potential confounds, and partly because investigations into the acquisition of person systems seldom probe the question of contrasts directly. Children acquiring tripartition languages do sometimes confuse first and second person in production, but second person is often the first to be mastered in comprehension; see, for example, Moyer et al. (2015, 2) and references cited therein, especially Oshima-Takane (1992). Considerably less work has been done on the acquisition of quadripartition languages.

Although the prospect is complicated by mismatches between comprehension and production and by the possibility of backtracking, the predictions for acquisition made by the contrastive-hierarchy approach show promise. Moreover, this view of how features are organized has broader implications for how questions about acquisition should be framed: to look at how learners acquire person or any analogous grammatical system, we should focus on acquisition of *distinctions* (à la Jakobson 1941) rather than of *items*.

Conclusion

In phonology, feature geometries are motivated not only by dependency relations among features, but by the fact that those dependencies are active in autosegmental processes (spreading and delinking). In other words, there is evidence that they are part of the structural representation of each segment. It remains open exactly how phonological contrastive hierarchies relate to phonological feature geometries, since they encode some of the same information in different ways. See Iosad (2012) for a proposal combining the SDA with Morén's (2003, 2006) Parallel Structures Model of feature geometry. Broadly speaking, contrastive hierarchies are paradigmatic, defining systems of oppositions, and feature geometries are syntagmatic, structuring combinations of features in phonological representations.

In morphosyntax, syntagmatic representations are phrase structure (and word structure) trees, and operations like Merge and Move apply to them. No clear evidence has yet emerged to suggest that the dependencies among morphosyntactic features are relevant to any of these operations. The dependencies that have previously been expressed in morphosyntactic feature geometries are real, but they are paradigmatic rather than syntagmatic.

Contrastive hierarchies offer a way of representing these dependencies that does not imply that morphosyntactic features should engage in the same kinds of spreading and delinking operations that apply to phonological autosegments. At the same time, contrastive hierarchies do other useful things that feature geometries cannot. They represent scope relations between features in a way that is neither redundant nor stipulative, and account for the fact that the interpretation of a feature depends in part on the domain in which it is contrastive. They are compatible with multiple views of the formal properties of features themselves, and in the case of privative features make it possible to express the dependence of one feature on the absence of another. For person features, we have shown how a contrastive-hierarchy approach can reduce the required formal complexity of the features themselves. Finally, they present an opportunity to shed new light on the acquisition of grammatical elements by framing the question as pertaining to contrasts rather than to Vocabulary items.

Notes

We are grateful to Neil Banerjee, Bronwyn Bjorkman, B. Elan Dresher, David Lightfoot, and Andrew Peters, and to the audiences at the 2016 Tromsø Hierarchies Workshop, the 2017 Georgetown University Round Table, and the 2017 Annual Meeting of the Canadian Linguistic Association, for helpful questions and discussion on this topic.

1 Or perhaps only the nonempty members of $P(\pi)$, as per Harbour's operation of restriction to D_e. Note, however, that for us this would be a restriction on the input to the SDA rather than a repair on its output, and that in any case both our system and Harbour's predict (plausibly enough) that if empty persons are conceptually possible at all (cf. Harbour 2016, 85–86), they will be referred to with the same forms as third persons (o_o).

2 This re-application of (potentially contrary values of) a single feature is similar to Harbour's (2011, 2014) treatment of grammatical number. For example, applying first [−minimal] and then [+minimal] picks out the minimal subregion of the nonminimal region of the ontological space.

References

Béjar, Susana. 2003. *Phi-Syntax: A Theory of Agreement.* PhD diss., University of Toronto.

Bonet, Eulàlia. 1991. *Morphology after Syntax: Pronominal Clitics in Romance.* Doctoral diss., Massachusetts Institute of Technology.

Burstynsky, Edward N. 1968. "Quelques observations de phonologie générative appliquées au français canadien." In *Recherches sur la structure phonique du français canadien*, edited by Pierre R. Léon, 9–17. Montréal: Marcel Didier.

Clements, G. N. 1991. "Vowel Height Assimilation in Bantu Languages." In *Proceedings of the Seventeenth Annual Meeting of the Berkeley Linguistics Society*, 25–64. Berkeley, CA: Berkeley Linguistics Society.

Clements, G. N., and Elizabeth Hume. 1995. "The Internal Organization of Speech Sounds." In *The Handbook of Phonological Theory*, edited by John Goldsmith, 245–306. Oxford: Blackwell.

Cowper, Elizabeth. 2005a. "The Geometry of Interpretable Features: Infl in English and Spanish." *Language* 81 (1): 10–46.

Cowper, Elizabeth. 2005b. "A Note on Number." *Linguistic Inquiry* 36 (3): 441–55.

Cowper, Elizabeth, and Daniel Currie Hall. 2014. "Reductiō ad discrīmen: Where Features Come From." *Nordlyd* 41 (2): 145–64.

Dresher, B. Elan. 2009. *The Contrastive Hierarchy in Phonology.* Cambridge: Cambridge University Press.

Dresher, B. Elan. 2014. "The Arch Not the Stones: Universal Feature Theory without Universal Features." *Nordlyd* 41 (2): 165–81.

Dresher, B. Elan. 2015. "The Motivation for Contrastive Feature Hierarchies in Phonology." *Linguistic Variation* 15 (1): 1–40.

Dresher, B. Elan. 2016. "Contrast in Phonology, 1867–1967: History and Development." *Annual Review of Linguistics* 2:53–73.

Dresher, B. Elan. This volume. "Contrastive Feature Hierarchies in Phonology: Variation and Universality."

Dresher, B. Elan, Christopher Harvey, and Will Oxford. 2014. "Contrast Shift as a Type of Diachronic Change." In *NELS 43: Proceedings of the Forty-Third Annual Meeting of the North East Linguistic Society* 1, edited by Hsin-Lun Huang, Ethan Poole, and Amanda Rysling, 103–16. Amherst, MA: GLSA.

Hall, Daniel Currie. 2007. *The Role and Representation of Contrast in Phonological Theory.* PhD diss., University of Toronto.

Hall, Daniel Currie. 2011. "Phonological Contrast and Its Phonetic Enhancement: Dispersedness without Dispersion." *Phonology 28* (1): 1–54.

Hall, Daniel Currie. 2017. "Contrastive Specification in Phonology." In *Oxford Research Encyclopedia of Linguistics*, edited by Mark Aronoff. Oxford: Oxford University Press, 2014. doi:10.1093/acrefore/9780199384655.013.26.

Halle, Morris. 1997. "Distributed Morphology: Impoverishment and Fission." *MIT Working Papers in Linguistics* 30:125–49.

Halle, Morris, and Alec Marantz. 1993. "Distributed Morphology and the Pieces of Inflection." In *The View from Building 20: Essays in Linguistics in Honor of Sylvain Bromberger*, edited by Kenneth Hale and Samuel Jay Keyser, 111–76. Cambridge, MA: MIT Press.

Harbour, Daniel. 2011. "Descriptive and Explanatory Markedness." *Morphology* 21 (2): 223–45.

Harbour, Daniel. 2016. *Impossible Persons.* Cambridge, MA: MIT Press.

Harbour, Daniel, and Christian Elsholtz. 2012. "Feature Geometry: Self-Destructed." MS, Queen Mary University of London and Technische Universität Graz.

Harley, Heidi. 1994. "Hug a Tree: Deriving the Morphosyntactic Feature Hierarchy." *MIT Working Papers in Linguistics* 21:289–320.

Harley, Heidi, and Elizabeth Ritter. 2002. "Person and Number in Pronouns: A Feature-Geometric Analysis." *Language* 78 (3): 482–526.

Iosad, Pavel. 2012. *Representation and Variation in Substance-Free Phonology: A Case Study in Celtic.* PhD diss., University of Tromsø.

Jakobson, Roman. 1941. *Kindersprache, Aphasie und allgemeine Lautgesetze.* Uppsala: Uppsala Universitetet.

Jakobson, Roman, Gunnar Fant, and Morris Halle. 1952. *Preliminaries to Speech Analysis: The Distinctive Features and Their Correlates.* Cambridge, MA: MIT Press.

Mackenzie, Sara. 2011. "Contrast and the Evaluation of Similarity: Evidence from Consonant Harmony." *Lingua* 121 (8): 1401–23.

Mielke, Jeff. 2008. *The Emergence of Distinctive Features.* Oxford: Oxford University Press.

Morén, Bruce. 2003. "The Parallel Structures Model of Feature Geometry." *Working Papers of the Cornell Phonetics Laboratory* 15:194–270.

Morén, Bruce. 2006. "The Division of Labor between Segment-Internal Structure and Violable Constraints." In *Freedom of Analysis*, edited by Sylvia Blaho, Patrik Bye, and Martin Krämer, 313–44. The Hague: Mouton.

Moyer, Morgan, Kaitlyn Harrigan, Valentine Hacquard, and Jeffrey Lidz. 2015. "2-Year-Olds' Comprehension of Personal Pronouns." In *BUCLD 39 Online Proceedings Supplement*, edited by Elizabeth Grillo, Kyle Jepson, and Maria LaMendola, 11 pp. Boston: Boston University. http://www.bu.edu/bucld/files/2015/06/Moyer.pdf.

Oshima-Takane, Yuriko. 1992. "Analysis of Pronominal Errors: A Case-Study." *Journal of Child Language* 19 (1): 111–31.

Spahr, Christopher. 2014. "A Contrastive Hierarchical Account of Positional Neutralization." *The Linguistic Review* 31 (3–4): 551–85. doi:10.1515/tlr-2014-0008.

Chapter 4

Allophonic Systems as a Variable within Individual Speakers

BETSY SNELLER
University of Pennsylvania

The introduction of the linguistic variable in Labov's 1966 "The Linguistic Variable as a Structural Unit" ushered in the new subfield of variationist linguistics, with the linguistic variable as the central unit of analysis. Labov's original formulation of the linguistic variable pertained primarily to phonological variation, and a longstanding definition of the linguistic variable since has been "saying 'the same thing' in several different ways" (Labov 1972, 271). While the early field of language variation debated whether syntax and morphology could be a linguistic variable (Lavandera 1978; Labov 1978; Romaine 1981), subsequent years of the study of language variation has settled on the linguistic variable operating within all levels of the grammar, from syntax (Kroch 1989; Santorini 1993) and morphology (Miller 2013; Krejci and Hilton 2017) to phonology (Sneller 2014; Trudgill 1974) and phonetics (Podesva 2007; Labov 1963).

While linguistic variables have been demonstrated for every level of the grammar, there is more to be said about the nature of phonological variables. Most studies of phonological variables involve a single segment variably replacing another segment, such as the change in Montreal French between [ʁ] and [r] for canonical /r/ (Sankoff and Blondeau 2007) or variation between a monophthong [u] and a diphthong [aʊ] in words like house in Buckie Scottish English (Smith, Durham, and Richards 2013). Often, this variation may be between more than one variant, as in the variation between [h], [θ], and [f] for word-initial /θ/ in Glasgow English (Stuart-Smith et al. 2013), or as may occur when phonetic lenition processes or loan word phonology interact with phonological variation (Sankoff and Blondeau 2007). The study of phonology more generally from a variationist perspective, however, encompasses far more than just variation between segments; for example, chain shifts such as the Northern Cities Shift or the Southern Shift (Labov, Ash, and Boberg 2006) describe a phonological change affecting an entire subset of a phonological inventory. From the very beginning, Labov's formal description of the linguistic variable conceived of variable nonrhoticity in New York English as a systemic variable: "It concerns the oscillations of entire phonemic categories: the set of ingliding phonemes appears and disappears as a whole" (1966, 6). In other words, Labov analyzed speakers as varying between one phonemic *system* that includes ingliding phonemes and a second system that does not include ingliding phonemes, rather than analyzing speakers as variably deleting a single segment /r/. Since Labov (1966), however, structural phonological units have typically not been the subject of analyses of intraspeaker variation, leaving some work to be done regarding the status of structural phonological targets as an intraspeaker variable.

In this chapter, I provide evidence that phonological variation does occur over a structurally abstract phonological unit: allophonic systems. This variation is found in speakers who grew up during a phonological restructuring of an allophonic split in /æ/ in Philadelphia. This chapter is structured as follows: First, I provide some linguistic background on the restructuring of /æ/ in Philadelphia. I then analyze the productions of forty-two speakers who grew up during this restructuring, finding evidence of allophonic variation in a subset of speakers, for whom I provide a more fine-grained analysis. Finally, I end with a discussion of the implications of finding intraspeaker allophonic variation on the fields of language variation and phonology.

Background: /æ/ in Philadelphia

In this section, I provide some background into the allophonic restructuring currently underway in Philadelphia. For a more in-depth analysis of this change, I refer the reader to Labov, Fisher, Gylfadottir, Henderson, and Sneller (2016).

Restructuring of /ae/ in Philadelphia

Beginning with the first treatments (Ferguson 1972), Philadelphia English has been described as producing a split in the low front vowel /æ/ into two distinct targets: tense and lax. The lax target is a nonperipheral low front vowel [æ] that is relatively shorter in duration (avg: 119 ms). The tense target is both fronted and raised along the front periphery, exhibits a longer average duration (130 ms), and is often produced with an inglide ([æᵊ], [ɛᵊ], [eᵊ], or [iᵊ]). For exposition, I follow the notation of Labov (1989), which denotes the lax allophone as *æ* and the tense allophone as *æh*. This traditional split is governed by a regular phonological rule, shown in (1) and henceforth referred to as PHL.

(1) PHL: æ → æh / __ [+ant] ∧ ([+nasal] ∨ [−voice +fricative])]σ

PHL is a phonologically regular rule triggered by a disjunctive set of phonological contexts: nasals or voiceless fricatives which are also anterior and syllable-final ({m, n, f, θ, s}), producing tense *æh* in *ham* but lax *æ* in *hammer*. In addition to the regular PHL rule, /æ/ in Philadelphia has also developed some lexical specificity, with some words (*mad, bad, glad*) produced as exceptionally tense and others (e.g., *and, ran, carafe*) produced as exceptionally lax. The unnatural class of phonological triggers and the existence of lexical exceptions have caused some scholars to classify this split as phonemic (Ferguson 1972; Labov 1989; Labov, Ash, and Boberg 2006). In this chapter, I follow the position of more recent work (Labov et al. 2016), as well as Kiparsky 1995, which find evidence that speakers of Philadelphia English born after 1985 treat this split as an allophonic distinction rather than a phonemic one. Additionally, following Yang (2016), I allow productive rules, including those that are allophonic, to list a finite number of lexical exceptions. The traditional Philadelphia PHL data, along with its lexical exceptions, falls well below the tolerance threshold for lexical exceptions and can therefore be considered to constitute a productive allophonic rule. However, the traditional PHL split is rapidly being replaced by the geographically widespread nasal allophonic split, henceforth NAS (Labov, Rosenfelder, and Fruehwald 2013; Labov et al. 2016), shown in (2):

(2) NAS: æ → æh / __ [+nasal]

NAS is a phonologically simple allophonic rule that tenses /æ/ before any nasal segment with no lexical exceptions. NAS has been spreading across many dialects of North America (Labov, Ash, and Boberg 2006; Becker and Wong 2009; Wagner et al. 2016), including into the geographic area surrounding Philadelphia. Labov et al. (2016) demonstrate that NAS is prevalent in the speech of younger Philadelphians who attended elite schools in Philadelphia, and argue that it therefore constitutes a change from above likely instituted through dialect contact. This position has been supported by computational simulations in Sneller, Fruehwald, and Yang (2017), who argue that NAS could not have been endogenously innovated in Philadelphia and that, instead, dialect contact with NAS speakers moving into Philadelphia best accounts for the change from PHL to NAS.

Competition between PHL and NAS

Both PHL and NAS result in tense and lax tokens that fall into roughly the same phonetic space. This is shown in Figure 4.1, which displays normalized F1 and F2 measurements of /æ/ tokens for a classic PHL speaker (left) and a new NAS speaker (right), classified into their tenseness categories according to their respective phonological rules.

Notably, PHL and NAS share some of the same conditioning factors. Indeed, because most /æ/ words fall under the elsewhere condition, the majority of tokens would be produced identically whether the speaker was adhering to PHL or to NAS. While PHL comprises two phonological triggers (tautosyllabic anterior nasals and tautosyllabic anterior voiceless fricatives) and NAS comprises only one (nasals), analyzing the production of the whole community requires breaking these triggers down into six main conditioning factors, which either are shared between PHL and NAS or would result in different productions from a PHL speaker and a NAS speaker. The six major phonological conditions, their reflexes under PHL and NAS, and their type and token frequency are shown in Table 4.1.[1]

Figure 4.2, which is adapted from Labov et al. (2016), traces these six conditioning factors over the history of recorded data from Philadelphia. The diagonal measure, F2-2*F1, acts as a measure of tenseness: the higher along the *y*-axis, the more raised along the front periphery the token is. Data is drawn from the Philadelphia

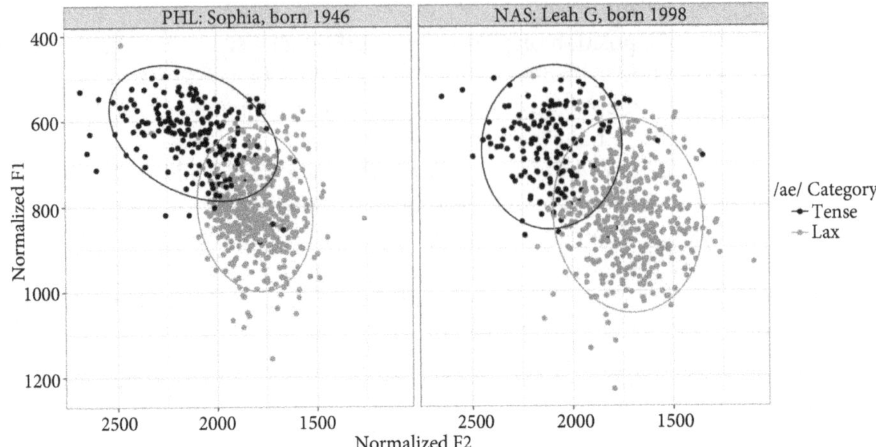

Figure 4.1. Phonetic similarities between tense and lax categories for PHL speaker (left) and NAS speaker (right)

Table 4.1. The six major phonological conditioning factors between PHL and NAS

Conditioning Factor	Example	PHL	NAS	Token freq	Type freq
Tautosyllabic anterior nasal	*hand*	**Tense**	**Tense**	.20	.19
Tautosyllabic anterior voiceless fricative	*class*	**Tense**	**Lax**	.16	.07
Intervocalic anterior nasal	*manage*	**Lax**	**Tense**	.06	.10
Velar nasal	*hang*	**Lax**	**Tense**	.03	.04
Lexical exceptions to tense	*mad*	**Tense**	**Lax**	.05	.001
Elsewhere	*cat*	**Lax**	**Lax**	.51	.60

Neighborhood Corpus (Labov and Rosenfelder 2013), as well as from the Influence of Higher Education on Local Phonology Corpus (Labov 2015). For each speaker, the mean measurement of each of the six conditioning factors is plotted. Figure 4.2 shows the long-lived stability of PHL, with the three traditionally tense categories consistently tense until the early 1980s, when some speakers begin to produce NAS. Labov et al. (2016) argued that PHL and NAS were allophonic systems in competition on the level of the community, with NAS winning out for speakers born at the end of our data set for 2000–2009.

While PHL and NAS are argued to compete on the level of the community, we are still left with the question of how this community-level pattern results from indi-

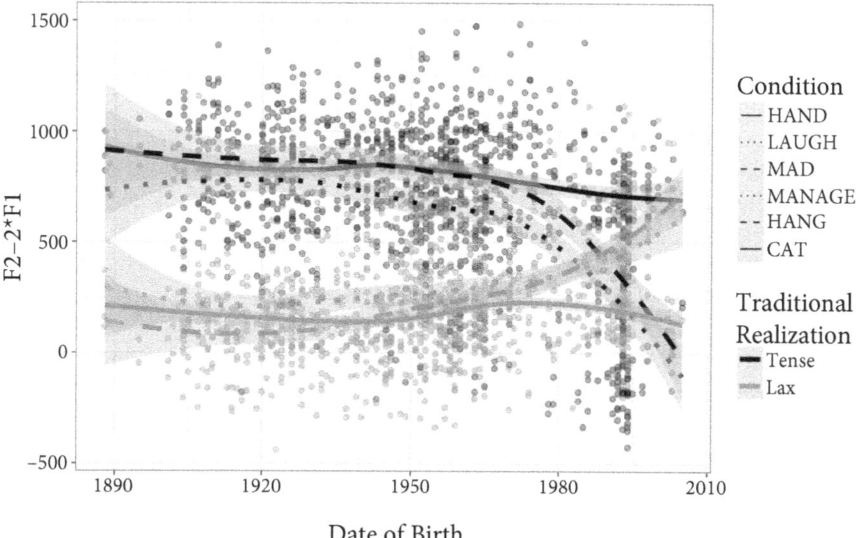

Figure 4.2 Mean values for each phonological conditioning factor for each speaker in the PNC and IHELP data

Source: Labov et al. 2016.

vidual speakers. One possibility, following from a strong reading of Fruehwald (2013) and Janda and Joseph (2003), is that speakers in Philadelphia acquire only one of either PHL or NAS, and stick to their one allophonic system throughout their entire life. This method of change would mean that Figure 4.2 simply shows that NAS is the allophonic system selected by a rapidly increasing number of Philadelphians. The second possibility—which is the central argument of the current chapter—is that individual speakers born during the community-wide transition from PHL to NAS have learned *both* PHL and NAS, and that these two allophonic systems act as a variable for these speakers, similarly to syntactic competition found in Kroch (1989) and posited for phonological change in Fruehwald, Gress-Wright, and Wallenberg (2013).

Individual Speaker Productions

To test whether PHL and NAS act as a single linguistic variable for individual speakers, I closely analyzed the production of forty-two speakers. Data were drawn from the IHELP corpus (Labov 2015), and analysis is restricted to white speakers born after 1980, which is the population displaying variation between the traditional PHL /æ/ split and the incoming NAS split.[2]

Analysis

To test whether PHL and NAS are both present as underlying systems for individual speakers, it is necessary to analyze individual tokens as having been produced by either PHL or NAS. In most cases of phonological change, particularly for changes involving vowel mergers or splits, classifying individual tokens as being produced by the old or the new phonological system is near to impossible due to the overlapping distributions of tokens. The allophonic restructuring from PHL to NAS, however, provides a rare opportunity to classify each individual word token as having been produced under one system or the other. Because both rules result in phonetically distinct tense and lax targets, it is possible to classify individual tokens as being either tense or lax. If these tokens fall under one of the four conditioning factors that distinguish PHL from NAS (shown in Table 4.1), they can then be classified as having been produced by one of the two allophonic rules.

Token classification was conducted as follows. First, each speaker's /æ/ tokens were split into training data and test data. Training data were composed of the two conditioning factors that are shared between PHL and NAS, with *hand* tokens classified as tense and *cat* tokens classified as lax. This allowed us to characterize speakers' individual tense and lax targets. An example is shown in Figure 4.3a, with 95 percent confidence ellipses drawn around the training data. Training tokens are plotted in gray. Test data were composed of the four conditioning factors that are different between PHL and NAS. A glm classifier was created in R (R Core Team 2017)—with fixed effects of F1 measurement, F2 measurement, F3 measurement, duration, and syllable stress, as shown in (3)—and fit to the training data. These coefficients were then used to predict the probability of tense or lax for the test data set, using the predict() function, as shown in (4).

(3) predmod <- glm(tense ~ F1*F2*F3*duration*stress)

(4) testdata$tenseProb <- predict(predmod)

Using the productions of the traditional PHL and NAS speakers from Figure 4.1 as a guide, probability thresholds of .2 were selected as cutoff points for test tokens preceding a nasal and .15 for all other test tokens; tokens with a probability of being tense above this threshold were classified as tense, and those below the threshold were classified as lax. After being classified as tense or lax, each test token was then categorized as either PHL or NAS, according to which system it conformed to. These tokens are then plotted over the set of training data, as shown in Figure 4.3b.

We can see in Figure 4.3 that, despite producing overwhelmingly NAS tokens, Leah still produces three tokens that were classified as PHL. I note that incongruent tokens are not altogether unexpected: Labov (1989) found PHL speakers to hypercorrect up to 15 percent of their tense *æh* tokens to lax in speech contexts that promote formal speech style, resulting in up to 15 percent of /æ/ tokens that are incongruous with PHL. Following Labov (1989), I consider speakers with 15 percent or fewer incongruous /æ/ tokens to be still conforming to a single /æ/ system. Since Leah produces only three out of her 256 test tokens as PHL, she is overall classified as an NAS speaker.[3]

Results

The majority of speakers in our data set produce tokens of /æ/ mainly consistent with either PHL (orange) or NAS (green), as shown in Figure 4.4.

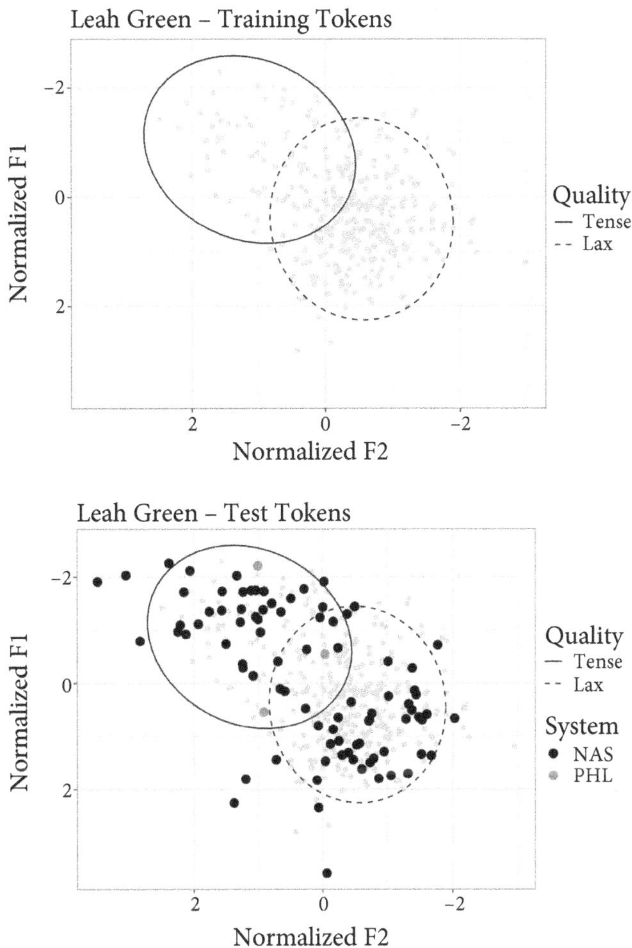

Figure 4.3. Training tokens (a) for Leah G, superimposed with test tokens (b).

Of the forty-two speakers analyzed, ten are clearly dominated by PHL and thirty-two by NAS. For these thirty-two speakers, their allophonic /æ/ system does not vary, or at least does not vary within the confines of their sociolinguistic interview. Speakers who produce tokens consistent with only one /æ/ system could work in the aggregate to produce the community-wide competition we see in Figure 4.2. However, these speakers are not the full story. The absence of variation among these thirty-two speakers does not mean that variation does not exist for anyone; indeed, the social pattern of NAS found in Labov et al. (2016) suggests that even when looking at speakers with a similar age range, we would expect some of these speakers (particularly the graduates of elite public schools) to have completed the change to

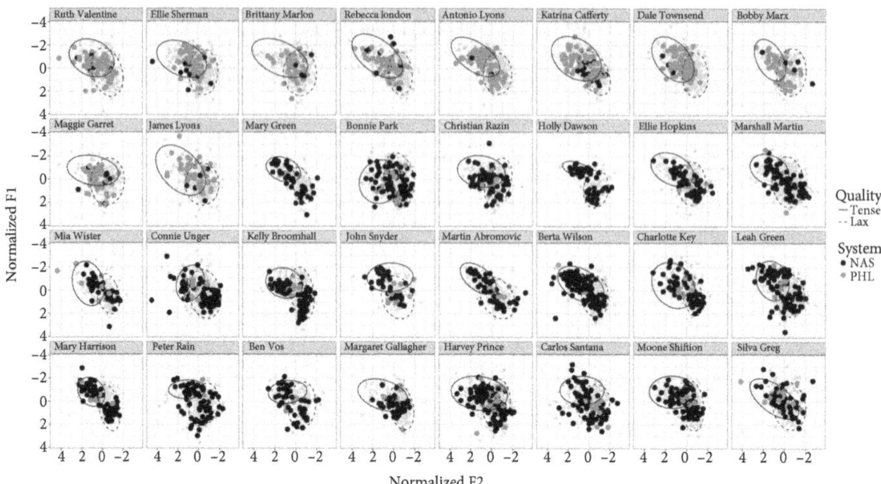

Figure 4.4. Thirty-two speakers in the dataset are classified as either PHL or NAS speakers, producing fewer than 15% incongruent tokens.

NAS while others (particularly the graduates of neighborhood Catholic schools) retain PHL. It is possible, then, that Figure 4.4 represents speakers from the parts of Philadelphia that either have already undergone the change from PHL to NAS or have not yet undergone it.

In support of this position, I also find several speakers producing clear variation between these two systems (Figure 4.5). These ten speakers vary in their /æ/ system, producing tokens that would be incongruous with PHL and tokens that would be incongruous with NAS. This surface-level variation between two allophonic systems suggests that the allophonic systems themselves may be a variable for these speakers. In the next section, I look closely at the productions of several of these speakers to determine the nature of the variation.

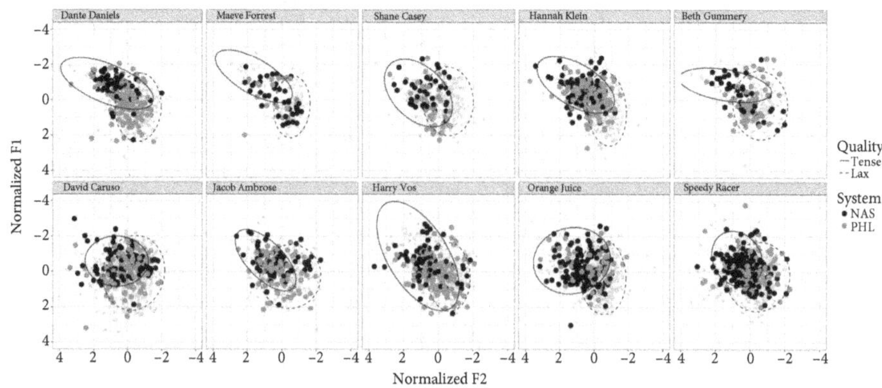

Figure 4.5. Variation between PHL and NAS

Variation between PHL and NAS

Finding surface-level variation between PHL and NAS within a single individual speaker points to the possibility of intraspeaker allophonic variation. However, before concluding that these speakers are producing variation between two allophonic systems, there are several alternative explanations that must first be falsified. In this section, we take a closer look at the productions of individuals who appear to produce variation between PHL and NAS, to investigate the nature of this variation.

Disjunction

Recall that PHL is composed of a disjoint set of phonological triggers. Indeed, while I have chosen to represent PHL as a single rule with disjoint triggers, it is also possible to represent the traditional system as two separate rules, shown in (5):

(5) a. PHL^1: æ → æh / __ [+ant] ∧ [+nasal]]σ
    b. PHL^2: æ → æh / __ [+ant] ∧ [−voice +fricative]]σ

If speakers represent the traditional input as two distinct rules rather than a single system, it is possible that the surface variation is simply the result of a speaker discarding one of the two rules. If, for example, a speaker rejected PHL^2, they would produce tense *æh* preceding anterior tautosyllabic nasals and lax tokens elsewhere. This means that tokens preceding intervocalic nasals (*manage*) and velar nasals (*hang*) would be produced lax, appearing as surface-level PHL tokens. This same speaker would also produce lax tokens preceding voiceless fricatives (*class*), which would appear as surface-level NAS tokens. If, however, speakers are producing true variation between the allophonic system PHL and the allophonic system NAS, we should see variation between PHL and NAS within each phonological conditioning factor.

Because the frequency of test /æ/ tokens in natural speech is relatively low, I will focus this section on the two speakers with the most speech data in order to maximize the likelihood of obtaining an accurate representation of those speakers' productions. Figure 4.6 displays the productions of two speakers, referred to as Orange Juice and Speedy Racer. The top row displays clearly PHL and NAS productions of both speakers' fricative category, while the bottom row displays PHL and NAS productions of both speakers' nasal test token category. We can see, for example, that Orange Juice produces tense tokens of the fricative category (*past*, *bathroom*) as well as lax tokens of this same category (*asshole*, *last*). This within-category shows that the surface-level variation found in Orange Juice's production is not the result of her eliminating the tense fricative condition from her PHL rule. Likewise, Orange Juice and Speedy Racer both produce tense and lax tokens within their intervocalic nasal condition (*damage*, *planet* for Orange Juice; *janitor*, *panicked* for Speedy Racer) and within their velar nasal condition (*angry*, *slang* for Orange Juice; *angry*, *strangle* for Speedy Racer). Taken together, the variation that we see within each of these categories for both speakers shows that the apparent variation in Figure 4.5 is not just the result of speakers abandoning one piece of the traditional PHL rule, but instead suggests that speakers are truly producing variation between the traditional PHL rule and the new NAS rule.

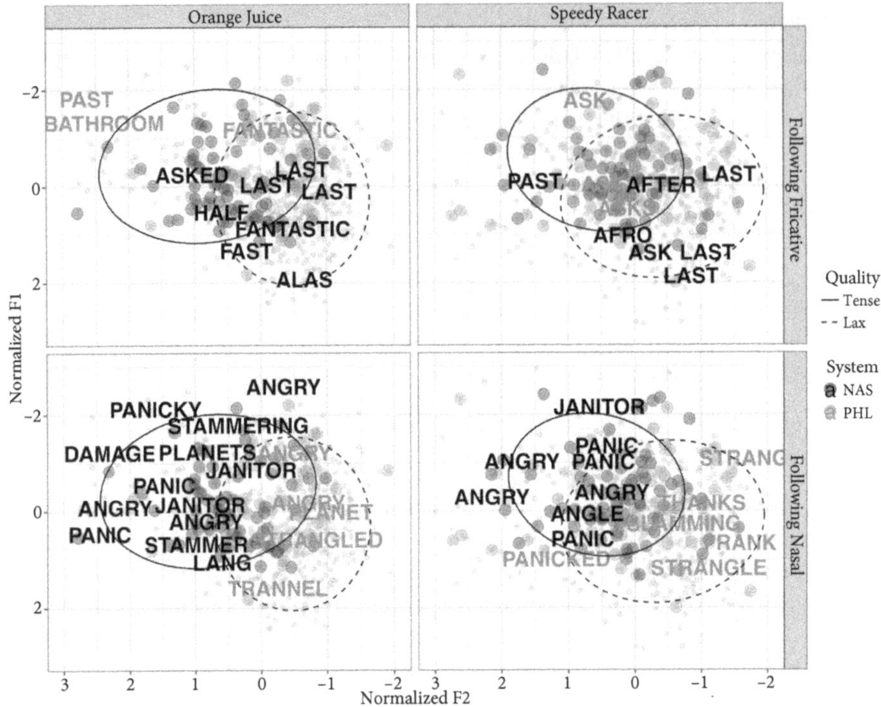

Figure 4.6. Variation between PHL and NAS within phonological category

Lexical Diffusion

With variation between PHL and NAS found within each phonological conditioning factor, this leaves us with one final alternative possibility before we can conclude that PHL and NAS are truly variable within speakers: lexical diffusion. Traditional PHL input requires speakers to memorize a list of lexical exceptions to tense and a list of lexical exceptions to lax. Furthermore, this list of exceptions has been shown to change over time, with *planet* joining the exceptionally tense class for many speakers born around 1990 (Brody 2011) and various words leaving the exceptionally lax class (e.g., *ran*, *swam*, *began* for speakers born around 1985). This raises the possibility that the variation within conditioning factors shown in Figure 4.6 is actually the result of lexical diffusion into and out of each list of exceptions. For example, if a speaker produced PHL but added *janitor* to their list of exceptionally tense tokens, this speaker would produce tense *janitor* and lax *manage*, appearing on the surface to be variation within the intervocalic nasal conditioning factor. If this same speaker added *hang* to the exceptionally tense and *class* to the exceptionally lax, the speaker would appear on the surface to produce variation within all conditioning factors between PHL and NAS. If, however, a speaker truly does produce variation between PHL and NAS overall, that speaker is expected to produce variation between PHL and NAS within a single lemma.

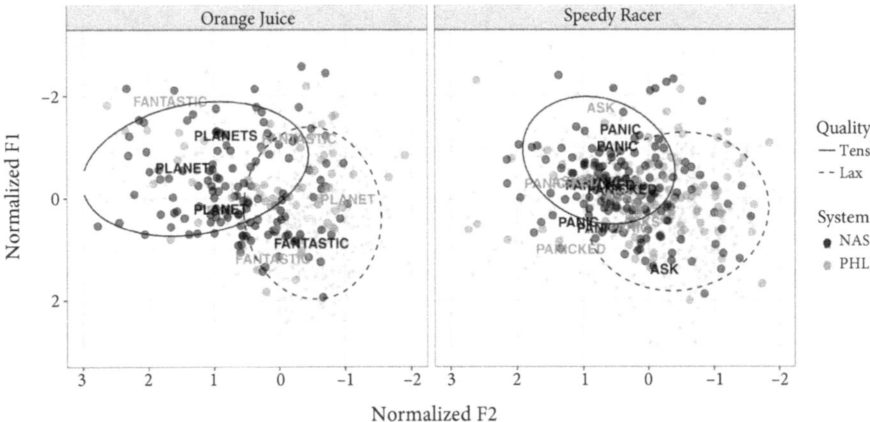

Figure 4.7 Variation between PHL and NAS within lexical item

Figure 4.7 presents a few highlighted tokens for both Orange Juice and Speedy Racer, selected for readability and for the relatively high number of tokens of each word. Orange Juice produces both tense and lax forms of the stressed vowel in *fantastic*, as well as in the word *planet*. Speedy Racer produces both tense and lax forms of *panic* and *ask*. The variation that we find within lemmas suggests that the surface-level variation between PHL and NAS for these speakers is not driven by the addition or subtraction of lexical items from the listed set of lexical exceptions. Speakers vary within phonological categories as well as within word types, leading to the conclusion that what appears on the surface to be allophonic variation is indeed intraspeaker variation between two allophonic systems.

Discussion

In this chapter, I have shown evidence that the structurally abstract unit of "allophonic rule" acts as a linguistic variable for some speakers during this allophonic restructuring of /æ/ in Philadelphia, supporting the initial position of Labov (1966). The implications of finding intraspeaker variation of this sort are relatively straightforward for the field of variation and change: namely, that allophonic systems may serve as the locus of linguistic variation and be the target of a variable rule. This finding carries with it the charge to consider the role of more abstract structures when investigating complicated surface-level variation, allowing allophonic systems themselves to be a potential variable for speakers.

I note also that the idea of phonological rules applying to abstract phonological structures is not altogether new. Fruehwald (2013) showed that diachronically, a phonological rule targeting the back raising diphthongs (/aw/, /ow/, /uw/) caused these three vowels to first front together, then back together. Chain shifts such as the Southern Shift can be analyzed as the result of a phonological rule or set of rules applying to an abstract target such as "front vowels" or "short vowels." The idea that rules can apply to an abstract phonological target is generally a widely accepted aspect of language variation; the main extension made here is to provide evidence that not only can abstract units such as an allophonic system be the target of a phonological rule, but these abstract units can also be a linguistic variant *within individual speakers*. I claim that these abstract units can be targeted by a variable rule.

This chapter demonstrates the oscillation of two separate allophonic systems within a single speaker; the identification of such intraspeaker variation raises further questions about the social stratification of this variation. It is clear that much larger bodies of data will be required to analyze the social distribution of this oscillation as compared to the general *fact* of oscillation. However, some preliminary work on the social stratification and evaluation of PHL and NAS may point in fruitful directions. The demographics of PHL and NAS in Philadelphia show social stratification between the two (Labov et al. 2016). It remains to be seen whether Philadelphians can assign social evaluation to PHL and NAS as a whole rather than just assigning social evaluation to particular aspects of each allophonic system (such as tense */æh/* preceding voiceless fricatives). Labov and Harris (1986) and Eckert and Labov (2017) argue that the abstract system is unavailable for social evaluation, although in other work (Sneller 2017), I find evidence of social evaluation following structural rather than phonetic lines. While this change from PHL to NAS is relatively new, the strong social stratification found in Labov et al. (2016) makes this abstract variable particularly likely to attract social evaluation if evaluation of abstract structures is possible. As this change propagates throughout the community, we may see whether the allophonic systems themselves are subject to social evaluation.

Finally, this intraspeaker variation of allophonic systems occurs during the course of a phonological change. While the focus of this chapter has been on the phonological and sociolinguistic implications of demonstrating that an abstract allophonic rule can be the target of intraspeaker variation, these results have implications for theories of language change as well. Finding intraspeaker competition between PHL and NAS suggests ultimately that abstract phonological and syntactic change may propagate both through a speech community and through a similar mechanism of intraspeaker competition.

Notes

The author gratefully acknowledges the support of the National Science Foundation (#BCS-1628408). Thanks especially to William Labov, Gene Buckley, and the audience at GURT 2017 for insightful comments and suggestions.

1 For this analysis, I have excluded PHL's lexical exceptions to lax (such as *ran* and *swam*) and pre-/l/ tokens (such as *Italian*), since these categories have shown inconsistent production even within fully PHL speakers in the PNC, making them uninformative as to the underlying system for any individual tokens.

2 While there is a shift to NAS for Black Philadelphians as well, the variation there is between the traditional Philly AAE neutral /æ/ and NAS; because the traditional Philly AAE /æ/ system has a single target for /æ/, it is not possible to determine the underlying system for any individual tokens, making this change uninformative as to the status of phonological competition within individual speakers.

3 Leah's tensest PHL token is a tense production of *Castor*, a street in her childhood neighborhood, and the other two are productions of and that were classified as lax.

References

Becker, Kara, and Amy Wing-mei Wong. 2009. "The Short-a System of New York City English: An Update." *University of Pennsylvania Working Papers in Linguistics* 15 (2): 1–12.

Brody, Stefanie. 2011. "Transmissions of Philadelphia Short-a: The Changing Gravity of 'Planets.'" Paper presented at *NWAV 38*, Ottawa.

Eckert, Penelope, and William Labov. 2017. "Phonetics, Phonology and Social Meaning." *Journal of Sociolinguistics* 21 (4): 467–96.

Ferguson, Charles. 1972. "'Short a' in Philadelphia English." In *Studies in Linguistics in Honor of George L. Trager*, edited by M. Estellie Smith, 259–74. The Hague: Mouton.

Fruehwald, Josef. 2013. "Phonological Involvement in Phonetic Change." PhD diss., University of Pennsylvania.

Fruehwald, Josef, Jonathan Gress-Wright, and Joel C. Wallenberg. 2013. "Phonological Rule Change: The Constant Rate Effect." In *Proceedings of the 40th Annual Meeting of the North East Linguistic Society*, edited by Seda Kan, Claire Moore-Cantwell, and Robert Staubs. Amherst, MA: GLSA Publications.

Janda, Richard D., and Brian D. Joseph. 2003. "Reconsidering the Canons of Sound Change: Towards a 'Big Bang' Theory." In *Historical Linguistics 2001: Selected Papers from the 15th International Conference on Historical Linguistics*, Melbourne, edited by Barry Blake and Kate Burridge, 205–19. Amsterdam: Benjamins.

Kiparsky, Paul. 1995. "The Phonological Basis of Sound Change." In *The Handbook of Phonological Theory*, edited by John Goldsmith. Oxford: Blackwell.

Krejci, Bonnie, and Katherine Hilton. 2017. "There's Three Variants: Agreement Variation in Existential There Constructions." *Language Variation and Change* 29 (2): 187–204. doi:10.1017/S0954394517000096.

Kroch, Anthony. 1989. "Reflexes of Grammar in Patterns of Language Change." *Language Variation and Change* 1 (3): 199–244.

Labov, William. 1963. "The Social Motivation of a Sound Change." *Word* 19 (3): 273–309. doi:10.1080/00437956.1963.11659799.

Labov, William. 1966. "The Linguistic Variable as a Structural Unit." *Washington Linguistics Review* 3:4–22.

Labov, William. 1972. *Sociolinguistic Patterns*. Oxford: Blackwell.

Labov, William. 1978. "Where Does the Linguistic Variable Stop? A Response to Beatriz Lavandera." *Working Papers in Sociolinguistics* 44:1–17.

Labov, William. 1989. "The Exact Description of a Speech Community." In *Language Change and Variation*, edited by Ralph Fasold and Deborah Schiffrin, 1–57. Amsterdam: Benjamins.

Labov, William. 2015. Influence of Higher Education on Local Phonology.

Labov, William, Sharon Ash, and Charles Boberg. 2006. *The Atlas of North American English: Phonetics, Phonology and Sound Change*. Berlin: Mouton de Gruyter.

Labov, William, Sabriya Fisher, Duna Gylfadottir, Anita Henderson, and Betsy Sneller. 2016. "Competing Systems in Philadelphia Phonology." *Language Variation and Change* 28(3): 273–305. doi:10.1017/S0954394516000132.

Labov, William, and Wendell A. Harris. 1986. "De Facto Segregation of Black and White Vernaculars." In *Diversity and Diachrony*, edited by David Sankoff, 1–24. Amsterdam: Benjamins.

Labov, William, and Ingrid Rosenfelder. 2013. *Philadelphia Neighborhood Corpus*. Philadelphia: Linguistics Laboratory.

Labov, William, Ingrid Rosenfelder, and Josef Fruehwald. 2013. "One Hundred Years of Sound Change in Philadelphia: Linear Incrementation, Reversal and Reanalysis." *Language* 89 (1): 30–65.

Lavandera, Beatriz R. 1978. "Where Does the Sociolinguistic Variable Stop?" *Language in Society* 7 (2): 171–82.

Miller, Karen. 2013. "Acquisition of Variable Rules: /s/-Lenition in the Speech of Chilean Spanish-Speaking Children and Their Caregivers." *Language Variation and Change* 25 (3): 311–40. doi:10.1017/S095439451300015X.

Podesva, Robert. 2007. "Phonation Type as a Stylistic Variable: The Use of Falsetto in Constructing a Persona." *Journal of Sociolinguistics* 11 (4): 478–504.

R Core Team. 2017. *R: A Language and Environment for Statistical Computing.* Vienna: R Foundation for Statistical Computing. http://www.r-project.org/.

Romaine, Suzanne. 1981. "The Status of Variable Rules in Sociolinguistic Theory." *Journal of Linguistics* 17 (1): 93–119. http://www.jstor.org/stable/4175571.

Sankoff, Gillian, and Hélène Blondeau. 2007. "Language Change across the Lifespan: /r/ in Montreal French." *Language* 83 (3): 560–88.

Santorini, Beatrice. 1993. "The Rate of Phrase Structure Change in the History of Yiddish." *Language Variation and Change* 5 (3): 257–83.

Smith, Jennifer, Mercedes Durham, and Hazel Richards. 2013. "The Social and Linguistic in the Acquisition of Sociolinguistic Norms: Caregivers, Children, and Variation." *Linguistics* 51 (2): 285–324. doi:10.1515/ling-2013-0012.

Sneller, Betsy. 2014. "Antagonistic Contact and Inverse Affiliation: Appropriation of /th/-Fronting by White Speakers in South Philadelphia." *University of Pennsylvania Working Papers in Linguistics* 20 (2). http://repository.upenn.edu/pwpl/vol20/iss2/19.

Sneller, Betsy. 2017. "On the Unobservability of Structure: Phonetic vs. Phonology in Experimental Data." Paper presented at the 2017 Annual Meeting of the Linguistics Association of Great Britain, Canterbury.

Sneller, Betsy, Josef Fruehwald, and Charles Yang. 2017. "The Nasal Invasion: Predicting Phonological Change in Dialect Contact." Paper presented at *NWAV 45*, Vancouver.

Stuart-Smith, Jane, Gwilym Pryce, Claire Timmins, and Barrie Gunter. 2013. "Television Can Also Be a Factor in Language Change: Evidence from an Urban Dialect." *Language* 89 (3): 501–36.

Trudgill, Peter. 1974. *The Social Differentiation of English in Norwich.* Cambridge: Cambridge University Press.

Wagner, Suzanne E., Alexander Mason, Monica Nesbitt, Erin Pevan, and Matt Savage. 2016. "Reversal and Re-Organization of the Northern Cities Shift in Michigan." *University of Pennsylvania Working Papers in Linguistics* 22 (2).

Yang, Charles D. 2016. *The Price of Linguistic Productivity: How Children Learn to Break the Rules of Language.* Cambridge, MA: MIT Press.

Chapter 5

A Label Theoretic Explanation of the Resultative Parameter

DANIEL MILWAY
University of Toronto

Variation in Secondary Predicates

It has long been observed that languages vary in regard to whether they allow resultative interpretation of secondary predicates. For instance, English allows resultatives (1), while French does not (2):

(1) She hammered the metal flat.
(2) *Il a marché les jambes raides.
He has walked the legs stiff
"He walked his legs off." (Washio 1997)

Both languages, however, allow secondary predicates with depictive interpretation (3–4):

(3) She ate the meat raw
(4) Il a mangé la viande crue.
He has eaten the meat raw
"He ate the meat raw."

This presents an acquisition puzzle as there is no reliable way to distinguish between the two constructions, yet one is variably acquired, while the other is universally acquired. Such a parameter cannot be directly acquired but must be indirectly acquired as a reflex of some surface parameter. Snyder (2012) argues that resultatives are strongly correlated with bare stem compounding.[1] That is, grammars that generate bare stem compounds also generate adjectival resultatives (5), while those that do not generate bare stem compounds do not generate adjectival resultatives (6).

(5) pocket watch chain
(6) *poche montre chaîne

Assuming, as Snyder does, that the compounding parameter and the resultative parameter are linked, our task, then, is to show that the setting of one can be derived from the other. This task is taken up in the following section, where I show that a modified version of Chomsky's (2013, 2015) label theory can predict Snyder's correlation.

The chapter is structured as follows: First, I give my theoretical assumptions, along with the analysis of resultatives and compounding that these assumptions yield. Following this is a discussion of label theory and proposed extensions to it. Finally, I demonstrate that, given my analysis of resultatives, the correlation between resultatives and bare stem compounding is predicted by the modified version of label theory I propose.

Background Assumptions

In this section, I discuss the theoretical assumptions I bring into this study, the structural analysis of adjectival resultatives that I assume, and my analysis of the bare stem compounding parameter.

Theoretical Assumptions

My basic theoretical commitments are essentially the uncontroversial tenets of the Minimalist Program in the Chomskyan tradition. I assume that the human language faculty consists of four components: A finite lexicon, a simple combinatory operation (Merge), an interface with the Sensorimotor system (SM), and an interface with the Conceptual-Intensional system (CI). Complex syntactic objects are constructed from the lexicon by iterations of Merge, but those objects are only licit linguistic expressions if they are interpretable at both interfaces.

I take Merge and the interfaces to be invariant across speakers, meaning the source of language variation is the lexicon. That is to say, I assume the Borer-Chomsky conjecture, as given in (7):

(7) The Borer-Chomsky Conjecture (Baker 2008)
All parameters of variation are attributable to differences in the features of particular items (e.g., the functional heads) in the lexicon.

The Structure of Resultatives

The structure I assume for resultatives is demonstrated in the structure of (8), next.

(8)

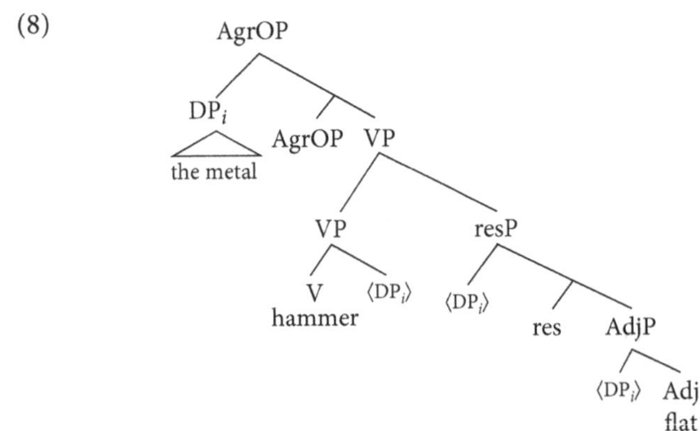

This structure is based on Kratzer's (2004) analysis of adjectival resultatives, but there are a few features that diverge from her analysis that bear noting. First, the resP is adjoined to the VP, whereas in Kratzer's analysis it is merged in [Comp V]. This change is required to have the object DP *the metal* merge in [Comp V] and be θ-marked by the verb. Second, a result of the first property, the object DP must move sideward from [Spec res] to [Comp V] (see Nunes 2001). Finally, although it is not represented in (8), I assume that res is a phase head, meaning the object DP must raise from the small clause (AdjP) to [Spec res] in order to move to the VP. These features will be important because, as I show later, the key to blocking resultatives in French-type languages is blocking the movement from the small clause to [Spec res].

The Lexical Basis of Bare Stem Compounding

Following the Borer-Chomsky conjecture, if there is parametric variation in the availability of bare stem compounding, then it must be derivable from variation in the lexicon. I propose that grammars that generate bare stem compounds are restricted to those whose lexicons contain category-determining heads without φ-features. My reasoning is as follows: in order to generate bare stem compounds, a language must generate bare stems. Adopting Snyder's (2016) definition, a bare stem is any form that (i) "could be used as an independent word," (ii) "is the form that inflectional morphology would combine with," and (iii) "does not yet bear any inflection." In current generative syntactic theory, a stem is an acategorial root merged with a category-determining head as demonstrated in (9):

(9) $dog \leftrightarrow \{n, \sqrt{DOG}\}$

Since roots are standardly assumed to lack any sort of formal feature, the presence or absence of inflection on a stem must be a property of the category-determining head. It is quite reasonable, then, to assume that bare stems are formed with category-determining heads that lack φ-features, while non-bare stems are formed with category-determining heads that have φ-features. So, English (and English-type languages) have "bare" category-determining heads (e.g., $n_{\varnothing}$, $adj_{\varnothing}$, $v_{\varnothing}$), while French (and French-type languages) have only "inflected" category-determining heads (e.g., n_{φ}, adj_{φ}, v_{φ}).

Label Theory

In this section I first describe label theory, a theory of syntax within the minimalist program, as proposed by Chomsky (2013, 2015) and propose two modifications of that theory.

Chomsky (2013, 2015)

Chomsky's starting point for label theory is the proposal that narrow syntax is reducible to simplest Merge, as in (10):

(10) Merge(X, Y) = {X, Y}

Syntax is reducible to this operation in that it accounts for most of the fundamental properties of natural language (e.g., structure-dependence of rules, displacement). It does not, however, account for projection/labeling. In other words, simplest Merge cannot explain why *see the girl*, the structure of which is given in (11), is a VP and not a DP.

(11) {*see*, {*the*, *girl*}}

Chomsky's proposal is that labels are assigned at the CI interface by a Labeling Algorithm (LA). In the simplest cases, LA is able to find a single head that is most prominent in a given syntactic object. These cases are restricted to objects consisting of a head merged with a phrase, and they are labeled as in (12):

(12) Head-phrase structures
LA({X, YP}) = X

The more difficult cases are those in which there is no single most prominent element in an object. For instance, in the case of "first merge," where two heads combine to form a phrase, LA has no structural way of picking a label. Chomsky, however, observes that only a particular subcase of these structures surfaces in language: head-root structures, which I previously identified with stems, and hypothesizes that roots, being featureless, are invisible to LA, meaning the category-determining head serves as the label, as in (13):

(13) Head-head structures
LA({X, $\sqrt{ROOT}$ } = X (Where X is not a root)

The one other case, and the case most relevant to this chapter, is the case of syntactic objects consisting of two phrases. As with the head-head structures, LA will be unable to pick a single most prominent element in these structures. Chomsky proposes that there are two subcases of these phrase-phrase structures that can be labeled. First, if one of the constituent phrases is a lower copy of a chain, then it is invisible to LA, meaning the label of the other constituent phrase "projects," as shown in (14):

(14) Phrase-phrase structures (subcase 1)
LA({<XP>, YP}) = LA(YP) (Where <XP> is a lower copy)

The second subcase consists of those phrase-phrase structures in which the two phrases agree for some feature (15). In this case, Chomsky proposes that the pair of agreeing features acts as the label of the structure.

(15) Phrase-phrase structures (subcase 2)
$\text{LA}(\{\text{XP}_F, \text{YP}_F\}) = <F,F>$

We can see the second subcase in subject-TP structures and *wh*-questions as demonstrated in (16) and (17):

(16) $\text{LA}(\{\text{DP}_\varphi, \text{TP}_\varphi\}) = <\varphi,\varphi>$
(17) $\text{LA}(\{\text{WhP}_Q, \text{CP}_Q\}) = <Q,Q>$

Labels, Chomsky proposes, are required for proper interpretation at the CI interface, meaning only those cases where a label can be assigned are convergent. The requirement for a label is associated with the CI interface by a process of elimination. It does not arise from a property of Merge, and there is no evidence of labels in externalization. This leaves the CI interface as the remaining logically possible locus for such a requirement. This raises the question of why labels would be needed for interpretation by the CI interface, which I address in the next section.

There are heads, according to Chomsky, that cannot serve as labels. Roots are, by definition, featureless and, by hypothesis, cannot label phrases. Chomsky also proposes that functional heads with only one set of features cannot label unless they agree with another phrase for those features. English finite T_{φ}, for instance, is proposed to have a single set of φ-features, and therefore needs a subject to agree with those features. Italian finite $T_{<\varphi,\varphi>}$, in contrast, is proposed to have a full set of φ-features, and therefore can label a phrase without an agreeing subject. This, Chomsky argues, explains why the extended projection principle (EPP) holds for English, but not for Italian. Implicit in this discussion is the proposal that functional heads without formal features, for instance English nonfinite $T_{\varnothing}$, are able to label without agreement.

Extensions to Label Theory

The extensions I will propose in this section take the form of answers to two questions left unanswered by Chomsky's (2013, 2015) proposals. The first question, a major one, is why labels would be needed for interpretation at the CI interface. The second, a minor question, is how host-adjunct structures are labeled. The answers to these questions will allow me to fully explain the resultative parameter.

Labels Determine Compositionality

Chomsky argues that syntactic objects must be labeled for proper interpretation at the CI interface. Assuming this to be correct, the next logical question is why it is correct; what necessary information does a label provide? I propose that the label of a syntactic object determines how that object composes semantically. This means that (contra Heim and Kratzer 1998) lexical items are not specified for semantic type, but rather their type is effectively determined dynamically (cf. Partee 1986). This can be formalized by saying that the CI interface interprets pairs consisting of a syntactic object (SO) and a label (L). Recall that the label can either be a head or a pair of features. Each of these types of labels is associated with a mode of composition. Head labels are associated with function application, as in (18), while pair labels are associated with operator-variable structures, as in (19):

(18) $[\![<\{D, NP\}, D>]\!] = [\![D]\!]([\![NP]\!])$
(19) $[\![<\{WhP, CP\}, <Q,Q>>]\!] = (Wh\ x)(\ldots x \ldots)$

Host-Adjunct Structures Are Unlabeled

Since resultative VPs are host-adjunct structures, a theory that explains them must entail a theory of adjuncts. Label theory, as proposed by Chomsky, however, does not adequately cover adjuncts. I propose to integrate adjuncts into label theory by placing them outside the domain of labeling. That is, I propose that host-adjunct structures are ignored by LA and, as a result, default to a null label.[2] I further hypothesize that a null label is associated with conjunctive interpretation as demonstrated in (20):

(20) $[\![<\{NP, AP\}, \varnothing>]\!] = [\![NP]\!](x)\ \&\ [\![AP]\!](x)$

If the host-adjunct structures are ignored by LA, then it is reasonable to assume that the adjunct itself is also ignored by LA. This would mean that the internal structure of the adjunct phrase is unlabeled unless it was independently labeled following its own derivation. I give concrete examples of this in the following section.

A Note on Unlabeled Tree Diagrams

The fact that Merge constructs unlabeled phrases is reflected in the tree diagrams in the remainder of this chapter. For example, the adjectival resultative structure introduced in (8) will be represented as in (21):

(21)

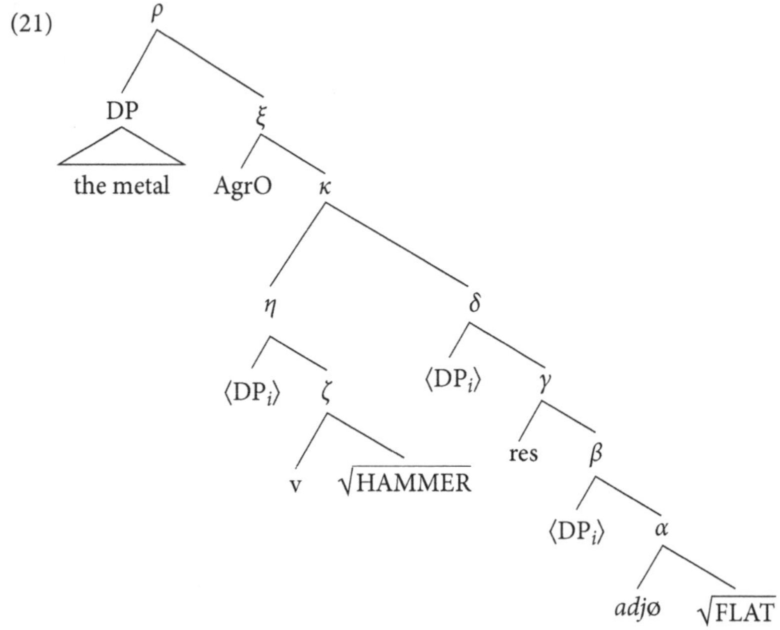

The use of Greek letters in these trees is not meant to signal any sort of analysis, but rather to allow us to refer to individual syntactic objects in our analysis. For example, the letter η refers to the syntactic object {DP, {v, $\sqrt{HAMMER}$ }}.

Deriving (*)Rresultatives

In this section I demonstrate how label theory, augmented with my hypotheses, can account for the link between bare stem compounding and adjectival resultatives. In the next section I will show how an adjectival resultative is derived in a language with $adj_{\varnothing}$ (i.e., English), and in the section after that I will show how an adjectival resultative fails to be derived in a language with adj_{φ} (i.e., French).

Deriving Resultatives in English-Type Languages

The first step in deriving resultatives is deriving the result phrase represented in (22), which adjoins to the VP.

(22)

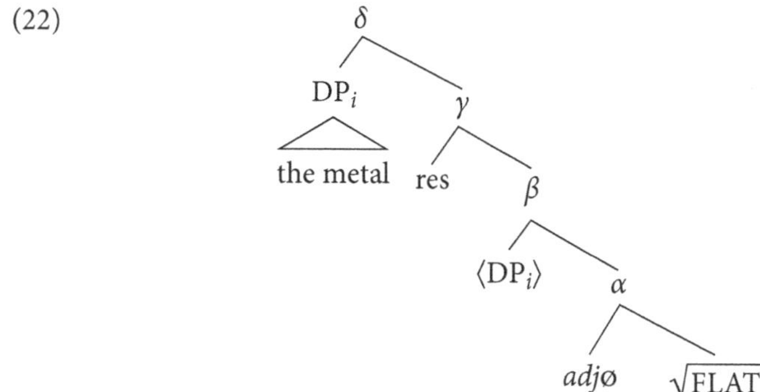

Upon building the structure in (22), β, the complement of res, which I take to be a phase head, will be transferred to the interfaces. At this point, β and α will be labeled by LA. Since α is a head-root structure, it will take the non-root, in this case *adj,* as its label. Since β is a phrase-phrase structure in which one of the phrases (the DP *the metal*) is a lower copy, the non-moved phrase provides the label (LA(β) = LA(α) = *adj*). The phrases γ and δ, having not been transferred, remain unlabeled.

The next step will be to build the VP that the structure in (22) will adjoin to. Before moving to the VP, however, we must Copy the DP *the metal* in order to move it sideward into the VP. The final (relevant) structure is given in (23):

(23)

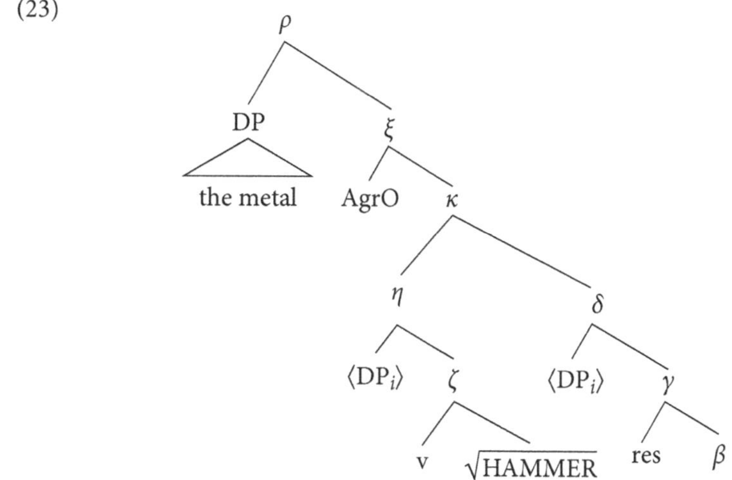

Note that the DP *the metal* has been remerged with the verb (represented here as ζ) in theme position and δ, the resulting phrase has been adjoined to the newly formed phrase. This creates a sideward movement structure, and the DP must move to a position that c-commands all of its instances in order to be linearized (Nunes 2001). In this case, the DP moves to its final position in [Spec, AgrO] forming ρ. The derivation of the sentence continues until a phase head is merged and its complement, which includes ρ, is transferred. Assuming the DP and AgrO agree for φ-features, ρ will be labeled by the pair of features <φ,φ>, and ξ will be labeled by

AgrO. The next structure, κ, is a host-adjunct structure, meaning LA will skip it and proceed to the next structure in the host, η. As a side effect of skipping the host-adjunct structure, the adjunct itself will also be skipped by the algorithm. Finally, since the DP member of η is a lower copy, it is invisible, and the label of η will be the label of ζ, which will be *v*.

So, adjectival resultatives can be derived when the result adjective bears no φ-features. In the next section I will show that attempts to derive adjectival resultatives with a φ-bearing adjective are predicted to fail.

Blocking Resultatives in French-Type Languages

If we assume that the principal difference between English-type languages and French-type languages is the presence or absence of category-determining heads without φ-features, then our theory of grammar should allow us to derive the ban on adjectival resultatives from the presence of φ-features on category-determining heads. In this section, I demonstrate that the theory of grammar I propose is able to do so. I make two attempts to derive an adjectival resultative with a φ-bearing adjective and show how each attempt is ultimately doomed.

First Attempt

First, I will show that deriving resultatives in the manner in which they are derived in English-type languages fails. The first step in this attempt is to derive the result phrase shown in (24). Note that the category-determining head in (24), unlike the one in (22), bears a set of φ-features.

(24)

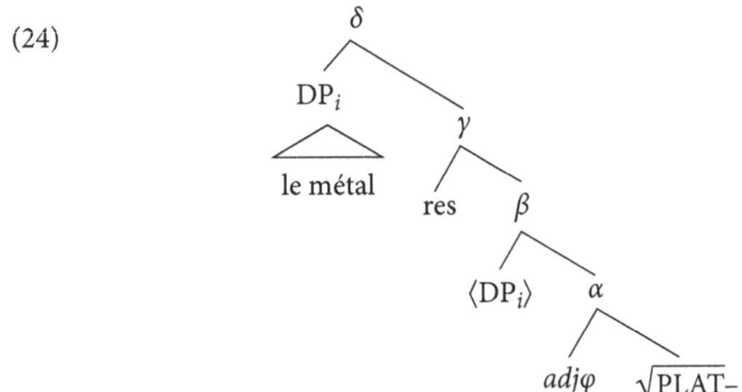

As in English-type languages, res is a phase-head, and therefore its complement β is transferred to the interface and labeled. The DP *le métal* has been moved, so it is invisible to LA. As a result, the label of β will be the label of α, which would be *adj*, if the category-determining head was strong enough to provide a label. By hypothesis, however, French-type *adj* bears a single set of φ-features, and therefore must be strengthened by agreement in order to provide a label. The DP, which would agree with *adj*, has moved and therefore cannot agree, meaning the category-determining head is unstrengthened and therefore too weak to label. This failure to label will lead to a crash, halting the derivation early.

So, resultatives cannot be derived in French-type languages by the same process as they are in English-type languages. In the next section I attempt a different process and show that it also fails.

Second Attempt

The previous attempt to derive resultatives in a French-type language fails because the DP *le métal* is moved from [Spec *adj*] before it can agree with *adj*. In this attempt, we will leave the DP in situ and show that this leads to issues further down the line.

So, again, we start with the result phrase represented in (25). Note that the DP has not moved.

(25)

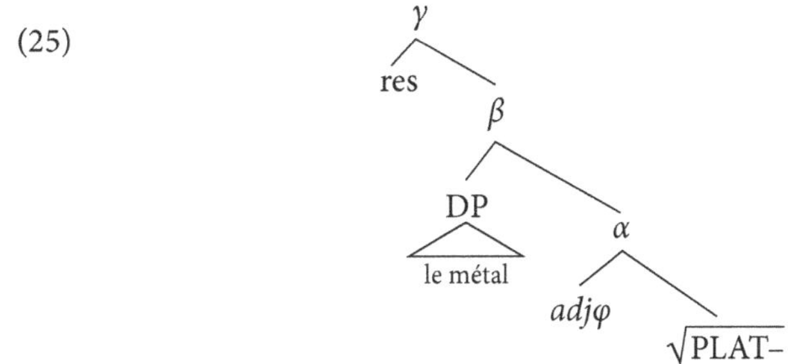

Again, the complement of res is transferred to the interfaces and labeled. The label of β will be <φ,φ> due to the φ-agreement between the DP and *adj*. The label of α will be *adj* because the category-determining head will have been strengthened by agreement with the DP. With the result phrase constructed, we can move on to the VP to which it will adjoin.

Recall that in order to merge the DP in theme position of the VP, it needs to be available. In the derivation of the English-type resultative, the theme DP is made available by a Copy operation. In that case, the DP was in [Spec res] and, therefore, had not been transferred. In this case, however, the DP was never moved to [Spec res] and has been transferred. This means that the DP is unavailable to be Copied and remerged with the verb. The second attempt at deriving adjectival resultatives in a French-type language, then, does not crash at the interfaces, but cannot be derived in the narrow syntax.

Summary

These two attempts at deriving adjectival resultatives in French-type languages fail because of conflicting requirements imposed by the grammar. In order to derive an adjectival resultative, we must move the object DP out of [Spec, *adj*], but in order for the derivation of the result phrase to converge, the object DP must remain in [Spec, *adj*]. Neither requirement can be satisfied without violating the other, so adjectival resultatives cannot be derived in French-type languages.

Conclusion

I began this chapter with a correlation observed by Snyder (2012): only grammars that generate bare stem compounds also generate adjectival resultatives. I went on to show that this correlation can, in fact, be derived in an extended version of Chomsky's (2013, 2015) label theory. The extensions to label theory came in the form of two hypotheses. First, I hypothesized that host-adjunct structures are ignored by LA, and second, I hypothesized that labels determine how a structure composes semantically. While this chapter demonstrates the potential empirical value of these hypotheses, it does not address their theoretical basis. Further study will be required to integrate these hypotheses into the broader theory of grammar.

Notes

1 This is merely the most refined version of Snyder's compounding parameter, which he first proposed in his 1995 dissertation. In its earliest form, the compounding parameter was about N-N compounding.

2 This proposal is inspired by Chametzky (1996) and Hornstein (2009), who propose that adjuncts and adjunction are separate from the base phrase structure component of the grammar.

References

Baker, Mark C. 2008. "The Macroparameter in a Microparametric World." In *The Limits of Syntactic Variation*, edited by Teresa Biberauer, 351–73. Amsterdam: Benjamins.

Chametzky, Robert. 1996. *A Theory of Phrase Markers and the Extended Base*. Albany: SUNY Press.

Chomsky, Noam. 2013. "Problems of Projection." *Lingua* 130:33–49.

Chomsky, Noam. 2015. "Problems of Projection: Extensions." In *Structures, Strategies and Beyond: Studies in Honour of Adriana Belletti*, edited by Elisa Di Domenico, Cornelia Hamann, and Simona Matteini, 3–16. Amsterdam: Benjamins.

Heim, Irene, and Angelika Kratzer. 1998. *Semantics in Generative Grammar*. Malden, MA: Blackwell.

Hornstein, Norbert. 2009. *A Theory of Syntax: Minimal Operations and Universal Grammar*. Cambridge: Cambridge University Press.

Kratzer, Angelika. 2004. "Building Resultatives." In *Event Arguments in Syntax, Semantics and Discourse*, edited by Claudia Maienborn and Angelika Wöllstein-Leisten. Tübingen: Max Niemeyer Verlag.

Nunes, Jairo. 2001. "Sideward Movement." *Linguistic Inquiry* 32 (2): 303–44.

Partee, Barbara. 1986. "Noun Phrase Interpretation and Type-Shifting Principles." In *Studies in Discourse Representation Theory and the Theory of Generalized Quantifiers*, edited by Jeroen Groenendijk, Dick de Jongh, and Martin Stokhof, 115–43. Dordrecht: Foris.

Snyder, William. 1995. "Language Acquisition and Language Variation: The Role of Morphology." Doctoral diss., Massachusetts Institute of Technology.

Snyder, William. 2012. "Parameter Theory and Motion Predicates." In *Telicity, Change, and State: A Cross-Categorial View of Event Structure*, edited by Violeta Demonte and Louise McNally, 279–99. Oxford: Oxford University Press.

Snyder, William. 2016. "Compound Word Formation." In *The Oxford Handbook of Developmental Linguistics*, edited by Jeffrey Lidz, William Snyder, and Joe Pater, 89–110. Oxford: Oxford University Press.

Washio, Ryuichi. 1997. "Resultatives, Compositionality and Language Variation." *Journal of East Asian Linguistics* 6 (1): 1–49.

Chapter 6

Adverbial -*s*: So Awks but So Natural!

NORBERT CORVER
Utrecht University

IT SEEMS FAIR TO say that the bound morpheme -*s* in languages such as Dutch and English is most familiar from possessive noun phrases such as *Freds auto* (Dutch) and *Fred's car*. As has been noted by traditional grammarians, however, the distribution of -*s* is much more widespread. Specifically, -*s* occurs abundantly in what are traditionally called adverbial expressions. Some illustrations of this so-called adverbial -*s* in Dutch and English are given in (1) and (2), respectively:

(1) *een*s "once," *ineen***s** "at once," *ergen*s "somewhere," *ander*s "differently," *ondergrond*s "underground," *strak*s "soon"
(2) indoor**s**, upward**s**, northward**s**, sideway**s**, sometime**s**, alway**s**

Although it may be tempting to analyze these examples as fixed, unanalyzable expressions, there are signs of morphosyntactic behavior that hint at a composite structure of these expressions. In Dutch, for example, *straks* can be split up by means of a diminutive morpheme: *strak-je-s* (soon-dim-s, "soon"). Also, the expression *ondergronds* exhibits a phrasal stress pattern rather than a word-like (compound) stress pattern. This is exemplified by *ondergronds* in (3a), which has the same stress pattern as the prepositional phrase *onder de grond*. As (3b) shows, compound stress typically falls on the first element of a compound.

(3)	a.	Deze bijen	wonen	onderGRONDS /	[$_{PP}$ onder de GROND].
		these bees	live	under-ground-s /	under the ground
	b.	De ONDERgrond	is	te	hard.
		the subsoil	is	too	hard

A similar argument can be given for English: *indoors* shows phrasal rather than compound stress; see (4a). The latter stress pattern we find in (4b), which notably lacks adverbial -*s*. The element *indoor* in (4b) behaves like an attributive adjectival modifier of *event*.

(4) a. We stayed indoors. (compare: in the HOUSE)
b. an indoor event.

If we are right in saying that the "adverbial" expressions in (1) and (2) have a composite syntactic structure, the question arises what the inner structure looks like and what grammatical role adverbial *-s* plays in this structure. In this chapter it will be proposed that *-s* is an affixal manifestation of the categorial heads n° and a°. Building on the idea that children are cue-based learners, I will suggest that children's Universal Grammar (UG)–based knowledge of the syntactic structure *[*$_{np/aP}$ *n/a [Root]]* will help them in parsing this hidden bound morpheme. Another issue that will be addressed concerns variation. It turns out that there is interdialectal variation as regards the appearance of adverbial *-s*. This chapter focuses on adverbial *-s* in Dutch. The proposed analysis can be extended to the English patterns in (2).

Two Case Studies on Adverbial -s

We saw earlier that there are signs of phrasal syntax in adverbial expressions featuring *-s*. I now present two case studies on adverbial *-s* in Dutch. With these two case studies I hope to show that adverbial *-s* is still an active part of Dutch grammar and not some sort of historical residue. Its active role is suggested, first, by its productive use in certain structural environments and, second, by its rule-governed behavior. The two types of adverbial expressions I will discuss are given in (5):

(5) a. Jan loopt *zachtje**s***.
Jan walks slow-dim-s
"Jan walks slowly."

b. Jan loopt *ander**s*** (dan Piet).
Jan walks different-s than Piet
"Jan walks in a different way than Piet does."

The discussion starts with the pattern *zachtjes* in (5a). As the gloss indicates, three components can be identified in this adverbial expression: the adjective *zacht*, the diminutive morpheme *-je*, and adverbial *-s*. As shown by the ill-formedness of (6a), the appearance of *-s* right after *-je* is obligatory. Furthermore, if *-je* is absent and we have a bare adjective, *-s* cannot appear; see (6b).

(6) a. Jan loopt *zacht-je*(-**s**)*.
Jan walks slow-dim(-s)

b. Jan loopt *zacht(*-**s**)*.
Jan walks slow(-s)
"Jan walks slowly."

Example (7) shows that the adjectival component can be complex; that is, it can have a phrasal syntax. This is straightforwardly shown by the fact that *zacht* can be accompanied by degree modifiers:

(7) Jan liep [*te/zeer/erg/even* zacht(je**s**)].
Jan walked too/very/very/as slow(dim-s)

Example (8) shows that the free comparative morphemes *meer* "more" and *minder* "less" can also modify the adjective:

(8) a. Ze zag [net iets meer bleek-je-s] (dan normaal).
she looked just a-little more pale-DIM-s than normally

b. Jan rijdt nu [minder zacht-je-s] (dan vorige keer).
Jan drives now less slow-DIM-s than last time

It is not possible, however, to have a bound comparative morpheme in combination with *zachtjes*. Both the sequence A-COMPAR-DIM-S in (9a) and the sequence A-DIM-s-compar in (9b) are ruled out:

(9) a. *Jan rijdt nu [nog zacht-er-tje-s]
Jan drives now even slow-COMPAR-DIM-s
"Jan drives even more slowly now."

b. ?*Jan rijdt nu [nog zacht-je-s-er].

Notice, finally, that, while a prepositional phrase (PP) complement can easily combine with the bare adjective *bang* in (10a), such a combination is less acceptable when we have the adverbial form *bangetjes* (i.e., *bang*-DIM-S); see (10b):

(10) a. [$_{AP}$ Bang [$_{PP}$ voor mijn kritiek]] kwam Jan schoorvoetend de kamer binnen.
afraid of my criticism entered Jan reluctantly the room PRT

b. ?*[$_{AP}$ Bange**tjes** [$_{PP}$ voor mijn kritiek]] . . .

The preceding data suggest that the appearance of adverbial *-s* and the inner morphosyntactic behavior of the adverbial expression is rule-governed. To this it can be added that the formation of the adverbial expression A-DIM-S is quite productive; many Dutch adjectives can fill the A-slot, both monosyllabic and polysyllabic ones: *boos-je-s* "angrily," *stil-etje-s* "silently," *gevoelig-je-s* "sensitively," *gezellig-je-s* "cosily," and so on.

Taking the aforementioned data as our empirical basis, let us next address the question as to what the internal syntax of these adverbial expressions is. The diminutive morpheme *-je* is, of course, best known for its suffixal attachment to nouns, as in *huis-je* "little house" and *tafel-tje* "little table." Attachment of the diminutive morpheme to the noun does not change the categorial status of the newly built complex object. Thus, *tafel-tje* constitutes a nominal object, just like *tafel*. This is further confirmed by the fact that it can be followed by a plural morpheme (in this case, *-s*), just like *tafel*: *tafels*, *tafeltjes*. From this grammatical behavior of the diminutive morpheme, it can be derived that it is a nominal bound morpheme. Having shown this, the next question arises: How does the diminutive morpheme combine with the adjective?

In the spirit of Déchaine and Tremblay's (1996) analysis of the English adverbial suffix *-ly*, given in (11b) (see also Baker 2003), I propose that the nominal bound morpheme *-je* is the head of a noun phrase that is modified by an attributive adjective phrase. Thus:

(11) a. $[_{NP}$ $[_{AP}$ zacht] $[_{NP}$ -je-s]]
b. $[_{NP}$ $[_{AP}$ slow] $[_{NP}$ -ly]]

The phenomena just discussed follow straightforwardly from this structure: First, the attributive modifier (AP) can be accompanied by a degree word; see (7) and (8). Second, the pattern in (10b) is excluded for the same reason that the ill-formed noun phrase **een bange man voor kritiek* (an afraid man of criticism, "a man afraid of criticism") is, namely: a PP-complement can never be extraposed out of an attributive modifier and be placed in the right periphery of the containing noun phrase. Schematically:

(12) a. *$[_{NP}$ $[_{NP}$ $[_{AP}$ t_i bang] $[_{NP}$ -etje-s]] $[_{PP}$ voor mijn kritiek$]_i$]
b. *[**een** $[_{NP}$ $[_{NP}$ $[_{AP}$ t_i bange] $[_{NP}$ man]] $[_{PP}$ voor mijn kritiek$]_i$]]

Third, the ill-formedness of (9b) follows from the fact that the bound comparative morpheme *-er* cannot attach to a nominal element: *[$[_{noun}$ *-je-s*]-er]. Compare in this respect the ill-formed pattern **een [$[_{noun}$ liefhebber]-der$_{COMPARATIVE}$] van jazz music*, where the comparative morpheme is attached to the (derived) noun *liefhebber* "lover/ fan" with the intended meaning: "a greater lover/fan of jazz music."

As for the ill-formedness of (9a), I tentatively propose it relates to a constraint quite similar to Myers's (1984) generalization, which states that zero-derived words do not permit the affixation of further derivational morphemes. For example, adjectives derived from passive verbs by the addition of a phonologically null adjectivizer (Ø) block *-ly* affixation, as in the ill-formed pattern **pleasedly*, which has the more abstract representation in (13a); see Pesetsky (1995, 91). The derived structure of the ill-formed surface pattern *zachter-tje-s* in (9a) also features the sequence "gap + bound derivational morpheme," the only difference with (13a) being that the gap in (13b) is the trace of an adjectival head that has undergone raising to the comparative Q-head *-er*. The overall generalization is then that derivational morphemes cannot combine with a unit that ends with an empty head.

(13) a. [[[[please $_V$] ed $_V$] $Ø_A$] (*-ly)]
b. *$[_{NP}$ $[_{QP}$ $zacht_i$-er $[_{AP}$ t_i]] $[_{NP}$ -tje-s]]

Let me finish this discussion of *zachtjes* with the observation that the English adverbial marker *-ly*, analyzed as a nominal element in (11b), displays the same morphosyntactic behavior as the diminutive morpheme in (11a). First, the attributive adjective phrase (AP) modifier can be complex (i.e., contain degree words); see (14a). Second, comparative formation is possible only with a free comparative morpheme; see (14b). Finally, *-ly* adverbs typically do not combine with a PP-complement; see (14c).

(14) a. John drove [[too/very/so quick] -ly]. (compare (7))
b. more quickly / *quick-ly-er / *quick-er-ly (compare (8) and (9))
c. fearful-ly (*of Bill) (compare (10b))

Having provided a first analysis of adverbial expressions such as *zachtjes*, let us now turn to the second case study: the adverbial expression *anders* in (5b). I start with some basic observations. First of all, *anders* exhibits properties of a comparative construction: it includes the bound comparative morpheme *-(d)er* (*an*-der-*s*) and it can co-occur with the comparative *dan*-phrase ("than"), as in (15):

(15) Jan gedroeg zich [anders *dan Piet*].
Jan behaved REFL different-s than Piet
"Jan behaved differently from/than Piet."

Second, *-s* is obligatorily present on *anders*. Thus, the *-s*-less form *ander* is excluded in (15). Notice that, in this respect, *anders* behaves differently from other comparative adjectival expressions featuring *-er*:

(16) Jan gedroeg zich [*vreemder(*-s)* dan Piet].
Jan behaved REFL stranger(-s) than Piet
"Jan behaved more strangely than Piet."

Third, the *-s* of *anders* is not an intrinsic part of the adverbial expression. Note, for example, that in its attributive use, as in (17a), it has the form *ander*, that is, without *-s*.

(17) a. Jan vertoonde [*ander(*s)* gedrag] (attributive use)
Jan exhibited other(s) behavior

b. Jan gedroeg zich *ander*(-s)*. (predicative use)
Jan behaved REFL different (-s)

Fourth, as we saw earlier, *anders* is an intrinsically (i.e., lexically) comparative adjective: it licenses a "*dan*-phrase." At the same time, *anders* can be modified by degree modifiers that are normally found only with positive degree adjectives. This is illustrated in (18a,b). As shown by (18c), comparative forms that are formed by a synthetic comparative formation rule do not permit modification by *heel erg* "very much."

(18) a. Jan loopt [heel erg hard].
Jan walks so very fast
"Jan walks very fast."

b. Jan loopt [heel erg *anders* dan Piet].
Jan walks so very different-s than Piet
"Jan walks so differently from Piet."

c. *Jan loopt [heel erg *harder* dan Piet].
Jan walks so very faster than Piet

From the preceding data, it can be concluded that the adverbial expression *anders* has a comparative meaning but does not display the full set of properties that we find with comparative adjectives that have a rule-based derivation, that is, a derivation in which the comparative form is derived by moving the adjectival head (A°) to a higher [+comparative] functional head (Q°), as in (19a); see Corver (1997). I propose that *anders* is an adjectival expression whose comparative meaning is lexically specified; that is, it is an intrinsic part of the lexical semantics of the adjective. Even though (with a trained linguistic eye) the comparative morpheme *-(d)er* is still identifiable in *an*ders, it is also clear that this element is no longer felt to be a discrete element within a more complex form *ander*. If it were a discrete item, one would expect there to be a positive form *an* and a superlative form *an-st*, as well. These forms, however, are nonexistent.

(19) a. [$_{QP}$ -er$_{[+comparative]}$ [$_{AP}$ vreemd]] (see (16))

b. [$_{QP}$ (heel erg) [Q° [$_{AP}$ anders$_{[+comparative]}$]] (see (18b))

Let me finish this discussion of *anders* with the observation that, in colloquial/dialectal Dutch, we find more examples of comparative-like adverbial expressions that end in *-s*. For example, the form *verders* (furth-er-s) is attested in colloquial/dialectal Dutch. Importantly, this form typically has the meaning: "in addition to what you have already told me"; see (20a). When it has the meaning "farther" (i.e., "more distant/farther away"), *verder* typically does not combine with *-s*.

(20) a. Heb je *verder(s)* nog nieuws.
have you further(s) any news
"Do you have any news in addition to what you've already told us?"

b. Jan gooide de bal *verder(*s).*
Jan threw the ball further(*s)
"Jan threw the ball further away."

On the basis of the morphosyntactic behavior of patterns such as *zachtjes* (5a) and *anders* (5b), I hope to have shown that the appearance of "adverbial" *-s* is rule-governed. The next question to be addressed is the following: What is the nature of so-called adverbial *-s*?

Adverbial -s as a Manifestation of Categorial n° and a°

In traditional grammar (Royen 1947–54), adverbial *-s* was analyzed as genitive case. Since genitive case appears on quite a large number of adverbial expressions, it was considered to be an adverbial marker. I adhere to the original idea that *-s* represents genitive case. With Emonds (1985) and Pesetsky (2013), however, I propose that Case is not a primitive category but rather an affixal realization of a part of speech. In other words, Case is a part-of-speech suffix, or in Emonds's terms: an "alternative realization" of a categorial head/feature. The question now arises as to what part of speech (i.e., category) genitive case is an affixal realization of. In generative-linguistic Case theory of the 1980s (Rouveret and Vergnaud 1980; Chomsky 1986), the assignment of genitive case was associated with the categories N(oun) and A(djective). A noun like *destruction* and an adjective like *proud* assign genitive case to their nominal complement, where genitive case surfaces as a semantically empty preposition *of* (*the destruction of the city*, *proud of John*) or as a bound morpheme *'s* (*the city's destruction*). Under an analysis that takes Case to be a part-of-speech affix, *'s* is a manifestation of a nominal or adjectival suffix (say: N_{aff} and A_{aff}). In (21), the process of genitive case assignment is illustrated for the noun phrase *the destruction of the city*.

(21) a. [$_{DP}$ the [$_{NP}$ [$_{N}$ destruction] [$_{DP}$ the city]]] base structure

b. [$_{DP}$ the [$_{NP}$ [$_{N}$ destruction] [N_{aff} +[$_{DP}$ the city]]]] assignment of case (= N)

c. [$_{DP}$ the [$_{NP}$ [$_{N}$ destruction] [of +[$_{DP}$ the city]]]] spell-out of affixal N

With Pesetsky (2013), I take there to be two ways in which Case can appear on a constituent: (i) syntactic case assignment, as, for example, in (21), and (ii) Case as a lexical property. As regards this last way of Case appearance, Pesetsky (2013, 8) makes the following statement:

> Every element that comes from the lexicon as a noun, determiner, verb or preposition could equally well be described as coming from the lexicon assigned to the corresponding case-categories. In other words, from the point of view of syntax, every noun can be described as "born genitive," every verb as "born accusative," every determiner as "born nominative," and every preposition as "born oblique."

According to this statement, one should be able to find overt manifestations of genitive Case (i.e., affixal N/A) on nouns and adjectives themselves. I will argue that this is exactly what we find with so-called adverbial -*s*. Adverbial -*s* is the manifestation (spell-out) of the "genitive property" with which N and A are born. But before elaborating on this, I would like to make one more theoretical step. In line with Marantz (1997), Borer (2005), and others, I assume that lexical categories (nouns, adjectives, etc.) have the form f-Root, where f is a categorial head and the Root (henceforth √) is unspecified as to category. Thus, the noun *city* has a composite structure: *[$_{nP}$ n° [$_{\surd P}$ √city]]*. For the above-mentioned approach to Case, this means that genitive case is an affixal n°/a°. This categorial affix can surface on a satellite constituent of the noun through case assignment, or it can surface on n° itself (the "n°-as-born-genitive" way).

Taking the preceding as our theoretical framework, let us return to the patterns *zachtjes* and *anders* in (5) and see how we can account for the appearance of -*s*. The first pattern was assigned the structure in (11a), repeated as (22a). Under an analysis in which nouns have the form *n°* + √, the pattern in (22a) can be reanalyzed as (22b):

(22) a. [$_{NP}$ [$_{AP}$ zacht] [$_{NP}$ -je-s]]

b. [$_{nP}$ zacht [$_{nP}$ n (= -s) [√-je]]]

In (22b), the diminutive morpheme is a root carrying the abstract meaning "way." In the spirit of Emonds (1985, 162–63), -*je* in (22) can be characterized as a "grammatical noun." Grammatical nouns, also called "disguised nouns" by Emonds, are an in-between class of nominals: "in-between" in the sense that they display characteristics of both lexical categories and functional categories. According to Emonds, the closed class of English grammatical nouns includes lexical items such as *self*, *one*, *thing*, *place*, *time*, and *way*, which can be part of more complex expressions such as *him+self*, *no+one*, *some+thing*, *any+place*, *some+times*, and *any+way*. These grammatical nouns are lexical items that are used frequently and whose semantics are "less explicit." The impoverished semantics of grammatical nouns can be easily demonstrated by means of a comparison of the lexical noun *thing*, as in *I bought a nice thing*, and the grammatical noun *thing*, as in *I bought something*. In the former example, *thing* can be replaced by a contentful noun like *bike* or *table*; in the latter example such a replacement is impossible. Notice also that the lexical noun *thing* can be pluralized (*I bought some nice things*), while the grammatical noun *thing* cannot (*I bought something(*s) nice*).

Taking *-je* in *zachtjes* to be a grammatical noun, let us return to the question as to what accounts for the obligatory appearance of "adverbial" *-s*, which we have reinterpreted as an affixal n°. I assume that, just like other roots that combine with n°, the grammatical noun *-je* raises to n°, creating the amalgam *[-je+n°]*. Suppose now that, due to the "morphological weakness" of the grammatical noun *-je*, this complex head needs "nominal support" from a dummy element. This nominal support is provided by spelling out the genitive property with which n° is born; that is, n° is spelled out affixally, yielding *[-je+n° (= -s)]*. In a way, spelling out n° as *-s* makes the "nouniness" of the amalgam visible and recoverable. The *-s*-less pattern *zacht-je* in (6a) is ill-formed because the grammatical noun *-je* is too weak to function on its own as the nominal head of the projection nP.

Let us now turn to the pattern *anders* in (5b). Recall from the preceding that *anders* was analyzed as an intrinsically (i.e., lexically specified) comparative form; that is, the comparative meaning is an intrinsic part of *ander*, and *ander* is not lexically decomposable into an adjectival part and a comparative part. With the comparative feature—strictly speaking, a functional property—being part of the lexical item *ander*, it does not seem implausible to analyze *ander* as a grammatical adjective in the sense of Emonds (1985). Just like *-je*, I take *ander* to have undergone head movement to the categorial head, in this case a°, forming the amalgam *[[ander]+a°]*. Being a grammatical adjective, *ander* is too weak to act as an independent externalized adjectival head. Also in this case, support is needed in the form of externalization of the "genitive property" with which a° is born; that is, a° surfaces affixally as *-s*: *[[ander]+a° (= -s)]*.

The externalization of the genitive property with which n°/a° are born has a last resort flavor: Externalization as a part-of-speech suffix, viz. *-s*, must happen in order to mark the nominal/adjectival nature of the amalgam [Root + n/a], where Root equals a grammatical noun or adjective. Another structural environment where externalization of n° as *-s* may be expected is one in which the root is phonetically empty, that is, an ellipsis environment. Consider, for example, the "adverbial" expression *ineens* (in+one+-*s*, "at once/all of a sudden") in (1). I propose it has the structure in (23a). The categorial head n° externalizes as *-s* in order to make the nominal nature of the nP-complement of the preposition *in* recoverable. When the root is overt and "substantive enough" (i.e., not a grammatical noun), *-s* support is not needed and, for reasons of economy, is excluded; see the ill-formed pattern *in één keer(*-s)* in (23b).

(23) a. [$_{PP}$ in [$_{QP}$ één [$_{nP}$ n (= -*s*) [$\surd_{\varnothing}$]]]]

b. [$_{PP}$ in [$_{QP}$ één [$_{nP}$ [√keer+n] (= *-*s*)] ~~[√keer]~~]]]

Possibly, the presence of the functional Q-head *één* also plays a role in blocking the appearance of *-s* in (23b). Being a functional head in the extended nominal projection, the nominal nature of the entire projection is recoverable on the basis of this head. I should add that presence of *één* cannot be a sufficient condition for expressing the nominal nature of a projection. If it were, the ellipsis pattern **in één* (meaning "at once") should be fine, but it is not.

Recall at this point the adverbial expression *ondergronds* "underground" in (3a). Here -*s* must be spelled out, as in (24a), in spite of the presence of *grond*. As was shown in (3b), the pattern *onder de grond* does not exhibit "adverbial" -*s* on *grond*; see (24b). I propose that this is due to the presence of the determiner phrase (DP) layer, specifically the functional D-head *de*. The nominal flavor of the entire projection is marked by *de*. Consequently, the last-resort -*s*-insertion operation need not take place and therefore does not take place.

(24) a. $[_{\text{PP}}$ onder $[_{\text{nP}}$ [√grond+n (= -*s*)] ~~[√grond]~~]] (ondergronds)

b. $[_{\text{PP}}$ onder $[_{\text{DP}}$ de $[_{\text{nP}}$ [√grond+n (*-*s*)] ~~[√grond]~~]]] (onder de grond)

A Note on Adverbial -*s* in Dutch Child Language

So far, I have tried to show that adverbial -*s* is still an active part of Dutch grammar. Its appearance is rule-governed and its use is quite productive. With its affixal status, -*s* is "glued" on a host and may therefore be hard to identify. Another factor that might contribute to its hidden character is its occurrence at the end of a pattern. The hidden nature of adverbial -*s* raises the question how children are able to acquire this element of Dutch grammar. Discovering the grammar of adverbial -*s* purely on the basis of its appearance in external E-language strings of elements seems like a very difficult task. Under an approach in which language-learning children scan the utterances in their linguistic environment for designated structures or cues (i.e., pieces of I-language structure) prescribed by Universal Grammar (UG), the identification and acquisition of "adverbial" -*s* seems more straightforward (Dresher 1999; Lightfoot 1999). The children's UG-based knowledge of the structure $[_{\text{nP/aP}}$ n/a [RP]] and their UG-based knowledge that n/a is born genitive help them in parsing adverbial -*s* as a manifestation (i.e., overt expression) of the categorial heads n/a in the structure $[_{\text{nP/aP}}$ n/a [RP]].

Since a detailed discussion of the acquisition of adverbial -*s* falls beyond the scope of this chapter, I restrict myself to giving some examples of patterns featuring adverbial -*s* in Dutch child language; data is drawn from the Van Kampen corpus (Van Kampen 2009; MacWhinney 2000):

(25) a. (i)k ook *es* die eten. (2 years;0 months.19 days)
I also once those eat
"I also want to eat/try these."

b. ik ga sakjes terusbrenge. (3;0.18)
I go soon-DIM-S return
"I will also return it soon."

c. nee kwil t andersom. (3;3.03)
no I-want it other-s-around
"No, I'd like to have it the other way around."

d. nee, nee dan gaan we eventjes sgoot. (3;8.15)
no no then go we just-dim-s ??

e. nee, dat is nietes! (3;11.16)
no that is not-e-s
"No, that's not true!"

These examples show that patterns featuring "adverbial" *-s* are present in the child's output at a quite young age.

Note that (25a) contains the temporal adverb *es* "once" (pronounced /əs/); (25b,d) exemplify the pattern A+diminutive+-*s*; (25c) displays the pattern *andersom*, where adverbial *-s* occurs at the end of *ander*; and (25e), finally, shows the pattern *nietes*. The meaning of the latter corresponds to "not true" (Dutch: *niet waar*), which suggests that *-es* (pronounced /əs/) stands for an adjectival expression, viz., aP. The underlying structures of these patterns are given in (26). In line with the analysis proposed earlier, I assume that the root moves to the categorial head. I take *-e* (i.e., schwa) in (26a) and (26d) to be a "filler" sound.

(26) a. $[_{nP}$ n (= *-s*) [√-e_{time}]]
b. $[_{nP}$ sak $[_{nP}$ n (= -s) [√-je]]]
c. $[_{aP}$ a° (= -s) [√$ander_{[+comparative]}$]]
d. $[_{aP}$ niet $[_{aP}$ a (= -s) [√-e]]

A Note on Adverbial *-s* and Variation in Grammars

Adjectives can be used attributively or predicatively. In (27a), for example, *zachte* is used attributively; it modifies the noun *manier*. In (27b), *zacht* is used predicatively; it directly modifies the verb (phrase) *landde*. What about *zachtjes* in (27c)? Although the entire expression *zachtjes* has a predicative relationship with *landde*, the adjective *zacht* functions as an attributive modifier of *-je*; see (22b).

(27) Het vliegtuig landde . . .
the plane landed

a. op $[_{DP}$ een $[_{aP}$ zachte] manier]
in a gentle way

b. $[_{aP}$ zacht].
gently/softly

c. zachtjes
gentle-DIMINUTIVE-S

Thus, phrases that are used adverbially and look quite similar at the surface—such as (27b) and (27c)—may have a quite different internal syntax. Another striking illustration of this is given in (28), where both *onverwacht* and *onverwachts* are acceptable for me.

(28) Jan kwam onverwacht(*-s*) thuis.
Jan came unexpected(-s) home
"Jan came home unexpectedly."

I propose that bare *onverwacht* is an adjectival expression (i.e., aP) that is used adverbially. The pattern *onverwachts*, however, is arguably a nominal expression that is used adverbially. Within that nominal expression, *onverwacht* functions as an attributive modifier of a noun that surfaces in a minimal way, namely through the affixal realization of n° as -*s*; see (29) and compare (23a). I assume that the empty root carries the abstract meaning "way."

(29) $[_{nP}\ [_{aP}$ onverwacht$]\ [_{nP}$ n (= -*s*) $[\sqrt{}_{\emptyset}\ ]]]$

It turns out that dialectal varieties of Dutch sometimes differ in the adverbial forms they use. For example, Standard Dutch uses the -*s*-less form *mondeling* in a sentence like (30), while Kempenland Dutch, a southern variety, uses the form *mondelings* in the same context (de Bont 1958):

(30) Jan lichtte het mondeling / mondelings toe.
Jan explained it orally PRT

Schuringa (1923) gives the forms *ainlieks* "finally" and *eerlieks* "honestly" for Veenkoloniën Dutch (Northern Dutch), where present-day Standard Dutch uses the -*s*-less forms *eindelijk* and *eerlijk*, respectively.

Interestingly, even though -*s*-bearing forms such as *mondelings* "orally" and *eindelijks* "finally" are ruled out in Standard Dutch, we do find patterns in Standard Dutch that feature the bound morpheme -*s* at the end, such as *dagelijks* (day-*elijk-s*, "daily"), *jaarlijks* (year-*lijk-s*, "yearly"), *beurtelings* (turn-*eling-s*, "in turn"), *ruggelings* (back-*eling-s*, "backwards"). Possibly, this -*s* is also a manifestation of an underlying categorial head. The fact that these forms can be used attributively (e.g., *het jaarlijk-s-e feest*, the yearly-s-agr party, "the annual party") suggests that -*s* in these patterns is a manifestation of a°. I leave an in-depth analysis of these patterns for future research.

In sum, Dutch varieties display variation as regards the presence of "adverbial" -*s*. It was proposed that these surface differences are the result of differences in the syntactic structures that are used to express a certain adverbial meaning.

Conclusion

This chapter has examined the nature of what is traditionally called "adverbial" -*s*. I proposed that this bound morpheme is an affixal manifestation of the categorial heads n° and a°, and that its appearance is not arbitrary and unpredictable, but rather rule-based and, therefore, predictable. I suggested that (UG-based) knowledge of nP and aP may help the child in parsing (in combination with knowledge of Case theory) and acquiring these categorical externalizations. I further argued that surface expressions with the same "adverbial meaning" may differ from each other as regards their underlying internal syntax. This structural difference is reflected at the level of externalization: an -*s*-bearing versus an -*s*-less form. In conclusion: "adverbial" -*s*: so awks but so natural!

This kind of variation is best seen as the result of parsing, of assigning structure to expressions of external language (the "E-language" of Chomsky 1986) in light of what UG permits. Binary parameters do not seem to be helpful in these contexts.

References

Baker, Mark. 2003. *Lexical Categories: Verbs, Nouns, and Adjectives*. Cambridge: Cambridge University Press.

Borer, Hagit. 2005. *In Name Only*, vol. 1 of *Structuring Sense*. Oxford: Oxford University Press.

Chomsky, Noam. 1986. *Knowledge of Language: Its Nature, Origin, and Use*. New York: Praeger.

Corver, Norbert. 1997. "*Much*-Support as a Last Resort." *Linguistic Inquiry* 28:119–64.

de Bont, A. P. 1958. *Dialekt van Kempenland. Meer in het bijzonder d'Oerse taol. Deel 1. Klank- en vormleer en enige syntactische bijzonderheden*. Assen: Van Gorcum & Comp. N.V.

Déchaine, Rose-Marie, and Mireille Tremblay. 1996. "Adverbial PPs and Prepositional Adverbs in French and English." In *Canadian Linguistics Association Proceedings*. Calgary: University of Calgary Working Papers in Linguistics.

Dresher, Elan. 1999. "Charting the Learning Path: Cues to Parameter Setting." *Linguistic Inquiry* 30:27–67.

Emonds, Joseph. 1985. *A Unified Theory of Syntactic Categories*. Dordrecht: Foris.

Fodor, Janet D. 1998. "Unambiguous Triggers." *Linguistic Inquiry* 29:1–36.

Lightfoot, David. 1999. *The Development of Language: Acquisition, Change and Evolution*. Oxford: Blackwell.

MacWhinney, Brian. 2000. *The CHILDES Project: Tools for Analyzing Talk*. 3rd ed. Mahwah, NJ: Lawrence Erlbaum.

Marantz, Alec. 1997. "No Escape from Syntax: Don't Try Morphological Analysis in the Privacy of Your Own Lexicon." *University of Pennsylvania Working Papers in Linguistics* 4:201–25.

Myers, Scott. 1984. "Zero-Derivation and Inflection." In *MIT Working Papers in Linguistics 7: Papers from the January 1984 MIT Workshop in Morphology*. Cambridge, MA: Department of Linguistics and Philosophy, Massachusetts Institute of Technology.

Pesetsky, David. 1995. *Zero Syntax: Experiencers and Cascades*. Cambridge, MA: MIT Press.

Pesetsky, David. 2013. *Russian Case Morphology and the Syntactic Categories*. Cambridge, MA: MIT Press.

Rouveret, Alain, and Jean-Roger Vergnaud. 1980. "Specifying Reference to the Subject." *Linguistic Inquiry* 11:97–202.

Royen, Gerlach. 1947–54. *Buigingsverschijnselen in het Nederlands*. 4 vols. Amsterdam: Noord-Hollandsche Uitgevers Maatschappij.

Schuringa, F. G. 1923. *Het dialect van de Veenkoloniën in verband met de overige tongvallen in de provincie Groningen*. Den Haag: Wolters.

van Kampen, Jacqueline. 2009. "The Non-Biological Evolution of Grammar: Wh-Question Formation in Germanic." *Biolinguistics* 2–3 (3): 154–85.

Chapter 7

The Acquisition of English Article Alternations: Variation, Competition, and the Default

MARJORIE PAK
Emory University

Alongside the familiar *a* ~ *an* alternation (1a), many English speakers have a similar alternation in the definite article (1b), with [ðə] before consonants and [ði] before vowels:

(1) a. a book, a young man ~ an apple, an old man
    b. [ðə] book, [ðə] young man ~ [ði] apple, [ði] old man

Both *a* ~ *an* (henceforth A(N)) and [ði ~ ðə] (henceforth TH(I)) are variable alternations—meaning specifically that speakers sometimes "overuse" the preconsonantal forms *a* and [ðə] in prevocalic contexts (%*a apple*, %[ðə] *apple*). The preconsonantal forms are also overused in acquisition: utterances like *I ate a apple* are common until age 6, even among children acquiring the "standard" pattern in (1).

The focus of this chapter is a previously unnoticed contrast between A(N) and TH(I): While both alternations are variable, it appears that TH(I) is *more variable* than A(N). For example, many speakers who never say *a apple* sometimes say [ðə] *apple*, and the reverse pattern (✓*a apple*, *[ðə] *apple*) is to my knowledge unattested. Building on earlier work (Pak 2016a), I attribute this contrast to the acquisition of A(N) and TH(I) as fundamentally distinct types of alternations—one allomorphic, one phonological.

(2) PROPOSAL:

a. Unlike A(N), TH(I) is a *phonological* alternation. Specifically, [ði] and [ðə] are derived from a single underlying form [ðɪ] by phonological Tensing and Vowel Reduction—the same rules that are responsible for weak-strong alternations in other English function words, for example, *to*.

b. When children first recognize TH(I) as a phonological alternation, they can analyze it in more than one way. One option is to simply apply the same Tensing rule to TH(I) that is already in use for *to*—a *stress-sensitive* rule for the speakers studied here. Another option is to adopt a slightly different Tensing rule for TH(I), recognizing that [i] can be tensed even when stressless (*happy*, *baby*, etc.). The coexistence of these two options—*both* viable strategies for unifying TH(I) with preexisting phonological patterns—is what causes TH(I) to be more variable than A(N). A(N), in contrast, is recognized from the outset as idiosyncratic and thus analyzed allomorphically; there is never a drive to unify it with "other" phonological patterns.

The Pattern: Variation in A(N) and TH(I)

There is an extensive body of previous work on variation in both A(N) and TH(I), including sociolinguistic studies (Ash and Myhill 1986; Britain and Fox 2009; Gabrielatos et al. 2010); corpus-based studies (Jurafsky et al. 1998; Keating et al. 1994; Pak 2016a; Todaka 1992); and experimental studies (Gaskell et al. 2003; Newton and Wells 1999; Raymond, Fisher, and Healy 2002; Raymond et al. 2009). Again, VARIATION is defined here—as in most previous work—as the apparent overuse of the preconsonantal forms *a* and [ðə] in prevocalic contexts:

(3) a. % a apple, % a old man

b. % [ðə] apple, % [ðə] old man

A glottal stop [ʔ] can be inserted between the article and the following word in (3) (*a ʔapple*). Glottal stops are also frequently inserted after the prevocalic forms *an* and [ði] (*I want an ʔapple*) (Pak 2016b). I will not include glottal stops in examples here since the current analysis is not affected by their presence or absence.

The Adult Pattern: More Variation in TH(I)

Prevocalic *a* is common in many "nonstandard" varieties of English, with reported frequencies up to 100 percent in Philadelphia African American English (Ash and Myhill 1986), around 75 percent among Bangladeshi adolescents in London Tower Hamlets (Britain and Fox 2009) and at somewhat lower levels in London Hackney and Havering (Gabrielatos et al. 2010). Lass (2002) also identifies prevocalic *a* as a feature of the "extreme" variety of South African English. See Gabrielatos et al. (2010) for a more detailed review of A(N) variation.

Prevocalic [ðə] is attested in "standard" as well as "nonstandard" varieties of English—for example, the Buckeye corpus of central Ohio speech (Raymond et al. 2009, 108), the Switchboard corpus of American English (Jurafsky et al. 1998, 3113), and the TIMIT corpus of read sentences in American English (Keating et al. 1994). This last study reports no prevocalic [ðə] in speakers over age 50, but 33 percent prevocalic [ðə] in younger speakers, suggestive of a change in progress.

Those studies that have looked at A(N) and TH(I) in tandem have shown either high variation in both alternations (e.g., Ash and Myhill 1986), or higher variation in TH(I) than in A(N). For example, Lass (2002) describes middle-class South African English as having variable prevocalic [ðə] but no prevocalic *a*. Other studies showing

Table 7.1. Previous studies of variation in A(N) and TH(I)

	Prevocalic [ðə]	Prevocalic *a*
NA-English speaking adults in CHILDES[1]	10%	4%
White adolescent boys in London Towers Hamlets[2]	35%	25%
Bangladeshi adolescent boys in London Towers Hamlets[3]	81%	75%
Buckeye corpus[c]	~40%	<8%

[1] Pak (2016a, Table 1).
[2] Britain and Fox (2009, 189–90).
[3] Raymond et al. (2002, 629).

this asymmetry are summarized in Table 7.1. Notably, *no* study to my knowledge has found variable A(N) with invariant TH(I).

The Pattern in Children: More Overuse Errors with A(N)

As noted in the introduction, young English-speaking children frequently "overuse" the preconsonantal forms *a* and [ðə] (Gaskell et al. 2003; Seliger 1979):

(4) a. Boba Fett is a animal. (3.9 years) (MacWhinney 1991, 47a1)
  b. I'm gonna buy all [ðə] action figures. (4.2 years) (MacWhinney 1991, 48b2)

While the utterances in (4) are superficially parallel to those in (3), this is not a simple mirroring of adult variation. Children actually overuse *a* more than they overuse [ðə]—in striking contrast to the adult pattern in Table 7.1.

Newton and Wells (1999), in an experiment eliciting A(N) and TH(I) in British three- to seven-year-olds, find the frequency of *an*—over all prevocalic *a(n))*—lagging behind the frequency of [ði] (over all prevocalic *the*) by 5 to 15 percentage points at every age. I identify a similar pattern in my CHILDES study of North American English (Pak 2016a, Table 2)—prevocalic *an* lagging behind prevocalic [ði] throughout early childhood—even though the adults in the same corpus had the reverse pattern. This contrast gives rise to an apparent paradox:

(5) Children seem to take longer to acquire prevocalic *an* than prevocalic [ði], even when their caregivers are more consistent in using prevocalic *an* than prevocalic [ði].

Table 7.2 shows this same contrast borne out within two individual families from CHILDES: MacWhinney (1991) and Braunwald (1993), a subset of the corpora studied in Pak 2016a. Both of these corpora have a span of at least three years of recorded naturalistic speech produced by children ages 2–7, plus copious speech produced by parents. Moreover, the parents in these two corpora have remarkably similar patterns with A(N) and TH(I) as well as with a third alternation, TO; this will be a point of focus in a later section. For now, the key points to be taken from Table 7.2 are:

Table 7.2. Frequency of prevocalic *an* and [ði] over a 3- to 5-year period in two families

	speaker	age	% an	an/(a+an)	% ði	ði/(ðə+ði)
Braunwald	parents		100%	106/106	85%	152/179
	child 1	4–5	36%	5/14	21%	5/24
		6–7	31%	5/16	90%	53/59
	child 2	2–3	12%	3/25	36%	13/36
		4–5	20%	1/5	38%	3/8
MacWhinney	parents		99%	238/240	84%	338/401
	child 1	3	40%	8/20	38%	18/47
		4–5	29%	9/31	48%	35/73
		6–7	93%	28/30	66%	37/56
	child 2	3	33%	5/15	24%	5/21
		4–5	21%	8/37	38%	50/131

- The parents in both families have near-categorical prevocalic *an*, but allow some variation with TH(I) (approximately 15 percent prevocalic [ðə]).
- All four of the children "overuse" prevocalic *a* and [ðə] to at least some degree.
- With TH(I), three of the four children show a clear developmental trend—increasing use of prevocalic [ði] with increasing age—and both older siblings use prevocalic [ði] the majority of the time by the end of the study periods.
- With A(N), only one of the four children (MacWhinney's Child 1) reaches more than 50 percent prevocalic *an* by the end of the study period. Assuming that the other three children did eventually acquire their parents' pattern, any developmental trend they followed must have been established later than the ages studied here.

In the next section I explain the contrast in (5) by proposing that A(N) and TH(I) are fundamentally distinct types of alternations: A(N) is allomorphic while TH(I) is phonological. (The analysis of A(N) and TH(I) presented here is taken more or less directly from Pak 2016a.) Then I return to the observation we started with—that among adults, TH(I) is more variable than A(N)—and show that a phonological treatment of TH(I) helps us explain this contrast as well.

A(N) Is Harder Because It Is Unprecedented

Stages of Acquisition

Let us assume that, in order to reach adultlike patterns with A(N) and TH(I), children must proceed through three steps:

(6) i. Recognizing the alternation (i.e., associating the variants as "two ways of saying the same word")
ii. Analyzing the alternation (e.g., as allomorphic or phonological)
iii. Consistently executing the alternation in production

Achieving even this first step is likely to be delayed with A(N) and TH(I), due to the way the definite and indefinite articles are distributed in discourse.

First, the distribution is skewed: the ratio of preconsonantal to prevocalic articles is 9:1 in the MacWhinney and Braunwald corpora, meaning that children hear far more preconsonantal forms (*a* and [ðə]) than prevocalic forms (*an* and [ði]) in the input.

Second, the articles are almost always deaccented. English syntax does not allow articles in positions where they would be assigned phrase-final stress, and while it is possible for articles to have contrastive or "focal" stress (7), such utterances seem to be infrequent in child-directed speech (I have yet to encounter one in my CHILDES corpus work).

(7) a. Mary is thé expert on bats.
b. I said I wanted á car, not two cars.

Consider, by way of contrast, the English preposition and infinitive marker *to*, which participates in a similar alternation [tu~tə] (henceforth TO). Unlike the articles, *to* can be phrase-final, and in this position, it is always assigned some stress and pronounced with a full vowel:

(8) a. I told John not [tə] go, but he really wants [tù].
b. He gave this present [tə] Sam; I don't know who he gave that one [tù].

Correspondingly, as we will see, the MacWhinney and Braunwald children acquire adultlike TO by age 3, with *no* initial stage of "overusing" [tə]. This means that the delay in acquiring A(N) and TH(I) is not due to an inability to analyze or control alternations (6ii or 6iii). More likely, the culprit is a failure to even notice that there *is* an alternation (6i), because the evidence is not phonologically salient.

I therefore assume that prior to step (6i), children simply have *a* and [ðə] as *nonalternating* forms of the indefinite article (D[−def]) and definite article (D[+def]), respectively (cf. Gaskell et al. 2003).

(9) Nonalternating *a* and [ðə]
a. D[−def] ↔ ə
b. D[+def] ↔ ðə

Acquiring adultlike A(N) and TH(I), then, involves "unlearning" the insertion rules in (9) and replacing them with rules that produce the relevant alternations. The crucial difference between A(N) and TH(I) arises at step (6)ii) (analyzing the alternation): Children analyze A(N) allomorphically, TH(I) phonologically.

Analysis of A(N)

With A(N), there appears to be an additional delay in reaching step (6)ii). Newton and Wells (1999, 72) show that even when repeating a short sentence like *Jane gave me an ice cream* directly after an adult, children fail to produce *an* 40 percent of the time (cf. 30 percent with [ði]). An example from MacWhinney (1991, 20a2) illustrates the same kind of error:

(10) Father: And then he said, "That's an elephant."
Child (2;6): "That's a elephant."

Such imitation errors, reminiscent of the famous *Nobody don't likes me* parent-child exchange from McNeill (1966, 69), can be interpreted as suggested there: "Children assimilate . . . adult models to their current grammars" and do not produce forms that are not part of their grammar, even in imitation.

The reason for this delay in analyzing A(N), as suggested by Pak (2016a), is that A(N) is unprecedented: this is the only context where [n] alternates with Ø in English. The only solution available to children is to learn A(N) by "brute force": memorizing and storing the two variants and their contexts as a case of suppletive allomorphy (see Joseph 1997; Kaisse 1985; Rotenberg 1978; among others, for precedent).

(11) D[−def] ↔ ən /__V
↔ ə elsewhere

A [ə] is identified as the "elsewhere" allomorph because it is selected in prepausal and isolation contexts (Rotenberg 1978), for example, *Let's call it a, a, a . . . urf* (MacWhinney 1991, 47ba). See Pak (2016a) for an account of other variants of the indefinite article, [ej] and [æn/ɛn].

An additional assumption I make is that allomorphy, normally a "word-internal" phenomenon, is enabled here by cliticization of the article onto the first word in its complement:

(12) Article Local Dislocation: [D[±def]]⌒ [X] → [D[±def] [X . . .]]

(See Embick 2008 for more on Local Dislocation.)

The final stage of acquiring A(N) (step 6iii) can be characterized as practicing—remembering to execute (11) instead of the earlier, nonalternating (9a)—until the target frequency is reached. In some dialects, (9a) and (11) continue to coexist (or "compete") through adulthood; these are dialects that allow *a apple* as well as *an apple* (see Table 7.1). (See Embick 2008; Kroch 1994; Sneller, this volume for more on competing grammars.) In other dialects, the nonalternating grammar (9a) becomes extinct, yielding categorical prevocalic *a*; this is presumably the case for the MacWhinney and Braunwald adults in Table 7.2.

Analysis of TH(I)

Despite its apparent similarity to A(N), I argue that TH(I) is a fundamentally different kind of alternation—phonological rather than allomorphic (Pak 2016a). Unlike A(N), TH(I) is *not* unprecedented: there are other contexts where full vowels alternate with [ə] in English, including TO (Chomsky and Halle 1968, 111ff; Jurafsky et al. 1998; Selkirk 1995).

(13) a. *Affixation:* beaut[i] ~ beaut[ə]ful, happ[i] ~ happ[ə]ly
b. *Function words:* tu ~ tə, kæn ~ kən, fɔr ~ fɹ̩

The parallel between the V ~ ə alternations in TH(I) and (13) helps explain why TH(I) is acquired earlier than A(N). With A(N), children are forced to create an ad hoc allomorphy rule from scratch. TH(I), by contrast, can be subsumed under a more general pattern that has *already been analyzed.*

Specifically, V ~ ə alternations can be attributed to phonological rules of *Tensing* and *Vowel Reduction*—"word-internal" rules adapted from Chomsky and Halle (1968, 111ff) that are enabled here by article cliticization (12). (The word-boundedness of Tensing and Vowel Reduction explains why, for example, *ver*[i] *interesting* does not alternate with *ver*[ə] *funny.*) Under this analysis, [ði] and [ðə] are derived from the same underlying form [ðɪ] (14)a). If [ðɪ] is prevocalic or noncliticized, Tensing applies, yielding [ði]; otherwise, Vowel Reduction applies, yielding [ðə] (14)b).

(14)		_ apple	_ book
a.	D[+def] ↔ ðɪ	ðɪ apple	ðɪ book
b.	Tensing: V[-low] → [+tense] / __{V,#}	ði apple	———
	Vowel Reduction: V[-stress -tense] → ə	——	ðə book

As with A(N), the rest of acquisition (step 6iii) involves practicing—remembering to execute grammar (14) (with underlying [ðɪ] and phonological Tensing/Reduction) instead of the earlier grammar in (9b) (with nonalternating [ðə])—until the target frequencies are reached for the given variety of English. Again, I use competing grammars to model adult variation: the Braunwald and MacWhinney parents, for example, retain grammar (9b) alongside grammar (14) and continue to employ it about 15 percent of the time.

TH(I) Is More Prone to Variation because It *Is* Precedented

We are now ready to address the question we started with: Why do adults have *more* variation in TH(I) than in A(N)? There is no a priori reason to expect this contrast, given that variation is found in both phonology and morphology (see Tamminga, MacKenzie, and Embick 2016, 319ff). Still, I will argue that TH(I) is more prone to variation than A(N) due in part to its phonological status—or more specifically, its "precedentedness." I propose that different speakers adopt different strategies in their quest to unify TH(I) with other V ~ ə alternations (e.g., TO).

As noted above, TO has been described as very similar to TH(I), with [tu] appearing before vowels and [tə] before consonants (Britain and Fox 2009; Ladefoged and Johnson 2015, 118).

(15) a. John wants [tə] see me. ~ John wants [tu] invite me.

b. I went [tə] Dallas. ~ I went [tu] Atlanta.

The MacWhinney and Braunwald adults, however, have a different pattern for TO than for TH(I): they do not show a preference for [tu] in *all* prevocalic contexts, but only if the following vowel is unstressed (e.g., *to Atlánta, to arríve*). If the following word starts with a stressed vowel (e.g., *to* ánimals, *to éat*), they prefer [tə]. A series of examples produced by the MacWhinney father illustrates this general pattern:

(16) before V[-stress] — you can count [tu] a thóusand? (62a1)
It's just hard [tu] achíeve. (61b1)

before V[+stress] — Then you can count [tə] éighty-five. (62a1)
Is it okay [tə] éat cookies? (60b1)

Moreover, as noted earlier, the MacWhinney and Braunwald children have the same TO pattern as their parents—unlike with TH(I), there is *no* initial stage of "overusing" [tə].

I attribute the pattern in Table 7.3 to the following *stress-sensitive* Tensing rule, which requires the underlying lax vowel in *to* to have at least some stress in order to be tensed:

(17) V[-low] → [+tense] / ______ {V, #}
[+stress]

If the vowel has no stress, or if it is preconsonantal, it will not undergo Tensing and will later be subjected to Vowel Reduction (as in 14).

This treatment explains why these speakers so often have [tu] before unstressed vowels (*to* is assigned stress here, to avoid a lapse) and [tə] before stressed vowels (*to* doesn't get stressed here, to avoid a clash). The apparent variability of Tensing by this hypothesis is actually variability in stress assignment.

(18) a. he really wants [tù] (100 percent [tu]; obligatory stress on *to*)
b. [tù] a thóusand (85 percent [tu]; stress lapse in the other 15 percent)
c. [tə] éighty-fíve (85 percent [tə]; stress clash in the other 15 percent)

Now, assuming that the MacWhinney and Braunwald children have acquired a rule like (17) by age 3, why don't they simply deploy this same rule when they are ready to analyze TH(I)?

There may in fact be speakers who do exactly this. Participants in the study by Raymond et al. (2009, 97–98) more frequently showed a preference for prevocalic [ðə] if the following word had first-syllable stress ([ðə] *ápple*) than if it had second-syllable stress ([ðə] *Américan*)—as we would expect if the stress-sensitive rule in (17) were simply extended to TH(I).

Table 7.3. Prevocalic [tu] (vs. [tə]) in MacWhinney and Braunwald

		Adults		*Children*	
		% tu	tu/(tu+ tə)	% tu	tu/(tu+ tə)
Braunwald	before V[-stress]	88	22/25	71	15/21
	before V[+stress]	16	20/122	18	11/63
MacWhinney	before V[-stress]	83	68/82	96	45/47
	before V[+stress]	11	24/210	20	25/126

The MacWhinney and Braunwald speakers, however, seem to have postulated a slightly different, *non*-stress-sensitive Tensing rule for TH(ɪ) (revised from 14b).

(19) ɪ → [+tense] / __{V,#}

The precedent for this distinction, I believe, comes from the unique status of [i] in many varieties of English. Unlike other tense vowels in English, [i] frequently bears no stress at all.

(20) happy, funny, silly, baby, coffee, copy, Annie, very, lovely. . .

The stresslessness of [i] in words like (20) can be established by the absence of aspiration on a preceding voiceless stop (21a), the obligatory flapping (in American English) of a preceding alveolar stop (21b), and the placement of the mid-tone in the vocative chant on the *final* syllable (in words with secondary stress somewhere before the final syllable, the drop to M-tone goes there instead) (21c):

(20) a.	*Aspiration:*	có[p]y, snár[k]y	*cf.* snów[ph]èa, bar[kh]èeper
b.	*Flapping:*	sée[ɾ]y (??see[d]y)	*cf.* thrée-[dì] glásses
c.	*Vocative chant*:	snárkier, cópier	*cf.* bárkèeper, síghtsèer
		H HM H HM	H M M H MM

So there is abundant evidence that [i] can be simultaneously [+tense] and [-stress] in English—unlike [u], for which there is little evidence (Chomsky and Halle 1968 list *voodoo*, *Hindu*, and *jujitsu* as isolated examples of stressless word-final [u]). The unique ability of [i] to be [+tense -stress] is, by hypothesis, why the MacWhinney and Braunwald speakers have analyzed a slightly different Tensing rule for TH(ɪ) (19) than for TO (17).

Summarizing the proposal so far: At the point when children are ready to analyze TH(ɪ), they have two options. Option (i) (possibly adopted by some of Raymond et al.'s participants) is to subsume TH(ɪ) under the existing stress-sensitive Tensing rule for TO, while Option (ii) (adopted by the MacWhinney and Braunwald speakers) is to postulate a slightly different Tensing rule for TH(ɪ) in recognition of the unique status of [i] in English phonology. Both analyses are grounded in aligning TH(ɪ) with some pre-established phenomenon, and thus both follow the spirit of the current proposal, where TH(ɪ) is analyzed phonologically because it is precedented.

(22) Option i: Same (stress-sensitive) Tensing rule for TH(ɪ) and TO

V[-low] → [+tense] / ______ {V, #}
[+stress]

[ðə] cat ~ [ðə] ápple ~ [ðì] umbrélla,
[tə] go ~ [tə] éat~ [tù] arríve

Option ii: Different Tensing rules for TH(ɪ) and TO

ɪ → [+tense] / ____ {V, #} [ðə] cat ~ [ði] apple ~ [ði] umbrella

ʊ → [+tense] / ______ {V, #} [tə] go ~ [tə] éat~ [tù] arríve
[+stress]

There is in fact a third logical possibility—treating both TO and TH(I) as *non-stress-sensitive*. This would result in a pattern where *to* is pronounced [tu] before *all* vowel-initial words, regardless of stress:

(23) Option iii: Same (non-stress-sensitive) Tensing rule for TH(I) and TO
V[-low] → [+tense] / ____ {V, #}
[ðə] cat ~ [ði] apple ~ [ði] umbrella,
[tə] go ~ [tu] eat~ [tu] arrive

This option is also attested: Britain and Fox (2009, 186–87) report more than 90 percent prevocalic [ði] *and* [tu] ([ði] *apple* as well as [tu] *Ipswich*) in Fens English.

I believe that the situation seen here—where there are multiple options that all enable speakers to unify TH(I) with some preexisting pattern—is the source of the increased variation we see with TH(I) compared to A(N). Notice that one of these options—Option (i)—will consistently yield *more* prevocalic [ðə] than the others. In a community where some speakers adopt Option (i) while others adopt Option (ii) or (iii), the nonalternating grammar from early childhood will end up being reinforced, thus perpetuating prevocalic [ðə] among all speakers.

To see how this works, imagine two speakers S1 and S2. Both have the early-childhood [ðə]-inserting grammar (24a) (repeated from 9b) coexisting with a grammar where [ði] and [ðə] are derived phonologically from [ðɪ] (24b). But they have slightly different versions of (24b): S1 has gone with Option (i), with stress-sensitive Tensing, while S2 has gone with Option (ii), Tensing before all vowels regardless of stress:

(24) a. D[+def] ↔ ðə (nonalternating grammar)
b. S1: V[-low] à [+tense] / ______ {V, #}
[+stress]
S2: ɪ → [+tense] / ____ {V, #}

Now suppose that S1, using their grammar (b), says *the apple*. *The* is not assigned stress in this context (to avoid a clash with á*pple*), and so Tensing does not apply. Subsequently, the vowel in *the* is reduced: [ðə] *apple*.

S2 cannot analyze [ðə] *apple* with their grammar (b); their Tensing rule would apply here, yielding [ði] *apple*. S2 can analyze [ðə] *apple* only with their *non*-alternating grammar (a). S1's utterance thus serves to reinforce S2's nonalternating grammar (a) (cf. Legate and Yang 2007).

Having (re-)confirmed that grammar (a) is viable, S2 later uses it to produce a sentence where [ðə] is pitch-accented: *Mary is* [ðə́] *expert on bats*. Since this utterance can be generated *only* by the nonalternating grammar (a) (none of the Tensing rules in Options (i)–(iii) would fail to apply here), grammar (a) will again be reinforced. And so on.

With A(N), this kind of situation would never arise. There are of course speakers with variable prevocalic *an*, and I explained this variation by adopting the same basic assumption as for TH(I): these speakers have a nonalternating (*a*-inserting) grammar coexisting with an alternating (*a ~ an)* grammar. The crucial difference between A(N) and TH(I) is that there is *only one approach* to analyzing the alternating *a ~ an* grammar: creating an ad hoc rule from scratch, because A(N) is recognized from the outset as idiosyncratic. The type of scenario just laid out, where the nonalternating grammar is indirectly reinforced by misanalysis of an alternating grammar, would arise only with alternations with more than one viable analysis.

Summary and Conclusion

The fact that A(N) and TH(I) both apply to articles, and under such similar conditions, provides an unusual testing ground for hypotheses about the morphology-phonology interface. The focus of this chapter has been: Why do we find more variation in TH(I) than in A(N)? While variation in allomorphy and phonology are both attested, this chapter proposes a reason why some phonological alternations may be more susceptible to variation than parallel allomorphic alternations.

Following on earlier work, I argued that while A(N) and TH(I) are quite similar at first sight, they have different analyses: A(N) is allomorphic; TH(I) is phonological. I then proposed that phonological nature of TH(I) makes it more prone to variation: If an alternation is phonological, it will be analyzed as part of some broader general pattern in the language, but it is not always clear which general pattern it is to be aligned with. In the case of TH(I), we saw three viable strategies that speakers could (and apparently do) adopt: two that treat TH(I) on par with TO, and one that recognizes the unique distribution of [i] in English. This kind of indeterminacy, I suggested, allows inter- and intraspeaker variation to perpetuate.

Note

Thanks to Ian Kirby, Orli Hendler, the Emory Program in Linguistics, and the audience at GURT 2017 for helpful discussion and support. Any errors are my own.

References

Ash, Sharon, and John Myhill. 1986. "Linguistic correlates of inter-ethnic contact." In *Current Issues in Linguistic Theory: Diversity and Diachrony*, edited by David Sankoff, 33–44. Philadelphia: Benjamins.

Braunwald, Susan R. 1993. "Differences in Two Sisters' Acquisition of First Verbs." ERIC, ED 358 935.

Britain, David, and Sue Fox. 2009. "The Regularisation of Hiatus Resolution in British English." In *Vernacular Universals and Language Contacts*, edited by Markku Filppula, Juhani Klemola, and Heli Paulasto, 177–205. New York: Routledge.

Chomsky, Noam, and Morris Halle. 1968. *The Sound Pattern of English*. New York: Harper & Row.

Embick, David. 2008. "Variation and Morphosyntactic Theory: Competition Fractionated." *Language and Linguistics Compass* 2 (1): 59–78.

Gabrielatos, Costas, Eivind Nessa Torgersen, Sebastian Hoffmann, and Susan Fox. 2010. "A Corpus-based Sociolinguistic Study of Indefinite Article Forms in London English." *Journal of English Linguistics* 38 (4): 297–334.

Gaskell, M. Gareth, Helen Cox, Katherine Foley, Helen Grieve, and Rachel O'Brien. 2003. "Constraints on Definite Article Alternation in Speech Production: To 'Thee' or Not to 'Thee'?" *Memory & Cognition* 31:715–27.

Joseph, Bryan. 1997. "On the Linguistics of Marginality: The Centrality of the Periphery." In *CLS 33: Papers from the Main Session,* 197–213. Chicago: Chicago Linguistic Society.

Jurafsky, Daniel, Alan Bell, Eric Fosler-Lussier, Cynthia Girand, and William Raymond. 1998. "Reduction of English Function Words in Switchboard." In *Proceedings of the 5th International Conference on Spoken Language Processing,* 3111–14. Sydney.

Kaisse, Ellen M. 1985. *Connected Speech: The Interaction of Syntax and Phonology.* Orlando, FL: Academic Press.

Keating, Patricia A., Dani Byrd, Edward Flemming, and Yuichi Todaka. 1994. "Phonetic Analysis of Word and Segment Variation Using the TIMIT Corpus of American English." *Speech Communication* 14:131–42.

Kroch, Anthony. 1994. "Morphosyntactic Variation." In *Papers from the 30th Regional Meeting of the Chicago Linguistic Society, Vol. 2,* 180–201. Chicago: Chicago Linguistic Society.

Ladefoged, Peter, and Keith Johnson. 2015. *A Course in Phonetics.* Stamford, CA: Cengage Learning.

Lass, Roger. 2002. "South African English." In *Language in South Africa,* edited by Rajend Mesthrie, 104–26. Cambridge: Cambridge University Press.

Legate, Julie Anne, and Charles Yang. 2007. "Morphosyntactic Learning and the Development of Tense." *Language Acquisition* 14 (3): 315–44.

MacWhinney, Brian. 1991. *The CHILDES project: Tools for Analyzing Talk.* Hillsdale, NJ: Erlbaum.

McNeill, David. 1966. "Developmental psycholinguistics." In *The Genesis of Language: A Psycholinguistic Approach,* edited by Frank Smith and George A. Miller, 15–84. Cambridge, MA: MIT Press.

Newton, Caroline, and Bill Wells. 1999. "The Development of Between-Word Processes in the Connected Speech of Children Aged between Three and Seven Years." In *Pathologies of Speech and Language,* edited by Ben Maassen and Paul Groenen, 67–75. London: Whurr Publishers.

Pak, Marjorie. 2016a. "How Allomorphic Is English Article Allomorphy?" *Glossa* 1 (1): 20.1–27.

Pak, Marjorie. 2016b. "Optimizing by Accident: *A/An* Allomorphy and Glottal Stop." In *Proceedings of the Linguistic Society of America Annual Meeting* 1:12.1–13.

Raymond, William D., Julia A. Fisher, and Alice F. Healy. 2002. "Linguistic Knowledge and Language Performance in English Article Variant Performance." *Language and Cognitive Processes* 17:613–62.

Raymond, William D., Alice F. Healy, Samantha McDonnel, and Charlotte A. Healy. 2009. "Acquisition of Morphological Variation: The Case of the English Definite Article." *Language and Cognitive Processes* 24:89–119.

Rotenberg, Joel. 1978. "The Syntax of Phonology." PhD diss., Massachusetts Institute of Technology.

Seliger, Herbert W. 1979. "On the Nature and Function of Language Rules in Language Teaching." *TESOL Quarterly* 13:359–69.

Selkirk, Elisabeth. 1995. "The Prosodic Structure of Function Words." In *Signal to Syntax: Bootstrapping from Speech to Grammar in Early Acquisition,* edited by James L. Morgan and Katherine Demuth, 187–214. New York: Lawrence Erlbaum.

Tamminga, Meredith, Laurel MacKenzie, and David Embick. 2016. "The Dynamics of Variation in Individuals." *Linguistic Variation* 16 (2): 300–36.

Todaka, Yuichi. 1992. "Phonetic Variants of the Determiner 'The.'" In *UCLA Working Papers in Phonetics* 81:39–47.

Chapter 8

Verb Second Word Order in Norwegian Heritage Language: Syntax and Pragmatics

MARIT WESTERGAARD
UiT The Arctic University of Norway and NTNU Norwegian University of Science and Technology

TERJE LOHNDAL
NTNU Norwegian University of Science and Technology and UiT The Arctic University of Norway

IN THIS CHAPTER, WE investigate verb second (V2) word order in Norwegian heritage language spoken in the United States, that is, in a situation where the heritage speakers have English as their dominant language. We show not only that the syntax of V2 may be affected in a heritage language situation, but that the number of contexts for this word order may also be severely reduced (i.e., non-subject-initial declaratives). V2 languages typically have a high proportion of non-subject-initial declaratives in spontaneous speech, while English declaratives are mainly subject-initial. The reduction of non-subject-initial declaratives (the context for V2) is thus argued to be the result of cross-linguistic influence from English. We also show that this correlates with non-target-consistent word order, in that the fewer contexts for V2 that speakers produce, the more non-target-consistent non-V2 word orders appear in their data. We also discuss to what extent there is a causal relationship between the two phenomena.

This chapter is structured as follows. The next section presents some basic properties of V2 languages and English, focusing on the interplay of verb placement and pragmatic structure. This is followed by a discussion of some previous research on word order and pragmatic structure in different populations. We then formulate our research questions and present our participants and methodology. The following sections contain the results of our investigation and a general discussion of our findings in relation to our research questions. The chapter is concluded by a brief summary.

V2 Syntax and Pragmatics

V2 word order is a relatively robust property of all Germanic languages except present-day English, which has an SVO grammar. Traditionally, V2 is defined as a requirement that the finite verb appear in second position in main clauses. Importantly, V2 word order is distinguishable from SVO syntax only in declaratives that start with a non-subject, such as in (1):

(1) I går **spiste vi** fisk til middag.
yesterday ate we fish to dinner
"Yesterday we had fish for dinner."

In subject-initial declaratives, in contrast, the V2 word orders will be identical to SVO. There is considerable discussion in the literature as to whether subject-initial clauses involve a different underlying structure than non-subject-initial ones (see Travis 1984, Zwart 1997, and many others for extensive discussion). In this chapter, we assume that only non-subject-initial declaratives provide a relevant cue for V2 syntax, and that these clauses involve movement of the verb to some left-peripheral position, following den Besten's (1983) original analysis, further developed by Haider and Prinzhorn (1986), Platzack (1986), Holmberg (1986), Diesing (1990), Sigurðsson (1990), Rögnvaldsson and Thráinsson (1990), Vikner (1995), and Holmberg and Platzack (1995). Subject-initial declaratives have a different structural representation, arguably involving verb movement to a lower position in the inflectional domain of the clause (Travis 1984; Rögnvaldsson and Thráinsson 1990; Zwart 1997; Westergaard, Lohndal, and Alexiadou 2016).

The pragmatic structure of declaratives can be said to be reflected in the type of element that starts the clause. In Germanic V2 languages, the proportion of non-subject-initial declaratives is relatively high, as approximately 30 to 40 percent of all declaratives start with a non-subject in spontaneous production; see, for example, Lightfoot (1999), Westergaard (2009a), or Bohnacker and Rosén (2008). In English, on the other hand, the proportion of non-subject-initial declaratives is much lower, as subjects are preferred in initial position. As Yang (2001, 242) observes, "Based on the Penn Treebank, a corpus of modern English, . . . less than 10% of all sentences have V<2 word order." This percentage includes both XSV and SXV orders, demonstrating that XSV is rare and that there is a clear preference for SVO in English.

Thus, the difference between Norwegian and English is both syntactic and pragmatic: English is SVO and prefers subjects in initial position, while Norwegian is V2 and typically has a high number of non-subject-initial declaratives (the context for V2). These properties make it especially interesting to study speakers where English and Norwegian are in contact. Norwegian heritage speakers in the United States are precisely such speakers, as they are bilinguals who are native speakers of Norwegian, while they are dominant in English.

Previous Research

V2 word order is attested in monolingual acquisition from a very early age: Finite verbs are found in second position from the earliest relevant utterances in corpora of Germanic V2 languages; see, for example, Clahsen (1990, 1991) for German, Blom (2003) for Dutch, Waldmann (2008, 2012) for Swedish, and Westergaard (2009a) for Norwegian. Examples from Norwegian child language are provided in (2) and (3), showing that the finite verb appears in front of the subject.

(2) der **er** **mann**. (Ina.01, age 1;8.20)
there be.pres man
"There is (a/the) man."

(3) så **tegne** æ mamma. (Ina.02, age 1;10.4)
then draw.pres I mommie
"Then I draw mommie."

Furthermore, the acquisition of verb movement has been shown to be a step-by-step rule-based process, attested in Norwegian, Swedish, and English child language (cf. Waldmann 2012; Westergaard 2009a, b). For example, V2 in Norwegian declaratives is typically attested first with the verb *be* and full DP subjects, while this word order lags behind in declaratives with pronominal subjects.

In L2 (or Ln) acquisition, the Norwegian V2 word order has been shown to be a challenge for certain learners whose previously acquired language(s) do(es) not have a V2 requirement (e.g., Brautaset 1996). Bohnacker and Rosén (2008) have found that if both the L1 and the L2 are V2 languages, learners do not have any problems with the syntax of V2. However, they show that V2 languages may vary considerably with respect to the pragmatic structure of declaratives, reflected in the type of elements typically appearing in initial position: For example, while German declaratives often have informationally heavy (rhematic) elements clause-initially, the corresponding position in Swedish is mainly filled by informationally light (thematic) elements (especially *det* "it"). In a study of L1 Swedish learners of L2 German, they find that, while V2 syntax is attested from early on, the learners transfer the pragmatic structure of Swedish into their L2 German for an extended period of time; that is, the distribution of initial element types in their L2 corresponds to the typical Swedish distribution. An example of a (written) sentence in German produced by one of these learners is illustrated in (4), while example (5) represents the same sentence after it has been corrected by a native speaker of German, who has placed a heavier element in initial position.

(4) **Es** ist in dem königlichen Zimmern, wo den Besuchern die Motive aus mittelalterem Märchen begegnen . . .
it is in the royal rooms where the visitors the scenes from mediaeval sagas encounter . . .

(5) **In den königlichen Zimmern** begegnen den Besuchern Motive aus mittelalterlichen Märchen . . .
In the royal rooms encounter the visitors scenes from mediaeval sagas . . .
"In the royal rooms visitors will encounter scenes from mediaeval sagas . . ."

In the history of English, the loss of V2 word order in declaratives correlates with a reduction in the number of non-subject-initial declaratives in historical texts.

This has typically been referred to as a development where the clause-initial position is increasingly defined as a subject position (e.g., Kemenade and Los 2006). This means the structure in (6a) becomes less frequent over time in English, being replaced by the structure in (6b).

(6) a. [XP – V_{fin} – S]
b. [S – V_{fin} – . . .]

It is unclear to what extent the two developments (loss of V2 syntax, reduction of non-subject-initial declaratives) are causally related, and if so, what is cause and effect. Speyer (2008) has argued that the loss of V2 syntax led to a reduction in non-subject-initial declaratives, due to what he calls the *Clash Avoidance Requirement*, a dispreference for two prosodically prominent elements in adjacent positions (thus excluding a structure with a relatively heavy initial element followed by a heavy subject, e.g., [XP – DP_{subj} . . .]). The opposite development is argued for by Kemenade and Westergaard (2012): loss of information structure effects and a corresponding reduction of non-subject-initial clauses led to fewer V2 contexts in the input to learners, and thus eventually to a loss of the syntax of V2.

Finally, we consider previous studies on heritage languages. When a property is attested in a heritage language that is different from the non-heritage variety of the language, this is typically referred to as the result of either attrition or arrested development (sometimes referred to as incomplete acquisition; see, e.g., Montrul 2008). In heritage Icelandic, heritage Danish, as well as heritage German, it has been shown that, although V2 syntax seems relatively robust, occasional examples of non-V2 word order are attested in contexts where this would be ungrammatical in the non-heritage variety of the language (Arnbjörnsdóttir, Thráinsson, and Nowenstein, 2018; Kühl and Heegård Petersen, 2018; Schmid 2002). This has also been attested in previous studies on heritage Norwegian (Strømsvåg 2013; Eide and Hjelde 2015; Johannessen 2015a; Larsson and Johannessen 2015; Khayitova 2016). In general, it seems fair to say that examples of non-V2 word order are relatively infrequent. An example is illustrated in (7).

(7) Og der **dem lager** vin.
and there they make wine
"And there they make wine."
Target: Og der **lager dem** vin. (Eide and Hjelde 2015, 89)

Research Questions

In this chapter, we ask the following research questions:

1. May the pragmatic structure of declaratives be affected in a heritage language situation, similar to what has been found for L2 acquisition?
2. If so, what is the relationship between the proportion of contexts for V2 (non-subject-initial declaratives) and the loss of V2 syntax?

3. Why do there seem to be only occasional examples of non-V2 in heritage language data?
4. Could the production of non-V2 in Norwegian heritage language be considered the result of arrested development?

To address these questions, we conduct a study of a spoken corpus of heritage Norwegian spoken in the United States.

Participants and Methodology

Current speakers of Norwegian in the United States are second- to fourth-generation Norwegian-Americans, that is, descendants of immigrants from Norway who arrived in the United States in the late nineteenth and early twentieth centuries. They learned Norwegian from birth in the home, from their parents and grandparents. For most of the current speakers, the community played a limited role, related to the decline of Norwegian communities in the United States (see Haugen 1953 and Lovoll 1999 for more on the general linguistic and social situation). These speakers acquired English at age 5 or 6, and from then on, English became their dominant language. The current speakers are quite old (age 70 to 90) and have not passed on their heritage language to the next generation. Thus, today Norwegian is used only for special occasions with a limited set of speakers. Furthermore, the heritage speakers have minimal or no literacy in Norwegian.

Our data come from the Corpus of American Norwegian Speech (CANS; Johannessen 2015b), which currently comprises transcribed data from fifty heritage speakers of Norwegian heritage language. So far, we have investigated sixteen of the informants (six female, ten male). We compare these data with data from two speakers of non-heritage Norwegian in the Nordic Dialect Corpus (NDC; Johannessen et al. 2009), which contains data from four hundred informants from approximately one hundred locations in Norway. The corpora are similar, in that both consist of transcribed speech collected through structured conversations and interviews. However, we have relatively sparse data per speaker.

Concretely, we investigated the transcribed files manually, as it is not possible to search the corpus based on syntactic function. Subject-initial and non-subject-initial declaratives were identified, and for the latter, the clauses were also sorted according to whether or not they exhibited a V2 or a non-target-consistent non-V2 word order. Importantly, well-known exceptions to the V2 rule were discarded, for example, initial *kanskje* "maybe"; see Eide (2011) and Bentzen (2014). All files have been checked by at least two speakers of Norwegian.

Results

Let us first consider the results from the NDC. Table 8.1 shows the percentage of non-subject-initial declaratives for two speakers. The two speakers are very similar and we assume that they are representative of the situation in Norwegian, whereby approximately 30 percent of all declaratives are non-subject-initial.

Table 8.1. Subject-initial and non-subject-initial declaratives in the Nordic Dialect Corpus (n = 2, one female)

	Subject-initial	Non-Subject-initial (all V2)	Total declaratives
dalsbygda_03gm	224	100 (30.9%)	324
dalsbygda_04gk	214	94 (30.5%)	308

Table 8.2 displays the findings for the sixteen speakers in CANS that we are considering in this chapter, sorted according to their proportion of non-subject-initial declaratives.

As the table shows, speakers differ quite substantially in terms of the proportion of non-subject-initial clauses that they produce. Furthermore, the table verifies the previous findings that some speakers also produce non-V2 structures, another domain in which there is considerable variability: the percentage ranges from only V2 to 42.1 percent non-V2. Examples from the corpus illustrating V2 and non-V2 are provided in (8) and (9), respectively.

Table 8.2. Subject-initial and non-subject-initial declaratives in the Corpus of American Norwegian Speech (n = 16, six females)

Speaker	Subject-initial	Non-Subject-initial (V2+non-V2)	% Non-V2	Total
westby_WI_02gm	68	31 (31.3%)	—	99
coon_valley-WI_07gk	115	33 (22.3%)	1/33 (3%)	148
westby_WI_06gm	178	45 (20.2%)	4/45 (8.9%)	223
westby_WI_01gm	509	160 (19.6%)	2/160 (1.3%)	669
zumbrota_MN_02gm	137	33 (19.4%)	—	170
coon_valley_WI_06gm	260	57 (18%)	2/57 (3.5%)	317
zumbrota_MN_01gk	326	62 (16%)	5/62 (8.1%)	388
fargo_ND_01gm	174	31 (15.1%)	6/31 (19.4%)	205
westby_WI_05gm	85	15 (15%)	—	100
westby_WI_03gk	350	57 (14%)	—	407
portland_ND_02gk	157	25 (13.7%)	—	182
webster_SD_02gm	52	8 (13.3%)	—	60
blair_WI_04gk	217	23 (9.6%)	3/23 (13%)	240
chicago_IL_01gk	483	49 (9.2%)	4/49 (8.2%)	532
blair_WI_07gm	199	19 (8.7%)	2/19 (10.5%)	218
webster_SD_01gm	330	19 (6.0%)	8/19 (42.1%)	349

(8) a. og da mamma # gikk der # så **møtte hun** faren min (chicago_IL_01gk)
and when mom went there then met she father my
"And when my mother went there, she met my father . . ."

b. han hadde ett **sa han** (westby_WI_01gm)
he had one said he
"He had one, he said."

(9) a. det er rart . . . i Norge **de ville** aldri møttes (chicago_IL_01gk)
it is strange . . . in Norway they would never meet
"It is strange . . . in Norway they would never have met."

b. Når jeg taler norsk, **jeg taler** . . . (blair_WI_07gm)
when I speak Norwegian, I speak . . .
"When I speak Norwegian, I speak . . ."

In order to consider the relationship between non-target-consistent word order and the number of contexts for V2, we ran a correlation test and found a significant correlation between the percentage of non-V2 and the proportion of non-subject initial declaratives ($t = -2.52$, $df = 14$, $p = .024$, $R^2 = 0.31$). This is illustrated in Figure 8.1. In other words, the lower the proportion of contexts for V2 word order, the more non-target-consistent non-V2 speakers produce. The next section discusses what this finding tells us about the relationship between pragmatic and syntactic structure in this heritage language.

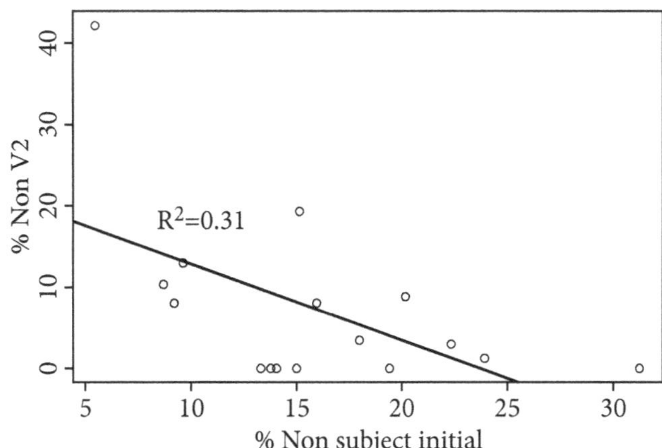

Figure 8.1. Non-Target-Consistent Non-V2 Correlates Statistically with Low Production of Context for V2 (Non-Subject-Initial Declaratives). $p < 0.05$.

Discussion

We formulated four research questions, which we discuss in turn here. The first research question concerns whether the pragmatic structure of declaratives may be affected in a heritage language situation, similar to what has been found for L2 acquisition. From the data presented in the previous section, we see that the initial element of declaratives in heritage Norwegian is quite different from what is found in the non-heritage variety, as there is a considerable reduction in the production of non-subject-initial clauses (the relevant contexts for V2). In the data of some speakers, the proportion of initial non-subjects is as low as 6 percent, which is similar to the distribution that is typical of English. A likely explanation for this reduction is that it is related to cross-linguistic influence from these speakers' dominant language. These heritage speakers are quite old and have been dominant in English throughout their adult lives. Thus, the typical distribution of initial elements in English declaratives overrides the pragmatic structure of Norwegian, the weaker language of these bilinguals. An alternative account of this finding could be that SVO word order is chosen because it is less complex than non-subject-initial declaratives and also leads to greater word order rigidity. This has been suggested for other heritage languages, for example, Russian or Spanish (Benmamoun, Montrul, and Polinsky 2013; Scontras, Fuchs, and Polinsky 2015), but in these cases, the majority language of the heritage speakers was also English, and it is thus impossible to distinguish between the two accounts.

Our second research question asks whether there is a relationship between the number of contexts for V2 and the loss of V2 syntax. According to the statistical analysis, there is a correlation between the two, in the sense that the fewer the contexts for V2 (non-subject-initial declaratives), the more non-V2 errors the speakers produce. Thus, the situation in heritage Norwegian is similar to what has been found for the history of English. Clearly, a correlation does not necessarily mean that the two findings are causally related: It is possible that the speakers' production is affected by their general proficiency in the heritage language and that the non-target-consistent production of V2 word order would also correlate with other deviant forms, for example, grammatical gender (Lohndal and Westergaard 2016). However, *if* the two phenomena are causally related, there are of course two possible scenarios, as in the history of English: (i) the loss of V2 syntax leads to a reduction in non-subject-initial declaratives, or (ii) the development is the other way around, in that the reduction in contexts for V2 leads to the loss of the syntax of V2.

We believe that there is some evidence against scenario (i): The heritage Norwegian speakers still use V2 syntax; note that even the speaker who produces only 6 percent non-subject-initial declaratives uses this word order close to 60 percent (cf. Table 8.2). Thus, the syntax of V2 is not lost from the I-language grammars of the heritage speakers, and it should be possible to retrieve it in cases where it would be necessary for prosodic Clash Avoidance (Speyer 2008). Furthermore, in the heritage speaker data—as in spontaneous spoken language in general (see, e.g., Westergaard 2010)—subjects are predominantly realized as pronouns, and in those cases, there is no prosodic clash, as the (heavy) initial element would be followed by a prosodically light subject. Thus, we find it more likely that the development is the other way around: Due to these speakers being unbalanced bilinguals (just like L2 learners; cf. Bohnacker and Rosén 2008), the pragmatic structure of their dominant language is affecting the distribution of initial elements in declaratives, causing them to produce a predominance of subject-initial clauses. This means that the context for V2 syntax is severely reduced in their own production, leading to this word order becoming vulnerable to further cross-linguistic influence from English. This means that the representation of V2 syntax is presumably (more or less) intact in the I-language grammar of these heritage Norwegian speakers, but due to lack of use of Norwegian and especially the context for V2 word order, the syntax of V2 becomes harder to retrieve in production.

We now turn to the third research question, which asks why there seem to be relatively few examples of non-V2 in heritage data. The answer to this question may be quite trivial. We have seen that the speakers who have the most problems with V2 syntax also produce very few contexts for V2 (i.e., declaratives with initial non-subjects). This means that these speakers in some sense avoid V2 syntax, and consequently, there will be few non-target-consistent examples in the data.

The last research question is concerned with whether the production of non-V2 in Norwegian heritage language is a result of (so-called) incomplete acquisition or arrested development, as has been argued for by Khayitova (2016). We consider it unlikely that V2 is not completely acquired in childhood, for two reasons: First, these heritage speakers were monolingual children until approximately age 6. Based on research on first language acquisition and V2, including work on Norwegian (Westergaard 2009a), we know that V2 is typically acquired early. Thus, there is no reason to think that these speakers of Norwegian heritage language did not acquire V2 target-consistently as children. One may question whether a change in the grammar could have already taken place, meaning that the input to the speakers in our corpus had examples of non-V2. It is not possible to determine this, since we do not have comparable data from the previous generation. However, as Eide and Hjelde (2015) argue, there is very little, if any, non-V2 in Norwegian heritage language data before the recordings in CANS. This suggests that the input to the speakers was relatively robustly V2.

The second argument that goes against arrested development is the fact that acquisition is typically a rule-based step-wise development. In Norwegian, V2 first appears with the verb *be* and a DP subject, and then later on, the child generalizes it to all verbs and all subjects, possibly with an intermediate stage allowing all subject types but restricted to the verb *be* (Westergaard 2009a, 2014). If V2 had been incompletely acquired, it is to be expected that some step is not acquired and that this emerges in production in a way that is rule-governed. The data we have so far for the sixteen American Norwegian speakers discussed in this chapter do not provide evidence of rule-governed production. Rather, the production of non-V2 seems to be unpredictable, which is more in line with the idea of *attrition* (cf. Lohndal and Westergaard 2016). This has also been argued for by Larsson and Johannessen (2015).

Conclusion

In this chapter, we have shown that not only purely syntactic properties such as V2 word order may be affected in a heritage language situation, but the distribution of contexts for this word order may also be severely reduced (i.e., non-subject-initial declaratives). We have argued that this is a result of cross-linguistic influence from English, the speakers' dominant language, since English has a different distribution with respect to pragmatics/information structure of declaratives, in that most declaratives are subject-initial. A reduction in the context for V2 word order subsequently leads to less activation of the syntax of V2, and as a result, this word order will be harder to retrieve in production. Thus, the two processes correlate, possibly one causing the other. If so, we would argue that the reduction of contexts for V2 word order affects V2 syntax in the sense that it becomes vulnerable to (nonrepresentational) cross-linguistic influence from English.

Note

This research was supported by a grant from the Research Council of Norway for the project MiMS (Micro-Variation in Multilingual Acquisition & Attrition Situations), project number 250857. We would like to thank Alexander Pfaff and Isabel Nadine Jensen for help with the heritage language data and Björn Lundquist for the statistical analysis.

References

Arnbjörnsdóttir, Birna, Höskuldur Thráinsson, and Iris Edda Nowenstein. 2018. "V2 and V3 Orders in North-American Icelandic." *Journal of Language Contact* 11 (3): 379–412.

Benmamoun, Elabbas, Silvina Montrul, and Maria Polinsky. 2013. "Heritage Languages and Their Speakers: Opportunities and Challenges for Linguistics." *Theoretical Linguistics* 39 (3–4): 129–81.

Bentzen, Kristine. 2014. "Verb Placement in Clauses with Initial Adverbial *Maybe.*" *Nordic Atlas of Linguistic Structures* (NALS) 1:225–39.

Blom, Elma. 2003. *From Root Infinitive to Finite Sentences: The Acquisition of Verbal Inflections and Auxiliaries.*" PhD diss., Utrecht University.

Bohnacker, Ute, and Christina Rosén. 2008. "The Clause-Initial Position in L2 German Declaratives: Transfer of Information Structure." *Studies in Second Language Acquisition* 30:511–38.

Brautaset, Anne. 1996. *Inversjon i norsk mellomspråk: En undersøkelse av inversjon i stiler skrevet av innlærere med norsk som andrespråk [Tromsø-studier i språkvitenskap 18]* [Inversion in Norwegian interlanguage: A study of inversion in essays written by L2 learners of Norwegian]. Oslo: Novus.

Clahsen, Harald. 1990. "Constraints on Parameter Setting: A Grammatical Analysis of Some Acquisition in Stages in German Child Language." *Language Acquisition* 1 (4): 361–91.

Clahsen, Harald. 1991. *Child Language and Developmental Dysphasia: Linguistic Studies of the Acquisition of German.* Amsterdam: Benjamins.

Den Besten, Hans. 1983. "On the Interaction of Root Transformations and Lexical Deletive Rules." In *On the Formal Syntax of the Westgermania*, edited by Werner Abraham, 47–131. Amsterdam: Benjamins.

Diesing, Molly. 1990. "Verb Movement and Subject Position in Yiddish." *Natural Language and Linguistic Theory* 8 (1): 41–79.

Eide, Kristin Melum. 2011. "Norwegian (Non-V2) Declaratives, Resumptive Elements, and the Wackernagel Position." *Nordic Journal of Linguistics* 34:179–213.

Eide, Kristin Melum, and Arnstein Hjelde. 2015. "Verb Second and Finiteness Morphology in Norwegian Heritage Language of the American Midwest." In *Moribund Germanic Heritage Languages in North America,* edited by B. Richard Page and Michael T. Putnam, 64–101. Leiden: Brill.

Haider, Hubert, and Martin Prinzhorn (eds.). 1986. *Verb Second Phenomena in Germanic Languages.* Dordrecht: Foris.

Haugen, Einar Ingvald. 1953. *The Norwegian Language in America. A Study in Bilingual Behavior.* Bloomington: Indiana University Press.

Holmberg, Anders. 1986. "Word Order and Syntactic Features in the Scandinavian Languages and English." PhD diss., Stockholm University.

Holmberg, Anders, and Christer Platzack. 1995. *The Role of Inflection in Scandinavian Syntax.* New York and Oxford: Oxford University Press.

Johannessen, Janne Bondi. 2015a. "Attrition in an American Norwegian Heritage Language Speaker." In *Germanic Heritage Languages in North America: Acquisition, Attrition and Change,* edited by Janne B. Johannessen and Joseph Salmons, 21–45. Amsterdam: Benjamins.

Johannessen, Janne Bondi. 2015b. "The Corpus of American Norwegian Speech (CANS)." In *Proceedings of the 20th Nordic Conference of Computational Linguistics,* edited by B. Megyesi. NEALT Proceedings Series 23.

Johannessen, Janne Bondi, Joel Priestley, Kristin Hagen, Tor A. Åfarli, and Øystein A. Vangsnes. 2009. "The Nordic Dialect Corpus—An Advanced Research Tool." In *Proceedings of the 17th Nordic Conference of Computational Linguistics (NODALIDA),* edited by Kristiina Jokinen and Eckhard Bick, 73–80. NEALT Proceedings Series 4.

Kemenade, Ans van, and Bettelou Los. 2006. "Discourse adverbs and clausal syntax in Old and Middle English." In *Handbook of the History of English,* edited by Ans van Kemenade and Bettelou Los, 224–48. Malden, MA: Blackwell.

Kemenade, Ans van, and Marit Westergaard. 2012. "Syntax and Information Structure: Verb-Second Variation in Middle English." In *Information Structure and Syntactic Change in the History of English,* edited by Anneli Meurman Solin, María José López-Couso, and Bettelou Los, 87–118. Oxford: Oxford University Press.

Khayitova, Sofiya. 2016. "V2 i amerikanorsk—ufullstendig innlæring eller språkforvitring?" [V2 in American Norwegian—Incomplete Acquisition or Attrition?]. MA thesis, University of Oslo.

Kühl, Karoline, and Jan Heegård Petersen. 2018. "The Position of Subject and Finite Verb in American Danish Sentences with a Fronted Element." *Journal of Language Contact* 11 (3): 413–40.

Larsson, Ida, and Janne Bondi Johannessen. 2015. "Incomplete Acquisition and Verb Placement in Heritage Scandinavian." In *Moribund Germanic Heritage Languages in North America: Theoretical Perspectives and Empirical Findings,* edited by B. Richard Page and Michael T. Putnam, 153–89. Leiden: Brill.

Lightfoot, David. 1999. *The Development of Language: Acquisition, Change, and Evolution.* Malden: Blackwell.

Lohndal, Terje, and Marit Westergaard. 2016. "Grammatical Gender in American Norwegian Heritage Language: Stability or Attrition?" *Frontiers in Psychology* 7:344. doi:10.3389/fpsyg.2016.00344.

Lovoll, Odd S. 1999. *The Promise of America: A History of the Norwegian-American People.* Rev. ed. Minneapolis: University of Minnesota Press.

Montrul, Silvina. 2008. *Incomplete Acquisition in Bilingualism: Re-examining the Age Factor.* Amsterdam: Benjamins.

Platzack, Christer. 1986. "COMP, INFL, and Germanic Word Order." In *Topics in Scandinavian Syntax,* edited by Lars Hellan and Kirsti Koch Christensen, 185–234. Dordrecht: Reidel.

Rögnvaldsson, Eiríkur, and Höskuldur Thráinsson. 1990. "On Icelandic Word Order Once More." In *Syntax and Semantics 24: Modern Icelandic Syntax,* edited by Joan Maling and Annie Zaenen, 3–40. New York: Academic Press.

Schmid, Monika S. 2002. *First Language Attrition, Use and Maintenance: The Case of German Jews in Anglophone Countries.* Amsterdam: Benjamins.

Scontras, Gregory, Zuzanna Fuchs, and Maria Polinsky. 2015. "Heritage Language and Linguistic Theory." *Frontiers in Psychology* 6:1545. doi:10.3389/fpsyg.2015.01545.

Sigurðsson, Halldór Ármann. 1990. "V1 Declaratives and Verb Raising in Icelandic." In *Syntax and Semantics 24: Modern Icelandic Syntax*, edited by Joan Maling and Annie Zaenen, 41–69. New York: Academic Press.

Speyer, Augustin. 2008. "Topicalization and Clash Avoidance: On the Interaction of Prosody and Syntax in the History of English with a Few Glances at German." PhD diss., University of Pennsylvania.

Strømsvåg, Sunniva. 2013. "Syntaktisk attrisjon i amerikanorsk" [Syntactic Attrition in American Norwegian]. MA thesis, NTNU Norwegian University of Science and Technology.

Travis, Lisa. 1984. "Parameters and Effects of Word Order Variation." PhD diss., Massachusetts Institute of Technology.

Vikner, Sten. 1995. *Verb Movement and Expletive Subjects in the Germanic Languages*. New York and Oxford: Oxford University Press.

Waldmann, Christian. 2008. "Input och output: Ordföljd i svenska barns huvudsatser och bisatser" [Input and Output: Word Order in Swedish Children's Main and Embedded Clauses]. PhD diss., University of Lund.

Waldmann, Christian. 2012. "Moving in Small Steps towards Verb Second: A Case Study." *Nordic Journal of Linguistics* 34 (3): 331–59.

Westergaard, Marit. 2009a. *The Acquisition of Word Order: Micro-Cues, Information Structure and Economy*. Amsterdam: Benjamins.

Westergaard, Marit. 2009b. "Usage-Based vs. Rule-Based Learning: The Acquisition of Word Order in Wh-Questions in English and Norwegian." *Journal of Child Language* 36 (5): 1023–51.

Westergaard, Marit. 2010. "Cue-Based Acquisition and Information Structure Drift in Diachronic Language Development." In *Diachronic Studies on Information Structure: Language Acquisition and Change [Language, Context and Cognition]*, edited by Gisella Ferraresi and Rosemarie Lühr, 87–116. Berlin: de Gruyter.

Westergaard, Marit. 2014. "Linguistic Variation and Micro-Cues in First Language Acquisition." *Linguistic Variation* 14 (1): 26–45.

Westergaard, Marit, Terje Lohndal, and Artemis Alexiadou. 2016. "The Asymmetric Nature of V2: Evidence from Learner Languages." Talk given at CGSW 31, Stellenbosch, December 2.

Yang, Charles. 2001. "Internal and External Forces in Language Change." *Language Variation and Change* 12 (3): 231–50.

Zwart, Jan-Wouter. 1997. *The Morphosyntax of Verb Movement: A Minimalist Approach to Dutch Syntax*. Dordrecht: Kluwer.

Chapter 9

Acquisition of Morphosyntax: A Pattern Learning Approach

HEIDI GETZ
Georgetown University

RECENT APPROACHES TO THEORETICAL linguistics propose that languages vary only in their lexicons. On this view, differences in morphosyntax across languages are captured by positing differences in the features of lexical items, such as functional heads (this is the Borer-Chomsky Conjecture; Borer 1984; Chomsky 1995). The features of lexical items must be acquired from exposure, but it is not clear what mechanisms enable this. How do learners identify the morphosyntactic features of words and morphemes in their language?

The present chapter examines the role of pattern learning, a kind of distributional analysis. Distributional patterns are what linguists capture using features. For example, in a language where Subjects normally occur first, the presence of a non-subject in first position might be captured by positing a Topic feature on the fronted constituent. Distributional patterns in natural languages tend to cluster, leading linguists to posit structures (functional projections) with positions for elements carrying different features. For example, languages with V2 word order such as German require verbs to be second in main clauses, which allow non-subjects to be first, but generally require verb-final in embedded clauses, where the subject must occur first. In addition, second-position verbs are morphologically inflected for finiteness, while verbs in final position are usually nonfinite. The relationship between fronting, verb position, and verb form is captured by positing a functional projection, CP, which has a set of features such that these surface contingencies follow.

In this chapter, I suggest that the features of functional projections like CP could be acquired by identifying and correlating concrete surface patterns. The process would work as follows. A child exposed to German might learn that (i) verbs may be second or final, and that second-position verbs take one set of endings, while final-position verbs tend to take a different set; (ii) subjects may be first, and when they are, the verb may be second or final; and (iii) non-subjects may be first as well, but the verb must be second. In fact, children learning V2 languages do know these facts quite early. Quantitative analyses of child language have revealed striking statistical contingencies among the relevant patterns (Poeppel and Wexler 1993). From this evidence, many generative linguists have inferred that children have adult-like representations of functional projections (e.g., Boser et al. 1992; Poeppel and Wexler 1993; Lust 1994). However, note that a child need not actually know what the patterns mean (e.g., that the verb endings encode the notions of finiteness or nonfiniteness) in order to place words in the correct position. That is, it is possible in principle for a child to learn correlations among patterns of word order and word form without actually representing those patterns in CP.

If this approach is right, then toddlers' knowledge of V2 languages may reflect knowledge of concrete distributional patterns, and not adult-like representations. This possibility has not been seriously considered in the generative literature. To the contrary, a widespread assumption in that literature is that acquisition of complex patterns is simply not possible without full linguistic representations. Poeppel and Wexler (1993), for example, note that "it is extremely difficult to see how such complex syntactic computations could be learned," and conclude that the only "realistic" representation of two-year-old Andreas's impressive knowledge of V2 word order is an adult-like transformational grammar including TP and CP.

However, the learnability of complex syntactic patterns is an empirical issue, and that is the focus of the present chapter. I explore the hypothesis that learners acquire linguistic contingencies by identifying and correlating concrete patterns of word order and word form. This is different in important ways from a constructivist approach (e.g., Freudenthal et al. 2007). Constructivist learning models posit that children memorize sentence templates but do not acquire any independent knowledge of the patterns inside them. In contrast, I suggest that the child does learn patterns, but may not initially represent them in an abstract adult-like way. Although the content of what is learned, on my approach, is inherently statistical—correlations or conditional probabilities between patterns of word order and word form—this mechanism is consistent with certain generative models of language acquisition. In particular, it fits naturally into cue-based models where the child is viewed as discovering linguistic structures in the input rather than evaluating grammars against a particular input (Lightfoot 1991, 2017; Westergaard 2009). On these approaches, the child uses representational primitives provided by Universal Grammar to "parse" input strings into pieces of structure. For example, knowledge of a statistical contingency between a topicalized (fronted) XP and a second-position finite verb might be stored as $[XP_{+TOP}\ [V_{+FIN}]]$. Other kinds of less structured representations (not posited by cue-based models) are also consistent with the pattern-learning approach, such as a simple list of facts ("the order of main clauses is XP-V where V has the ending F") or sets of conditional probabilities ($p(V2_{+F} \mid XP) = 1.0$). All of these are consistent with a pattern-learning mechanism because they allow for representation of incomplete knowledge. The child can accumulate pieces of structure (as in cue-based models), facts, or probabilities as she continues to identify and correlate new patterns in the input. Representing one set of distributional facts does not entail full knowledge of the entire grammar. This piecemeal approach to acquisition is importantly different from other generative approaches, where knowledge of V2 patterns is assumed to be possible only with fully adult-like linguistic representations.

A pattern-learning approach, then, is not incompatible with highly structured forms of grammatical knowledge. It is a possible mechanism by which knowledge might be acquired. This chapter takes a first step toward exploring how this might work. The most basic goal, motivated by the learnability concerns of Poeppel and Wexler (1993) and many others, was to find out whether a complex cluster of patterns can be learned in the laboratory at all, given minimal semantic and pragmatic information and relatively little exposure to the language. A second goal was to understand whether it is possible to learn those patterns without full linguistic representations. If so, a number of important questions will remain for future work. What specific statistical computations are learners using to identify and correlate patterns? Are patterns represented as (incomplete) pieces of tree structure, as in a cue-based model, or in some other form? Are there any limits on the kinds of patterns people can acquire? Do learners preferentially acquire the kinds of pattern clusters that are attested cross-linguistically? These are important and intriguing questions, but before we can answer them, we must ask whether a pattern-learning mechanism is viable at all. That is the question addressed by this chapter.

Methods

Our experimental approach was to create a miniature language containing a complex set of morphosyntactic patterns, and to ask which aspects of this language are readily acquired by learners. We chose the patterns that make up V2 word order—verb form, verb position, and fronting—for two reasons. First, this is a relatively well-known example of a canonical functional projection (CP). Second, it is exactly this contingency that Poeppel and Wexler (1993)—among many others in the literature—cite as too difficult to learn. The miniature language methodology allows us to test this claim empirically, as well as to ask whether learners need to represent the full structure of the language in order to acquire its morphosyntactic patterns.

Design

Miniature Language Structure

The structure of our language is summarized in Table 9.1. The basic sentence structure was S-Adv-O-V. We derived complex sentences by applying two rules: (1) front a nonverb (S, Adv, or O), and (2) place the verb second. These constraints allow sentences with initial Subjects to have either Vfinal or V2, while sentences with initial Objects or Adverbs require V2. The language's tiny vocabulary (Table 9.2) included a short, unstressed, meaningless "inflection" that occurred as a suffix on second-position verbs, but not final-position verbs.

Table 9.1. Structure of the miniature language.

	"Moved" words		"Unmoved" words				Types
Basic structures (12)			S	Adv	O	V-∅	6
			S		O	V-∅	6
Complex structures (26)	S	V-ka		Adv	O		4
	S	V-ka			O		4
	O	V-ka	S	Adv			5
	O	V-ka	S				5
	Adv	V-ka	S		O		8

Note: Complex sentences were derived by fronting a non-verb, placing the verb second, and adding the inflection -ka.

The sentences of the language contain a number of distributional patterns. Verbs vary in form (inflected or uninflected) and position (second or final), and nonverbs may occur either in the positions they occupy in the basic structure, or at the front of the sentence. As in natural V2 languages, there is a contingency between verb form and position and a further contingency between fronting non-Subjects and verb form/position. These patterns are produced by the transformational rules of the language, but they could in principle be learned independently from those rules. That is, the fact that verbs are second when Objects are first is an empirical fact that can be observed through distributional analysis and does not require knowing the position from which those elements moved (or even that there was movement at all). Teasing apart knowledge of concrete patterns from knowledge of the language's transformational grammar was the aim of this experiment.

Two-Alternative Forced-Choice Test

We designed a two-alternative forced-choice (2AFC) test in order to tease apart knowledge of the language's distributional patterns from knowledge of its trans-

Table 9.2. Vocabulary of the miniature language

Category	Word	Meaning
Noun	flugit	bee
	daffin	giraffe
	mawg	lion
Verb	zemper	hug
	nim	head-butt
Adverb	spad	slowly
	lapal	twice
Inflection	-ka	(none)

formational rules. On each of fifty-eight trials, participants heard one grammatical and one ungrammatical sentence. The grammatical choice occurred first or second equally often, in random order. Each ungrammatical sentence contained one of four types of errors.

Verb position errors were included to measure subjects' knowledge of the possible positions of the verb. The foils contained a verb in first position or third position, either with or without the V2 inflection. When the foil contained an inflected verb (*V1-ka and *V3-ka), the grammatical choice was an inflected Subject-initial V2 sentence. When the foil contained an uninflected verb (*V1-∅ and *V3-∅), the grammatical choice was a Subject-initial, verb-final, uninflected sentence.

Verb form errors tested participants' knowledge of the verb form/position contingency. Ungrammatical foils contained a verb in an allowable position, but incorrectly inflected (*V2-∅ or *Vfinal-ka). All grammatical sentences and ungrammatical foils were Subject-initial. There were two possible corrections for each inflection error: the verb either could be moved to a different position (keeping its inflection unchanged) or could remain in the same position but change its inflection. Foils were tested against both possible corrections, such that both types of foils were tested against all four grammatical Subject-initial structures.

Fronting errors were the most complex. In our language, initial Subjects could occur with V2 or Vfinal, while initial Objects and Adverbs required V2. We tested knowledge of this fronting restriction by pairing grammatical Object-first or Adverb-first V2 sentences with three types of ungrammatical foils: (i) V2 without inflection (*XP-V2-∅, e.g., *OV∅S); (ii) Vfinal with inflection (*XP-Vfin-ka, e.g., *OSVka); or (iii) Vfinal without inflection (*XP-Vfin-∅, e.g., *OSAV∅). Type (iii) is most crucial. Subjects could reject (i) and (ii) based on knowledge of the verb form/position contingency, but rejecting (iii) requires knowing that although the verb is correctly inflected for its position, the sentence is ungrammatical because initial Objects and Adverbs require V2.

Unlike other test items, which were designed to ask whether participants learned V2 patterns, the Transformational Rules test items allowed us to ask whether participants had fully acquired the language's transformational grammar. We first tested whether participants recognized the underlying (basic) structure (SAOV∅) by pairing it with a scrambled version (*SOAV∅). We also asked whether participants could distinguish between complex structures that either could or could not be generated by the rules of the language. Grammatical V2 sentences were created by applying the two rules, Fronting and Verb Movement, to the basic structure (SVkaAO, OVkaSA, and AVkaSO). To create foils, we rearranged the order of the remaining (unmoved) words, producing structures that could not be generated by the language's grammar (*SVkaOA, *OVkaAS, and *AVkaOS).

There are a variety of ways to succeed on the Rules test. Most importantly, if participants fully represent the language's transformational grammar, they should recognize that the ungrammatical foils cannot be generated by the rules of the language. However, there is other, less abstract knowledge that they could also draw on. Participants could succeed by rejecting ungrammatical bigrams, since each of the foils contained a bigram that never appeared in their input (*OA, *OS, or *AS). They could also succeed by simply memorizing the seven sentence structures as unique constructions. Success on this test therefore would not reveal what kinds of representations are required to learn a V2 language. However, *failure* on this test—if it accompanies successful learning of the restrictions on verb form/position and fronting non-subjects—would be informative: this would reveal that V2 patterns are learnable without full linguistic representations.

Materials

Audio recordings of individual exposure and test sentences were synthesized using MacInTalk in the Sharon voice from InfoVox iVox.[1] For each sentence, the input to MacInTalk included a string of words separated by 150 milliseconds of silence. Sentences were paired with videos from an existing corpus of miniature language stimuli (Austin 2010). In each video, one puppet approached a second puppet and performed a transitive action. The Agent and Patient of the action were always the syntactic subject and object, respectively. Our V2 language contained adverbs, so we created two modified versions of the videos where the action took place either twice or slowly. The videos in which the action took place twice were created by applying iMovie's Rewind function, then duplicating the video, such that the Agent appeared to perform the action, return to a standing position, and then reperform the action. The videos in which the action occurred slowly were created by applying iMovie's slow-motion function (25 percent slower).

The exposure set consisted of thirty-eight unique sentence types (four to eight sentence types for each of the seven sentence structures in Table 9.1).[2] Twenty-six of these sentences (68 percent) were complex (V2) sentences, while the remaining 32 percent (12/38) had basic sentence structure (Vfinal). Subject-initial sentences were a slight majority (53 percent). When selecting sentence strings, care was taken to ensure that the distribution of lexical items was even, both across and within sentence structures. For each sentence structure, sentence types were selected such that half used one verb and half used the other; each of the three nouns appeared as subject and object at least once with each verb; and, for sentences containing adverbs, each adverb occurred equally often with each verb.

Exposure was staggered across four blocks. Pilot experiments suggested that beginning exposure with a block of Basic structures led to better learning overall. We suspect this provides a stable word order to aid in learning vocabulary and categorizing lexical items, particularly Adverbs and Verbs, which might be misperceived as belonging to a single predicate category. In the first block, therefore, only Basic sentences were presented. Of the 12 Basic sentence types, half occurred once and half occurred twice in this block (in random order), such that participants heard a total of eighteen Basic sentences in the first block. In subsequent blocks, a mixture of six Basic and thirty Complex sentences were presented, such that each sentence type occurred a total of three times across the entire exposure phase. The order of sentences was randomized within each block for each participant.

Participants

Eight students at Georgetown University (ages 18–20, mean 18.6) participated in this study. Potential participants were screened via email. Individuals who reported having taken a course on language acquisition or language structure (e.g., Syntax) or any exposure to a V2 language were not invited to participate. Participants received $10 in exchange for participating.

Procedure

Participants were told that they would be learning a made-up language called SillySpeak by playing a computer game. The game was programmed in PsiTurk, a platform for conducting online experiments through Mechanical Turk (Gureckis et al. 2016) because earlier versions of this experiment were run through Mechanical Turk. Written instructions were provided on the screen. The experimenter was not present for any portion of the exposure or test phase.

The experiment began with explicit training of single nouns. An image of one puppet was displayed on the screen. Written instructions prompted participants to click the picture to hear the puppet's name and to repeat it aloud. At the end of this and all subsequent blocks, a refresher screen displayed images of all three puppets. Participants were invited to listen to and repeat the puppets' names again if they could not remember them. Next, participants entered the four-block Exposure phase. On each trial, participants listened to a sentence from the language and were instructed to repeat it. Each sentence was accompanied by a video of two puppets participating in a transitive action (e.g., "lion head-butts bee slowly"). Each block concluded with the refresher screen to ensure that participants had ample opportunities to review the three puppets' names. The entire exposure phase took approximately thirty minutes. The 2AFC test began immediately afterward. Participants were informed that there would be two new puppets, a Dog and an Elephant, who would each try to say what was happening in the video. The participant's job was to decide who said the best sentence in SillySpeak. The 2AFC trials were identical to the Exposure trials except that images of the two new puppets appeared below the movie, and a star appeared underneath each of the two images. Participants clicked each image to hear the two sentence alternatives. They indicated their choice by clicking the star underneath the puppet that said the best sentence.

Results

Test trials were designed to measure participants' knowledge of verb position, the verb form/verb position correlation, restrictions on fronting non-subjects, and the rules for generating sentences in the language. The design of the test was described in detail previously. Accuracy was measured as the proportion of times participants chose the grammatical alternative on the 2AFC test. The results for the concrete patterns of V2 word order were presented first, followed by the results for the transformational rules of the language.

Successful Acquisition of V2 Patterns

The patterns of V2 word order—verb position, verb form, and fronting restrictions—were readily acquired (Table 9.3 and Figure 9.1). On trials testing verb position, participants reliably chose grammatical V2 or Vfinal sentences over sentences where the verb occurred first or third, regardless of how the misplaced verb was inflected. On trials testing knowledge of the verb form/position contingency, participants reliably chose correct Subject-initial V2 or Vfinal sentences over sentences where the verb was second and bare or where it was final and inflected.

The most complex aspect of the language concerned the restrictions on fronting: initial Subjects allowed either V2 (inflected) or Vfinal (uninflected), while initial Objects or Adverbs required V2 (inflected). Participants in our study largely acquired these restrictions. Consistent with their knowledge of the verb form/contingency, participants chose correctly inflected Object- or Adverb-first V2 sentences over sentences where the verb was second but incorrectly inflected or where the verb was inflected but occurred sentence-finally. Crucially, participants also chose correct Object- or Adverb-first V2 sentences over Object- or Adverb-first sentences where the verb was final and uninflected. On those items, the verb was correctly inflected for its position, so choosing the correct item requires knowing that only one of the two verb positions is grammatical when an Object or Adverb occurs first.

Participants did not completely acquire the fronting restrictions. On trials where the foil was an Adverb- or Object-initial-inflected V3 sentence, participants chose the grammatical V2 sentence and the ungrammatical V3 sentence equally often. This contrasts with the result for Subject-initial sentences, where V2 was preferred over V3. These results suggest that participants may have learned a fronting restriction

Table 9.3. Choice of the correct structure on the two-alternative forced-choice test.

Ungrammatical item error type	Choice of grammatical item: Average (SD)
Verb position	
*V1-ka	.78 (.36)
*V1-Ø	.84 (.27)
*V3-ka	.69 (.37)
*V3-Ø	.63 (.44)
Verb form	
*V2-ka	.77 (.23)
*Vfinal-Ø	.73 (.26)
Fronting non-subjects	
*XP-V2-Ø	.79 (.26)
*XP-V3-ka	.47 (.31)
*XP-Vfinal-ka	.81 (.24)
*XP-Vfinal-Ø	.73 (.23)
Transformational rules	
Incorrect basic	.48 (.14)
Incorrect complex	.50 (.46)

Note: Participants learned the V2 patterns without fully acquiring the language's structure.

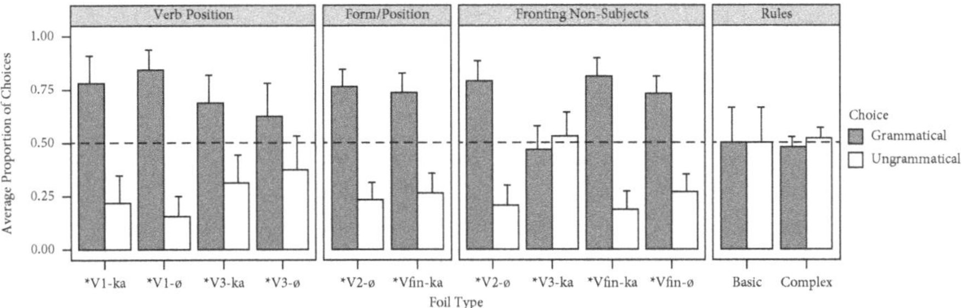

Figure 9.1. Average Choice of Grammatical or Ungrammatical Sentences on the 2AFC Test
Note: Participants readily acquired the distributional patterns, but not the generative rules of the language.

something like "if a non-Subject is first, the verb is medial," where the location of the verb was not specified in absolute terms.[3] In general, however, participants were easily able to learn the V2 patterns.

Failure to Learn the Full Grammar of the Language

The results reported so far demonstrated excellent learning of the surface properties of V2 word order. When knowledge of these same properties is evident in children's speech, many linguists have inferred that children have acquired a transformational grammar, where complex sentences are derived from a basic structure via a set of movement operations. Our methodology enables us to determine empirically whether a transformational grammar is required to learn V2 patterns, by asking participants to choose between sentences that could or could not be generated by the rules of the language. On these test items, participants chose the grammatical sentence only half the time, indicating that they did not acquire the language's transformational grammar (Table 9.3). That is, although participants readily acquired the surface patterns of our V2 language, this did not depend on full knowledge of the language's underlying structure.

Discussion

After approximately thirty minutes of exposure to our miniature V2 language, adult participants learned the two possible positions for the verb (second or final), the correlation between the verb's form and its position, and the restrictions on fronting (initial Subjects allowed V2 or Vfinal while initial Objects or Adverbs required V2). That is, they successfully acquired the central patterns of V2 word order. In children, this accomplishment has been argued to require knowledge of the full structure of the language. However, our participants could not distinguish sentences that could be generated by the language's transformational rules from those that could not be, as long as the foils did not contain violations of the V2 patterns. These results show that it is possible to learn V2 patterns without having full linguistic representations.

In fact, learning those patterns may counterintuitively be easier than learning other more basic properties of the language.

Children's Knowledge of V2 Patterns

The patterns that our adult participants acquired are exactly those that are acquired early by children learning V2 languages. Could children's early knowledge of V2 structures similarly reflect strong pattern-learning abilities, rather than adult-like representations? Children master V2 patterns at an age when it is not feasible to directly test whether their grammars rule out certain structures (before age 2). However, it is possible to ask whether children ever produce sentences like the ones our participants erroneously accepted. These were of two kinds. The first were the foils on our Rules test, where the restrictions on verb placement, verb form, and fronting are respected but there is an error in word order elsewhere in the sentence (e.g., *SVkaOA instead of SVkaAO). This kind of error in fact is attested for children learning a variety of V2 languages, including Dutch (Schlichting 1996), Norwegian (Westergaard 2008), and Swedish (Waldmann 2011; Santelmann 1995). The second kind of error was that participants did not prefer V2 over V3 structures when a non-Subject had been fronted (e.g., they accepted both *OSVkaA and OVkaSA). This error has also been attested in children learning V2 languages (Santelmann 1995). Waldmann (2011) notes that English-learning children make a similar kind of V3 error in wh-questions (e.g., *What you can do?*). In terms of errors, then, the evidence from child language is at least consistent with the hypothesis that children's knowledge of V2 patterns reflects strong pattern-learning abilities, and not adult-like representations.

It was noted earlier that the pattern-learning approach is compatible with generative models of acquisition that allow for a piecemeal learning process, particularly cue-based models (Lightfoot 1991, 2017; Westergaard 2009). In this regard, note that cue-based models easily capture adults' poor performance on our Rules test. Suppose a child has acquired the structure $[XP_{+TOP}\ [V_{+FIN}]]$ but does not yet represent that structure as derived from a more basic one. In that case, the learner has no reason to prefer, for example, O-V_{+FIN}-Adv-S over O-V_{+FIN}-S-Adv. Our participants' failure to reject Adverb- or Object-initial V3 sentences is more difficult to account for on a cue-based model. In future work, it will be important to determine whether this is an error that children learning miniature languages make as well, or if instead it is attested only by adult learners.

Conclusion

Functional projections manifest differently in different languages. In this chapter, I have argued that learners could begin acquiring the morphosyntax of their language by identifying and correlating concrete distributional patterns. I presented evidence that adults can acquire a complicated set of patterns without knowing the full structure of the language. Knowledge is consistent with "cue-based" models of acquisition, in which knowledge of distributional facts is represented as pieces of a linguistic tree, and with other forms of representations such as a list of rules. These results raise the possibility that children acquiring natural languages might also begin by learning patterns, without necessarily representing them in an adult-like linguistic tree. Ongoing work asks whether children are able to learn complex patterns as well as adults. If so, pattern learning could be an important mechanism enabling learners to acquire the morphosyntax of different languages.

Notes

Many thanks to Elissa Newport and David Lightfoot for valuable comments and discussion; to Kathleen Coughlin, Alannah Connolly, and Jaclyn Horowitz for assistance with data collection; and to the Newport Learning and Development Lab and the Feldstein Veron Fund for Cognitive Science for supporting this research.

1 http://www.assistiveware.com/product/infovox-ivox
2 We arrived at this distribution of type frequencies after extensive piloting. Preliminary results suggested that participants failed to extend a generalized "fronting" rule to adverbs when the AVSO structure had the same token frequency as the others.
3 For these test items, both alternatives contained an inflected verb (V2-ka or *V3-ka). However, it is not the case that participants were at chance on trials where both verbs were inflected: they strongly preferred V2-ka sentences over *Vfin-ka, regardless of whether Subjects, Objects, or Adverbs appeared first.

References

Austin, Alison C. 2010. *When Children Learn More Than What They Are Taught: Regularization in Child and Adult Learners.* PhD diss., University of Rochester.

Borer, Hagit. 1984. *Parametric Syntax.* Dordrecht: Foris.

Boser, Katharina, Barbara Lust, Lynn Santelmann, and John Whitman. 1992. "The Syntax of V2 in Early German Grammar: The Strong Continuity Hypothesis." In *Proceedings of NELS 22*, 51–65.

Chomsky, Noam. 1995. *The Minimalist Program.* Cambridge, MA: MIT Press.

Freudenthal, Daniel, Julian M. Pine, Javier Aguado-Orea, and Fernand Gobet. 2007. "Modeling the Developmental Patterning of Finiteness Marking in English, Dutch, German, and Spanish Using MOSAIC." *Cognitive Science* 31 (2): 311–41.

Gureckis, Todd M., Jay Martin, John McDonnell, Alexander S. Rich, Doug Markant, Anna Coenen, David Halpern, Jessica B. Hamrick, and Patricia Chan. 2016. "psiTurk: An Open-Source Framework for Conducting Replicable Behavioral Experiments Online." *Behavior Research Methods* 48 (3): 829–42.

Lightfoot, David W. 1991. *How to Set Parameters: Arguments from Language Change.* Cambridge, MA: MIT Press.

Lightfoot, David W. 2017. "Discovering New Variable Properties without Parameters." In *Parameters*, edited by Simin Karimi and Massimo Piattelli-Palmarini, special issue, *Linguistic Analysis* 41 (3–4): 409–44.

Lust, Barbara. 1994. "Functional Projection of CP and Phrase Structure Parameterization: An Argument for the Strong Continuity Hypothesis." In *Heads, Projections and Learnability*, 85–118, vol. 1 of *Syntactic Theory and First Language Acquisition: Cross-Linguistic Perspectives*, edited by Barbara Lust, Margarita Suñer, and John Whitman. Hillsdale, NJ: Lawrence Erlbaum.

Poeppel, David, and Kenneth Wexler. 1993. "The Full Competence Hypothesis of Clause Structure in Early German." *Language* 69 (1): 1–33.

Santelmann, Lynn Marie. 1995. *The Acquisition of Verb Second Grammar in Child Swedish: Continuity of Universal Grammar in Wh-Questions, Topicalization, and Verb Raising.* PhD diss., Cornell University.

Schlichting, Johanna Elisabeth Paulina Theresia. 1996. *Discovering Syntax: An Empirical Study in Dutch Language Acquisition*. Nijmegen: Nijmegen University Press.

Waldmann, Christian. 2011. "Moving in Small Steps Towards Verb Second: A Case Study." *Nordic Journal of Linguistics* 34 (3): 331–59.

Westergaard, Marit. 2008. "Verb Movement and Subject Placement in the Acquisition of Word Order." In *First Language Acquisition of Morphology and Syntax*, edited by Pedro Guijarro Fuentes, María Pilar Larrañaga, and John Clibbens, 61–86. Amsterdam: Benjamins.

Westergaard, Marit. 2009. "Usage-Based vs. Rule-Based Learning: The Acquisition of Word Order in Wh-Questions in English and Norwegian." *Journal of Child Language* 36 (5): 1023–51.

Chapter 10

How to Be Faithful to the Input in a Situation of Language Contact

ALICIA AVELLANA
Universidad de Buenos Aires and Conicet

LUCÍA BRANDANI
Universidad de Buenos Aires and Universidad Nacional Gen. Sarmiento

HANNAH FORSYTHE
Michigan State University

CRISTINA SCHMITT
Michigan State University

AS CHILDREN ACQUIRE A language, they accomplish at least two tasks: they construct a grammar from the input they receive, and they also learn the ways in which the community uses this system socially. These two tasks are independent, but we have plenty of evidence that typically developing children accomplish both of them early and efficiently. Children quickly discover the underlying rules of their language, and from a very early age they also match the frequency distributions of their speech communities and its different registers (Smith, Durham, and Fortune 2009; Nardy, Chevrot, and Barbu 2013).

Most work on the acquisition of grammar assumes an idealized scenario in which there is only negligible variability in the speech community. Under this scenario, children successfully acquire the grammar of their parents, predicting that languages should not undergo change (Keenan 2002).

But the fact is that languages do change. Somehow children end up internalizing a different system than their parents. Assuming that the human capacity to acquire language remains constant across generations, it must be that what changes is the input. To examine the role that children play in language change, we need to relax the methodological assumption of the homogeneous, stable speech community and delve into more realistic environments.

One common source of linguistic instability is population migration, which brings different languages and dialects into contact. This produces a clear rupture between what the migrant adults were exposed to and what their children are exposed to. In such cases, careful comparison of children's speech with that of their parents and that of the host culture can reveal the extent to which children's grammar "drifts" in one direction or the other. The particularities of this mismatch may even tell us something about how properties of the input determine the grammar that the child builds.

Since we have no reason to believe that the language acquisition mechanism is any different whether it finds itself in a contact environment or not, we have to assume that the child will always attempt to construct the grammar(s) to best fit the input that surrounds him or her. In doing so, the child must navigate the tension between remaining faithful to the input and making generalizations about it, a tension that is heightened in situations of contact, where the input is composed of utterances from more than one underlying grammar. In this chapter, we explore the idea that this tension is resolved by making generalizations in a modular fashion.

We focus on Paraguayan children living in Villa 21, an immigrant neighborhood of Buenos Aires, Argentina. These children are exposed to two mutually intelligible varieties of Spanish: the host variety (Rioplatense Spanish, henceforth RpS), and their parents' variety (Paraguayan Spanish, henceforth PS), learned either as a first or as a second language. They are also exposed to varying amounts of L1 and L2 Guaraní, which is Paraguay's second official language. The two dialects of Spanish are mutually intelligible and make use of the same lexicon and morphology but have underlying grammars that assign the morphological pieces slightly different interpretations and distributions. We take advantage of this situation to observe how children navigate the tension between these different grammars.

The Linguistic Background

Agreement

In RpS, agreement is categorically marked. Determiners, adjectives, and nouns agree in number and gender, and verbs agree in person and number with their subject, as illustrated in (1). In PS, however, agreement is subject to sociolinguistic variation, as well as variation due to individual speakers' proficiency in Spanish (Granda 1988; Krivoshein and Corvalán 1987; Dietrich 1995; Penner, Acosta, and Segovia 2012). Examples (2) and (3) are taken from our corpus. PS subject-verb agreement is not always marked (2). Nominal number agreement is often marked only once in the noun phrase, typically only when it adds semantic information. The presence of across-the-board lenition of syllable final /-s/ (3) contributes to the general tendency against overt realization of agreement.

(1) a. Las casas lindas están limpias.
The.F.PL house-F.PL pretty-F.PL be-3PL clean-F.PL
"The pretty houses are clean."

b. Nosotros hablamos español.
we speak-1PL Spanish
"We speak Spanish."

(2) a. **Está** todo(s) lo(s) dibujo(s).
be-3sg all-PL DEF-M-PL drawing-PL
"All the drawings are here."

(3) a. Hay **mucho** animales en la casa.
have **many-sg** animal-PL in DEF.F.SG house.
"There are many animals in the house."

b. Eso son lo(s) **zapato.**
this are DEF-M-PL **shoe.m-sg**
"These are the shoes."

Agreement in PS is an ill-studied phenomenon and it is not clear what its linguistic representation is, but for our purposes it suffices that agreement is obligatorily marked in RpS but not in PS.

Object Realization

In both RpS and PS, direct objects are realized with the same forms, but these forms are distributed differently over the semantic space. In RpS, object realization is sensitive to case, number, gender, animacy, and referential status. Referential direct objects may be realized as either (4a) full DPs (accompanied by the differential object marker *a* when animate); (4b) accusative clitic pronouns, which inflect for gender and number; or (4c) both a clitic and a DP, if the referent is animate. (Only animates are true clitic-doubling structures in RpS, according to Di Tullio, Saab, and Zdrojewski, forthcoming.) Null objects are also attested, but they are largely restricted to nonreferential uses, such as when the referent is an indefinite nonspecific (5), in contrast to cases like (6), where the referent is definite and specific. (However, in certain highly specified contexts such as (7), null objects with specific referents are permitted; see Masullo 2013.)

(4) a. Vi a Juan/la película (I) saw a Juan/the movie. b. Lo vi/la vi (I) saw him/her. c. Lo vi a Juan (I) him saw a Juan

(5) Vi bananas y compré.
"I saw bananas and bought (them)."

(6) a. ¿Trajiste el libro?
"Did you bring the book?"

b. Sí, lo traje.
"Yes, I brought it."

*c. *Sí, traje.*
"Yes, I brought (it)." (from Choi 2000, 534)

(7) Apaga ∅ [i.e. la luz, la televisión, etc.]
Turn off ∅ (cf. Turn it off/Turn off the light/the TV)
[Two persons leaving a room, one says to the other] (Masullo 2013)

In Paraguayan Spanish, the picture is quite different. First, null objects are permitted in definite specific contexts like (6), and the examples in (8) from our corpus show that they are also permitted in anaphoric contexts.

(8) a. El mozo agarró la rana y está llevando ∅ para afuera.
The waiter grabbed the frog and was taking (it) outside. [it = the frog]

b. Yo no trabajo por el momento porque no tengo adonde dejar a mi hijo, no quiero dejar ∅ con e(x)traño.
I am not working at the moment because I don't have where to leave my son, I don't want to leave (him) with strangers. [him = my son]

According to Choi (2000), null objects account for over 90 percent of anaphoric objects in the speech of both monolingual and bilingual Paraguayan speakers. Second, PS exhibits *leísmo. Leísmo* is the substitution of masculine and accusative clitics by the dative clitic *le*, which erodes the accusative-dative distinction, as well as gender distinctions, since *le* inflects only for number—and even that is inconsistent, given widespread lenition of syllable-final /s/.

While in RpS *leísmo* is dispreferred and socially marked (Ordóñez 2012; Kany [1945] 1969), in PS it is a common feature of all social classes and is consistently used for animate referents. Third, according to the literature, accusative clitics are nearly absent, being reserved for inanimate direct object referents (Choi 1998, 2000; Schwenter 2006; Usher de Herreros 1976; Palacios Alcaine 2000). Thus, the distribution of (non-DP) direct objects in PS appears to be sensitive only to animacy, with *le(s)* reserved for animate referents and either null objects or the (fairly rare) accusative clitics for inanimate referents. These differences are summarized in Table 10.1.

(9) Yo no le conozco a lo(s) animale(s).
I not LE know to DEF-M-PL animal.M-PL
"I don't know the animals."

Table 10.1. Properties of Rioplatense and Paraguayan Spanish

Grammatical property	Rioplatense	Paraguayan
Obligatory subject verb agreement marking	categorical	non-categorical
Definite referential null objects	restricted	widespread
Accusative clitics with gender and number	yes	rare
Use of *le* for direct objects	no	yes
Clitic doubling with accusative	yes	no

Hypotheses and Predictions

The hypotheses outlined in this section rest on the assumption that learners are equipped with both (i) a linguistically restricted hypothesis space and (ii) the ability to track statistical patterns in the input, which they use to calculate the probability of each hypothesis being true, along the lines proposed in Yang (2002). We also assume with Yang (2016) that the impulse to generalize is subject to economy principles. That is, children make hypotheses about how their input was produced only if making such a generalization is more efficient than simply memorizing the data it was meant to capture. With these assumptions in mind, we make the following hypotheses about how language acquisition will proceed when contact between dialects produces noisy or contradictory statistical patterns in the input.

Hypothesis 1: Faith in the input We hypothesize that children will treat the input they receive as informative. Since the learner does not know a priori that her linguistic environment contains patterns generated by different language systems, she will attempt to make the best generalizations she can to efficiently and faithfully reproduce these patterns. She will not, for example, attempt to simplify the rules of subject-verb agreement or discard forms or morphological features of vocabulary items in direct object position, provided there is enough evidence for these rules or features in one or the other dialect.

Hypothesis 2: Generalizations are modular We hypothesize that children construct the best fit for the data they are exposed to given the property being acquired. The learner does not attempt to make a wholesale choice about which dialect is a better match. Instead, she attempts to make generalizations by considering one subset of the input at a time. Convergence toward one dialect in the realm of subject-verb agreement, for example, does not imply convergence toward that dialect in the realm of object realization.

We will spell out more specific predictions in the next section where we examine children's production of subject-verb agreement and direct objects. In general terms, however, we predict no simplification and no adherence to one or the other dialect.

Corpus Data and Results

Subjects and Data

We report production data from a small corpus (approximately forty-seven thousand words) of three mother-child (MOT-CHI) dyads: (i) SF, a Paraguayan child who receives L2 PS input from her mother and RpS input at school, (ii) ML, a Paraguayan child who receives L1 PS input from her mother and RpS input at school, and (iii) TH, a native-born Argentinian child of comparable age and socioeconomic status, residing in the same neighborhood, who serves as a control. Subjects were recorded with their mothers and with an investigator narrating a picture book (*Frog Goes to Dinner*, Mayer 1974) and playing with toys (dolls, a kitchen set). The data presented here (Table 10.2) are part of a much larger, ongoing study of the acquisition of Spanish by Paraguayan immigrants in Buenos Aires. As such, the results reported here should be considered preliminary.

Table 10.2. Corpus size and speaker characteristics

CHI	Age	MLU	# Words	Input from MOT	MOT	# Words	MOT L1	# years in Buenos Aires
SF	4;7	3.2	6,494	PS (L2)	MG	15,126	Guaraní	15
ML	4;10	2.5	2,522	PS (L1)	RT	9,859	PS	8
TH	4;7	4.5	5,348	RpS	AN	7,426	RpS	lifetime

Agreement

Faced with a mixture of obligatory (RpS) and optional (PS) agreement, the learner can do one of the following:

(i) Simplify the input: end optionality by generalizing to a default form (e.g., 3sg).
(ii) Regularize the input: end optionality by generalizing to categorical agreement.
(iii) Match input frequencies: mimic the frequency at which agreement is produced, using a grammar that allows variability.

The first option would reduce both the set of agreement forms and the set of features that determine their distribution. The second option would amount to using all the features and forms in the input. The third option would amount to a variable rule for the realization of agreement identical to the adults.

Transcripts were reviewed by hand and any subject-verb agreement errors were noted, including cases where a null subject was used but its person and number features were obvious from context (thirty tokens total). Error types reported in Table 10.3 are

Table 10.3. Distribution of agreement errors

Subject	Verb	MG (L2 PS)	SF	RT (L1 PS)	ML
1SG	3SG	8	0	0	0
1PL	1SG	1	0	0	0
2SG	3SG	16	0	1	0
3SG	1SG	1	1	2	0
	2SG	3			
	3PL	2	3		
3PL	3SG	15	5	15	2
Total # of errors		46	9	18	2
# Finite verbs produced		2965	1364	1965	389
# of errors / 100 finite verbs		1.55	.66	.92	.51

organized by the person and number features of the subject and the verb. The RpS dyad did not produce any errors.

Perhaps unsurprisingly, the L2 mother is responsible for most of the errors. Her errors consist mostly of using a third singular form when agreeing with different kinds of subjects, consistent with the use of the unmarked zero form. The two children produced fewer errors per one hundred finite verbs than their mothers. These consist mostly of substituting third plural for third singular (five out of eleven errors; see example 10a) or third singular for third plural (five out of eleven errors; see example 10b). The latter type may simply be due to lenition of plural /s/ on the subject.

(10) a. lo(s) elefante(s) y lo(s) monito(s) se quenía [: querían] ir con la nena, con la nenita. (SF, 4;7.13)
b. Y esto cómo se llamaban (.) xxx? (SF, 4;7.13)

In sum, the children appear to be using agreement quite consistently. While their mothers display a small amount of optionality, the children display even less, with errors that are both fewer in number and unlikely to be the result of some default rule. While they do not remain completely faithful to their input, they nevertheless choose to generalize in the direction that allows them to be *more* faithful. This result also resonates with the well-known sociolinguistic fact that use of agreement primes agreement (Scherre and Naro 1991, 2013): as children are exposed to more agreement, they tend to use more agreement as well.

Object Realization: Overall Distribution of Verbal Complements

In the realm of direct object realization, children are faced with conflicting messages about the features responsible for the distribution of forms, in particular, pronominal forms (accusative clitics, dative clitics, and null objects). On the one hand, the PS grammar is approaching a system in which animate referents are realized with numberless, genderless, and caseless *le*, and inanimates are realized with the similarly undifferentiated null object. On the other hand, the RpS grammar presents a system of consistently number-, gender-, and case-marked accusative clitics, using alternate means to mark animacy (doubling, differential object marker *a*) and severely restricting the use of the null object. Faced with a mix of these distributions, children can choose to do one of three things:

(i) Simplify the input: The child can "finish" the work started by the PS grammar and create a strictly binary opposition between animate *le* and inanimate null objects.
(ii) Regularize the input: The child can converge toward the RpS grammar, ignoring or reinterpreting input from referential null objects as well as from direct-object uses of the dative *le*.
(iii) Reorganize the input: The child can preserve all the forms and features for which the RpS input provides evidence but reorganize the distribution to more closely match the mixed input.

The first option would require a massive break with the input, discarding not only all accusative clitics but also the need for underlying case, number, and gender distinctions. The second option is what we would predict if we take children's behavior with agreement to be indicative of their "preferred dialect." However, as mentioned before, it is not likely that children are aware of the need for such a choice given that they cannot possibly know a priori that their input is heterogeneous. The last possibility is more open ended, and here we suggest that such reorganization takes place in a modular fashion. That is, we suggest that children's use of some forms may converge to one dialect, but their use of others may converge to the other dialect.

As a first-pass analysis of the children's object realization, we will look at the distribution of verbal complements. Identifying null objects can be tricky, as it is not necessarily clear how to separate examples where a null object is intended from those in which the speaker intends an intransitive use of the verb—if indeed they even should be analyzed differently (see Pérez-Leroux, Pirvulescu, and Roberge 2017)—and while it may be ideal to focus exclusively on obligatorily transitive verbs, there are in practice too few of these to produce enough data. Even more difficult is the task of separating the different interpretations that speakers assign to null objects. However, so long as the *overall* occurrence of verbs and semantic contexts is roughly similar across speakers, we would expect PS speakers to produce a significantly greater number of verbs lacking an overt complement. We refer to these as zero complements in the results that follow.

From the Spanish MCDI MacArthur-Bates Communicative Development Inventories (Jackson-Maldonado et al. 2003), we identified all verbs that (i) accept direct objects and (ii) are known by at least half of typically developing children by the age of 2;6. We included both obligatorily and optionally transitive verbs, and we did not attempt to distinguish between transitive and intransitive uses of these verbs. Instead, we coded each verb token as having either (i) no overt direct object (zero, which subsumes both null objects and absence of an object), or (ii) having a DP, clitic, or clausal complement. We excluded reflexives, auxiliary uses, frozen expressions (e.g., *dale* "ok," *ya ves* "you see," etc.), and idiomatic uses (e.g., *a ver* "let's see . . . ," *tomar frío* "to catch a cold," etc.).

The overall distribution of complement types is shown in Figure 10.1 for each mother and child, as well as for the RpS-speaking investigators appearing in the same recordings (aggregated across investigators). Clitics are divided between accusative (*lo, la, los, las*) and dative (*le, les*) forms. Clitic doubling structures are classified with DP complements for the moment.

For both Paraguayan children, the overall distribution of DP, clitic, zero, and clausal complements is significantly different from the distribution of the investigators (SF: $\chi(3, N = 503) = 20.40, p < .0002$; ML: $\chi(3, N = 168) = 8.16, p = .043$), who produce fewer zero complements, and not significantly different from their mothers (SF: $\chi(3, N = 664) = 6.69, p = .08$; ML: $\chi(3, N = 388) = 4.30, p = .23$). Within the clitic category, however, the children match the investigators, producing either no *leísmo* (ML) or much less than their mothers (SF: $(1, N = 89) = 4.6, p = .032$).

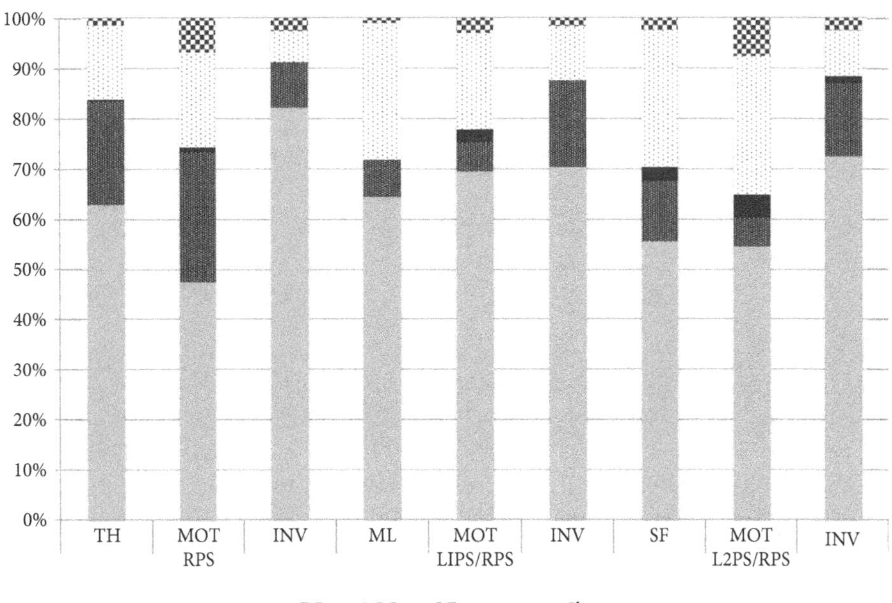

Figure 10.1. Distribution of Verbal Complement Types for the Children, Their Mothers, and the Investigators

In sum, the first-pass analysis suggests that children are converging on the PS dialect with respect to null objects and the RpS dialect with respect to the almost absence of *leísmo*. In the sections that follow, we provide a more fine-grained analysis of the distribution of first *leísmo* and then of null objects in children's speech.

A Closer Look at Leísmo

To increase the amount of clitic data, we used CLAN's Kwal command (MacWhinney 2000) to extract *all* tokens of accusative clitics (*la*, *lo*, *las*, *los*), as well as dative clitics in direct object position (*le*, *les*), coding for animacy and the presence/absence of a doubled DP.

In Table 10.4, we see that, consistent with the linguistic descriptions, the Argentinian mother produces almost no *leísmo* (four tokens out of eighty-six direct object clitics), while the Paraguayan mothers produce plenty; in fact, the majority of their direct object clitics are examples of *leísmo*. Turning to the children, Th produces a surprising amount of *leísmo*, but further inspection reveals that six out of the nine are tokens of the same verb *llamar* "to call/name" and may simply be a case of fossilization. Ml produces almost no *leísmo*, similar to the RpS-speaking investigators (χ (1, N = 50) = 1.06, p = .30) and significantly different from her mother (χ (1, N = 72) = 23.93, p < .001). Sf is the only child to produce a fair amount of *leísmo*, but she too produces significantly less than her mother (χ (1, N = 78) = 8.95, p < .003).

Table 10.4. Frequency of direct object dative (*le*) and accusative (*lo/la*) clitics

	TH -MOT-INV (MOT L1 RpS)			ML -MOT-INV (MOT L1 PS)			SF -MOT-INV (MOT L2 PS)		
	lo/la	**le**	**% *leísmo***	**lo/la**	**le**	**% *leísmo***	**lo/la**	**le**	**% *leísmo***
CHI	69	9	11.5%	18	2	10.0%	27	10	27.0%
MOT	82	4	4.7%	12	40	76.9%	15	26	63.4%
INV	30	0	0.0%	30	0	0.0%	27	1	3.6%

Next, we turn to the distribution of these clitics with respect to animacy and doubling (Table 10.5). For the Paraguayan mothers, *leísmo* is nearly exclusively reserved for animate referents, consistent with descriptions in the literature, and the few accusative clitics that they produce are mainly (though not exclusively) inanimate. SF is the only Paraguayan child who produces a fair amount of *leísmo*, and she initially also appears to reserve *leísmo* for animate referents and accusative clitics for inanimate referents—until we realize that she also uses doubling to achieve the same distinction. For SF, animates are exclusively doubled (thirteen out of thirteen dative and accusative tokens) and inanimates are nondoubled (twenty-three out of twenty-four tokens).

In sum, neither Paraguayan child is converging toward the simplified system in which accusatives disappear and *le* becomes an animacy marker. Both children produce plenty of accusative clitics, and even the child who displays some *leísmo* appears to be using it differently from her mother. While the numbers are small, her concurrent use of doubling and *leísmo* for animate referents appears to be an intriguing mix of the PS and RpS systems.

Table 10.5. Animacy and doubling of *leísmo* and accusative clitic tokens

	TH (Mot L1 RpS)		ML (Mot L1 PS)		SF (Mot L2 PS)	
	CHI	MOT	CHI	MOT	CHI	MOT
LE for animate, doubled	3	0	0	18	10	5
LE animate, non-doubled	5	4	2	19	0	21
LE inanimate, doubled	0	0	0	1	0	0
LE inanimate, non-doubled	1	0	0	2	0	0
ACC animate, doubled	1	5	5	0	3	1
ACC animate, non-doubled	0	10	5	3	0	5
ACC inanimate, doubled	0	3	1	0	1	2
ACC inanimate, non-doubled	68	64	7	9	23	7

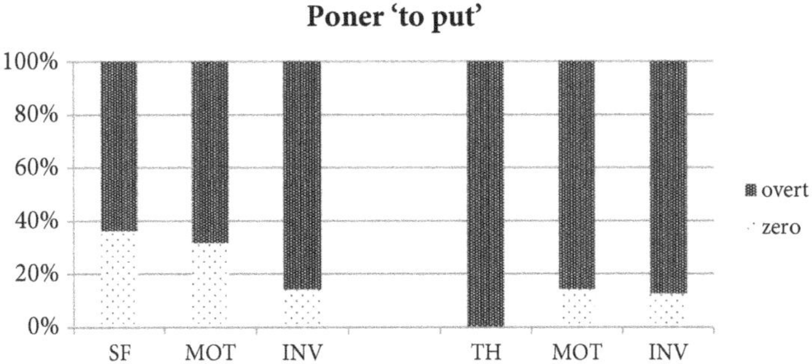

Figure 10.2. Distribution of Zero and Overt Complements for *poner*

A Closer Look at Null Objects

In this section we apply two different techniques to get a more fine-grained look at how children use null objects. One, as mentioned before, is to look at their distribution of zero complements of obligatorily transitive verbs, where we can be fairly certain that a zero complement constitutes a null object. Of course, the intended interpretation of these null objects (generic, anaphoric, etc.) may or may not be discernible from context. A second technique is to focus exclusively on the distribution of zero complements in the preterite, which encourages referential interpretations. Here, we can be fairly certain that a number of these zero complements will be anaphoric, and therefore ungrammatical in RpS. The rate at which children produce such complements will then hopefully tell us the extent to which they are entertaining the PS grammar.

For the first analysis, we look at the two most frequently occurring obligatorily transitive verbs from our first-pass analysis: *poner* "to put" (Figure 10.2) and *agarrar* "to grab" (Figure 10.3). Only SF and the Argentinian child produced enough tokens to analyze. For both verbs, the Paraguayan child aligns with her mother rather than the investigators, producing approximately 30 percent zero complements.

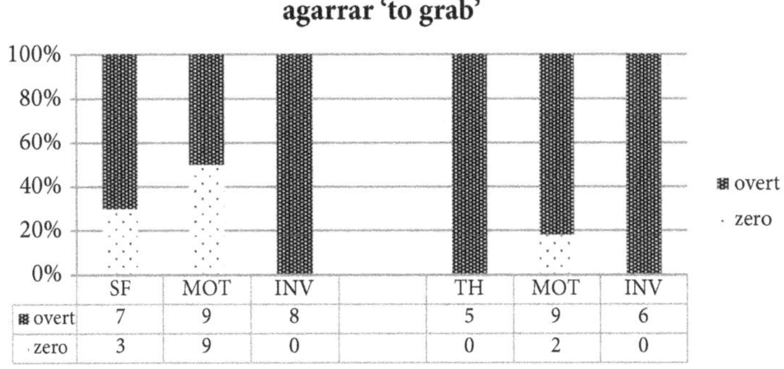

	SF	MOT	INV		TH	MOT	INV
overt	7	9	8		5	9	6
zero	3	9	0		0	2	0

Figure 10.3. Distribution of Zero and Overt Complements for *agarrar*

Table 10.6. Null objects produced and their acceptability in RpS

	Th	MOT	Ml	MOT	Sf	MOT
Unacceptable zero objects in RpS	0	0	2	2	5	23
Total zero objects	2	4	4	3	7	25

For the second analysis, we used CLAN's Combo function to extract all verbs in the preterite not immediately followed by an overt complement. These were then categorized by hand to extract all instances where a null object was used to refer to an object (rather than a proposition). Of these totals, reported in Table 10.6, the first and second authors identified those tokens that were ungrammatical according to their own native RpS intuitions. While the native-born dyad did produce some null complements, they were all deemed grammatical in RpS. In contrast, nearly all of the null complements produced by the Paraguayan dyads were deemed ungrammatical in RpS.

These more fine-grained analyses support the suggestion from our initial analysis that the Paraguayan children permit a wider distribution of null objects than would be allowed in RpS. They produce null objects at a greater rate than the RpS-speaking investigators and in contexts deemed by native RpS speakers to be ungrammatical, in contrast to the Argentinian child, whose use of null objects is limited but grammatical. Experimental methods (see Pérez-Leroux et al. 2017) will be necessary to distinguish the full range of semantic contexts in which children produce null objects.

Discussion

The children exposed to mixed PS-RpS Spanish do not choose one dialect over the other, but instead choose a mix of dialects. We suggest that these modular decisions are what allow them to remain faithful to the input. In the realm of agreement, children converge toward RpS (not surprisingly) because of the overwhelming evidence for this rule. In the realm of clitic realization, children converge toward the RpS dialect, preserving all the case, gender, and number distinctions for which their RpS input provides evidence. And in their use of null objects, children converge toward PS, which allows them to remain faithful to the positive evidence in their input that null objects are permitted in referential contexts. If children were to choose either dialect wholesale, they would be required to discard either forms or features that appear in their input. Yet by making piecemeal decisions, they are able to remain maximally faithful.

Note

This data was collected with the support from the National Science Foundation BCS 1656133 and HARP-MSU to Cristina Schmitt. We thank the research assistants, Marisol de los Ríos, Juan José Arias, Estefanía

Baranger (UBA), Anita Primucci, and Alan Munn, and the Language Acquisition Lab at MSU. We offer special thanks to Padre Toto, and to the children and parents at Casa Social and Casa de la Cultura.

References

Choi, Jinny K. 1998. *Languages in Contact: A Morphosyntactic Analysis of Paraguayan Spanish from a Historical and Sociolinguistic Perspective.* PhD diss., Georgetown University.

Choi, Jinny K. 2000. "[-Person] Direct Object Drop: The Genetic Cause of a Syntactic Feature in Paraguayan Spanish." *Hispania* 83:531–43.

Di Tullio, Ángela, Andrés Saab, and Pablo Zdrojewski. Forthcoming. "Clitic Doubling in a Doubling World. The Case of Argentinean Spanish Reconsidered." In *The Syntactic Variation of Spanish Dialects*, edited by Ángel J. Gallego. Oxford: Oxford University Press.

Dietrich, Wolf. 1995. "El español del Paraguay en contacto con el guaraní: Ejemplos seleccionados de nuevas grabaciones lingüísticas." In *Lenguas en contacto en hispanoamérica*, edited by Klaus Zimmermann, 203–16. Frankfurt/Madrid: Vervuert/Iberoamericana.

Granda, Germán de. 1988. *Sociedad, historia y lengua en el Paraguay*. Bogotá: Instituto Caro y Cuervo.

Jackson-Maldonado, Donna, Donna J. Thal, Larry Fenson, Virginia A. Marchman, Tyler Newton, and Barbara T. Conboy. 2003. "MacArthur Inventarios del Desarrollo de Habilidades Comunicativas (Inventarios): User's Guide and Technical Manual." Baltimore: Brookes.

Kany, Charles E. (1945) 1969. *Sintaxis hispanoamericana*. Madrid: Editorial Gredos.

Keenan, Edward L. 2002. "Explaining the Creation of Reflexive Pronouns in English." In *Studies in the History of the English Language: A Millennial Perspective*, edited by Donka Minkova and Robert P. Stockwell, 325–54. Berlin/New York: Mouton de Gruyter.

Krivoshein de Canese, Natalia, and Graziella Corvalán. 1987. *El español del Paraguay en contacto con el guaraní*. Asunción: Centro Paraguayo de Estudios Sociológicos.

MacWhinney, Brian. 2000. *The CHILDES Project: Tools for Analyzing Talk*. 3rd ed. Mahwah, NJ: Lawrence Erlbaum.

Masullo, Pascual José. 2013. "Clitic-less Definite Object Drop in River Plate Spanish." Presentation at the *33rd Linguistic Symposium on Romance Languages, Bloomington, Indiana.*

Mayer, Mercer. 1974. *Frog Goes to Dinner*. New York: Dial.

Nardy, Aurélie, Jean-Pierre Chevrot, and Stéphanie Barbu. 2013. "The Acquisition of Sociolinguistic Variation: Looking Back and Thinking Ahead." *Linguistics* 51 (2): 255–84.

Ordóñez, Francisco. 2012. "Clitics in Spanish." In *The Handbook of Hispanic Linguistics*, edited by José Ignacio Hualde, Antxon Olarrea, and Erin O'Rourke, 423–53. Oxford: Blackwell.

Palacios Alcaine, Azucena. 2000. "El sistema pronominal del español paraguayo: Un caso de contacto de lenguas." In *El español en contacto con lenguas indígenas*, edited by Julio Calvo Pérez, 123–43. Fankfurt: Vervuert.

Penner, Hedy, Soledad Acosta, and Malvina Segovia. 2012. *El descubrimiento del castellano paraguayo a través del guaraní: Una historia de los enfoques lingüísticos*. Asunción: Centro de Estudios Antropológicos de la Universidad Católica (CEADUC).

Pérez-Leroux, Ana Teresa, Mihaela Pirvulescu, and Yves Roberge. 2017. *Direct Objects and Language Acquisition*. Cambridge: Cambridge University Press.

Scherre, Maria Marta Pereira, and Anthony J. Naro. 1991. "Marking in Discourse: Birds of a Feather." *Language Variation and Change* 3 (1): 23–32.

Scherre, Maria Marta Pereira, and Anthony J. Naro. 2013. "Sociolinguistic Correlates of Negative Evaluation: Variable Concord in Rio de Janeiro." *University of Pennsylvania Working Papers in Linguistics* 19 (2).

Schwenter, Scott A. 2006. "Null Objects across South America." In *Selected Proceedings of the 8th Hispanic Linguistics Symposium*, edited by Timothy L. Face and Carol A. Klee, 23–36. Somerville, MA: Cascadilla Proceedings Project.

Smith, Jennifer, Mercedes Durham, and Liane Fortune. 2009. "Universal and Dialect-Specific Pathways of Acquisition: Caregivers, Children, and t/d Deletion." *Language Variation and Change* 21 (1): 69–95.

Usher de Herreros, Beatriz. 1976. *Castellano-paraguayo: Notas para una gramática contrastiva castellano-guaraní*. Asunción: Centro de Estudios Antropologicos.

Yang, Charles. 2002. *Knowledge and Learning in Natural Language*. Oxford: Oxford University Press.

Yang, Charles. 2016. *The Price of Linguistic Productivity*. Cambridge, MA: MIT Press.

Chapter 11

Variation and Mental Representation

GREGORY R. GUY
New York University

KNOWING HOW TO SPEAK a language includes at a very basic level knowing the words and how to pronounce them—that is to say, knowing the lexicon and the phonology. Linguists have conventionally conceived of the lexicon as a set of mental representations of words that represent the phonological content of the word as a string of phonemes. Complex words that contain multiple morphemes can be treated as having lexical entries that reflect this internal structure, or as being the products of a derivational process that builds them up from the constituent morphemes.

Finally, actual utterances are generated by applying additional phonological and articulatory phonetic constraints or processes to strings of words to produce speech. Notably, such processes are frequently variable, so that a given word or phrase can have multiple surface realizations that do not change its lexical identity. In this model, lexical entries are static and invariant, while variability is a surface output of phonological processes. This model is illustrated in (1):

(1) Conventional model

	UR	Surface variation
and	/ænd/	[ænd ~ æn]
band	/bænd/	[bænd ~ bæn]
banned	/bæn#d/	[bænd ~ bæn]

Such an architecture accounts for many important facts about phonology and the lexicon. But complications arise in accounting for an elementary observation about the surface variability of lexical items: their distribution is significantly conditioned by properties of the word that are not incorporated into the simple string-of-phonemes representation. This fact has motivated alternative architectures, such as the usage-based phonology or exemplar theory articulated by Bybee (2001) and others. In this approach, the mental representation of words incorporates memory traces of previous productions of the word. This exemplar cloud will hence replicate the variability that the speaker has encountered, and the statistical distribution of the variants. New utterances of the word are generated by drawing stochastically from the exemplar cloud, rather than from the single underlying representation postulated in conventional models.

I will survey some of the evidence bearing on these issues that has been discovered in studies of phonological variation. Specifically, I will look at findings regarding lexical frequency, lexical exceptions, morphological constraints on variability, and priming. I will argue that the facts suggest a need for richer and fuzzier mental representations than the conventional model, but more constrained than the exemplar model.

Before turning to the data, however, I want to note that this problem has ancient roots in the history of linguistics. It is foreshadowed in the nineteenth century debate over the Neogrammarian hypothesis. The Neogrammarians argued for exceptionless sound change, operating on phonemic units; words were mere strings of phonemes, so they all necessarily underwent whatever change affected their constituent sounds. The contrary view was articulated in the slogan: "Each word has its own history." The conventional model of the lexicon that I just described is a direct descendant of Herman Paul's formulation of the Neogrammarian position, while exemplars invoke the idiosyncratic potential of each word.

Lexical Frequency

One kind of constraint that is a characteristic of the word as a whole, rather than as a string of phonemes, is its frequency of use. Some words are common, some are rare, and a variety of evidence shows that speakers treat rare words differently from high-frequency forms; for example, they are articulated more slowly, and are less likely to undergo lenition processes. With respect to linguistic variation, several studies have found significant frequency effects, such that higher-frequency forms behave differently from lower-frequency forms.

Two examples from my own work on English involve coronal stop deletion and the *-ing/-in* alternation. In Guy, Hay, and Walker 2011, looking at the New Zealand English Corpus at the University of Canterbury, we found a strong log linear frequency effect, such that more common words were deleted more often (see Figure 11.1). This is of course a lenition process, the kind of operation that occurs more often in faster speech.

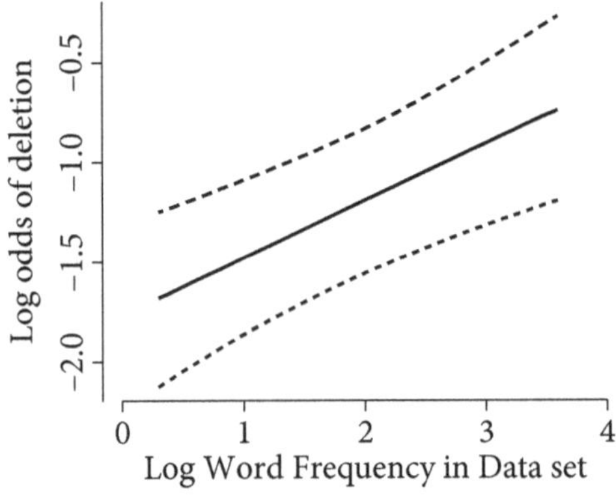

Figure 11.1. Coronal Stop Deletion Increases with Lexical Frequency. p=.0005.

Source: From Guy, Hay, and Walker 2008.

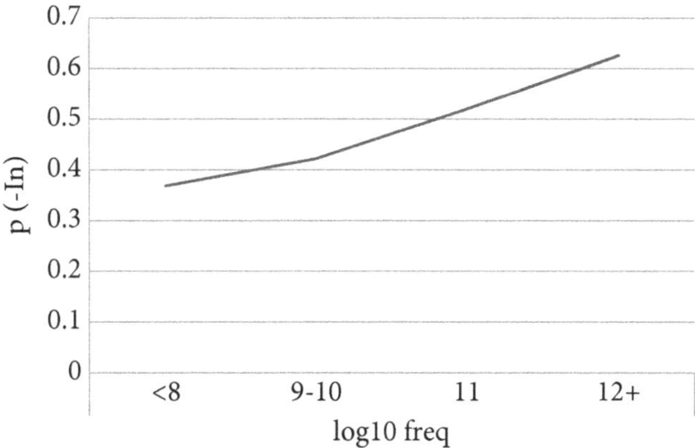

Figure 11.2. [-in] for *-ing* Increases with Lexical Frequency
Source: From Laturnus, de Vilchez, Chaves, and Guy (2016).

Similarly, the alveolar realization of the *-ing* suffix in English—*talkin'* instead of *talking*—is also favored in higher-frequency words. Figure 11.2 shows the frequency effect found in Laturnus et al. 2016. It is not clear that this is a lenition effect, although in a typological sense, alveolar nasals are certainly less marked than velars.

In these two cases, frequency effects were straightforward and significant. But in other studies, the results are different. Some studies of lexical frequency show no significant effects. The lenition of coda /s/ (sometimes characterized as "aspiration and deletion") is a common process in Caribbean Spanish. It involves shortening of duration and lowering the spectral makeup of the fricative noise. Erker's (2008) study of coda /s/ lenition in a corpus of Caribbean Spanish speech looked at both of these acoustic properties. However, neither is significantly associated with lexical frequency; Erker found a correlation coefficient of –0.02 (p = .74, n.s.) for center of gravity and 0.07 for duration (p = .136, n.s.).

What does this imply for the mental representation of words? Such results clearly indicate that quantitative information related to frequency of use is encoded in the lexical entry. Some phonological processes that are operative in the production of variable realizations must interact with or be sensitive to such information. I suggest that the most straightforward account of how the whole system works is effectively equivalent to a mixed effects probabilistic model, with fixed effects for the general constraints and random factors associated with individual words. Through experience, speakers learn that specific words are more or less likely to undergo a given phonological process and encode this in the lexical entry. Such individuation clearly requires an accumulation of evidence—hence it will be most evident in high-frequency words.

Bybee's usage-based phonology (2001, 2002) provides an alternative theory of frequency effects. Exemplar models preserve frequency information by storing in memory all exemplars of the word that the speaker has uttered or heard. But in such a model the interaction between frequency and a variable process requires an additional postulate. Bybee hypothesizes that lenition processes involve a kind of gradual erosion, advancing each time a word is uttered, so the cumulative effects are to make more frequent words appear more lenited:

> Given a tendency for reduction during production, the phonetic representation of a word will gradually accrue more exemplars that are reduced, and these exemplars will become more likely to be chosen for production, where they may undergo further reduction, gradually moving the words of the language in a consistent direction. The more frequent words will have more chances to undergo online reduction and thus will change more rapidly. (Bybee 2002, 271)

The problem with this model is that it overpredicts. Erker's study is a clear example of a gradual lenition process, and as we have seen, no frequency effect is evident. This suggests that "the reductive effect of articulatory automation" is not, in fact, automatic. Lexical frequency is a possible, but not automatic, constraint on phonological or phonetic processes.

Lexical Frequency and Morphology

Frequency also interacts with the second kind of constraint on variation that we will consider, namely morphology. It is well documented that many variable processes are sensitive to the morphological structure of forms. A well-known example is the *-in*/*-ing* alternation in English. Many studies (e.g., Houston 1985; Labov 1989; Tamminga 2014, 2016), have shown that the alveolar /n/ realization is much more common in verbal forms—*talkin'*, *runnin'*, and so forth—than in nominal forms (e.g., *ceiling, a building*). Laturnus et al. (2016) find that verbs are realized with alveolar *-in* in 55 percent of cases (N = 485, factor weight = 0.53), while nouns are realized with *-in* in only 38 percent of cases (N = 79, factor weight 0.32). The exceptional *something* and *nothing* exhibit alveolar *-in* 67 percent of the time (N = 81, factor weight = 0.51).

Another much-studied example is coronal stop deletion (Guy 1980, Guy and Boyd 1990). Guy (1991) finds that underived words systematically have the highest rates of deletion (38.1%, N = 658), and regular past tense forms have the lowest rate (16%, N = 181). For most English speakers, the irregular past tense forms, like *kept, told, lost*, have intermediate rates of deletion (33.9%, N = 56).

The interaction between morphological structure and frequency emerges when we look at frequency effects on each morphological category separately. Table 11.1 shows the results of such an analysis of coronal stop deletion, from Myers and Guy 1997. When we look at just the monomorphemes, lexical frequency has a significant

Table 11.1. Frequency interacts with morphology: coronal stop deletion in English

	Monomorphemic Words		**Regular Past Tense Verbs**	
	N	% deleted	N	% deleted
Low frequency	151	18.5	96	7.3
High frequency	573	33.9	220	8.2
	p < .01		p > .70	

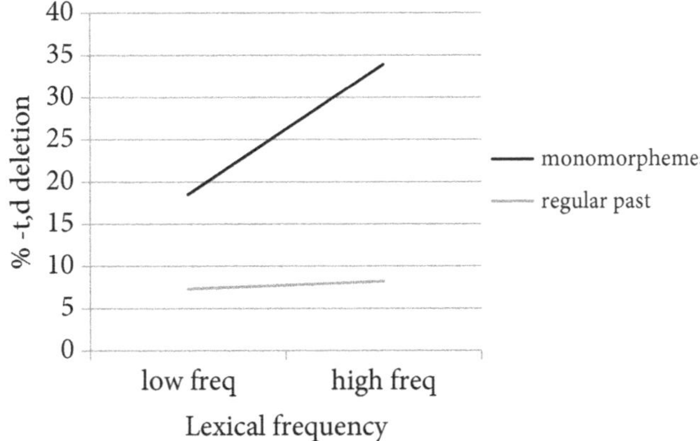

Figure 11.3. Morphology Interacts with Frequency: Coronal Stop Deletion in English

effect, as we saw earlier. But when we consider just the past tense verbs, there is no frequency effect.

Figure 11.3 shows a graphical display of these results. The line for the past tense verbs is basically flat with frequency, while the monomorphemes show the increase in deletion rate that was seen in Figure 11.1.

A continuous treatment of frequency yields a more refined picture of this effect. An unpublished study by Fruehwald, shown in Figure 11.4, examines coronal stop deletion rate in four lexical classes according to frequency treated as a continuous

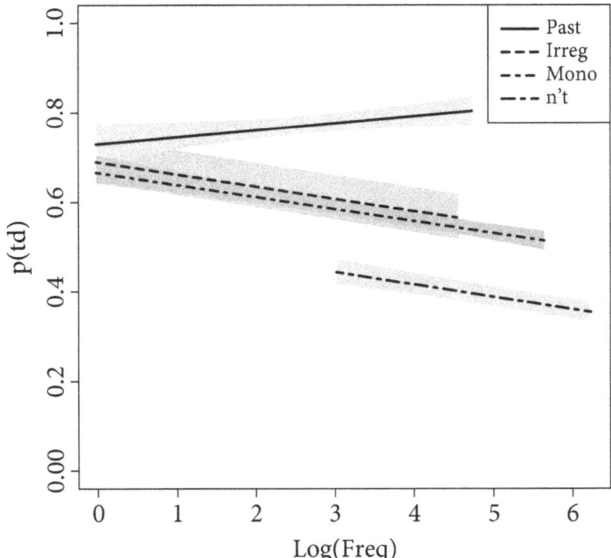

Figure 11.4. Frequency Interacts with Morphology

Source: From Fruehwald (2009).

variable. These data are presented in terms of stop retention instead of deletion, so the directionality of the graph is inverted: more deletion = lower down in the figure. The past tense verbs are the top line, showing modestly decreasing deletion rates as they get more frequent. But the monomorphemes, third from the top, show the same behavior as in the Myers and Guy study, with deletion increasing with higher frequency.

These findings have further implications for mental representations. It is clear that variable processes do not see words as mere strings of phonemes. Rather, they are sensitive to aspects of the morphology. In previous work (Guy 1991), I have argued from the perspective of lexical phonology that variable phonological processes actually penetrate the morphological operations involved in derivation and word formation. But at the very least the mental representations of words that provide the input to production must distinguish between derived and underived forms. These facts about the interaction between morphology and frequency are particularly notable: they appear to be inconsistent with Bybee's usage-based phonology. Bybee's model of progressive lenition with more frequent repetition suggests that frequency effects should be orthogonal to and independent of morphology; every uttered word is stored as an exemplar and available as a model for new productions, so more frequently uttered words should presumably be candidates for greater lenition, regardless of their morphology. The data presented here are more consistent with the model advanced by Pinker and others, that derived forms are not stored in the mental lexicon, but rather generated on the fly. (We can allow that especially high-frequency derived forms do acquire lexical entries, as Bybee 1985 argues, by the same process that allows the acquisition of irregular derived forms, such as *leave-left*, *sell-sold*, *think-thought*. But these would count as lexical exceptions, as in the next section.)

Lexical Exceptions

Further evidence on the nature of mental representations can be obtained from the study of lexical exceptions. Various strands of research on how variation affects individual words have demonstrated the existence of clearly exceptional words, which undergo phonological processes in idiosyncratic ways. We will consider four such cases: the English conjunction *and*, the Portuguese first person plural verbal morpheme *-mos*, Salvadoran Spanish discourse markers, and the pronouns *I*, *my* in Southern American English.

The first case is the word *and* in English. Like all English words terminating in a consonant cluster with final -t or -d, *and* is susceptible to coronal stop deletion (CSD). But this word appears with the final /d/ absent at an extraordinarily high rate in all studies that have investigated it. Table 11.2 shows the figures from the Guy et al. New Zealand English study. As we saw in Figure 11.1, high-frequency words are

Table 11.2. Coronal stop deletion in Early New Zealand English: exceptional *and*

	N	% final stop deletion
and	597	80%
other words	3348	29%

Table 11.3. Coronal stop deletion in Early New Zealand English by following context (18 speakers from the ONZE corpus at University of Canterbury)

	Other words		and	
Following Context:	N	% del	N	% del
__C	1339	58.3	315	87.9
__V	1477	10.4	182	75.3
Range:	47.9%	>	12.6%	

expected to show high deletion rates, but *and* is exceptional even when we control for its high lexical frequency.

Notably, *and* is relatively insensitive to other constraints on the deletion process: the contextual constraints on CSD are significantly attenuated for this word. For example, the following segment in the speech stream is a powerful constraint on this process. Before a consonant, deletion rates are much higher than before a vowel: *west side* favors deletion, *west end* disfavors. But this constraint is much weaker for *and*: "*ham 'n' eggs*"—with deletion before a vowel—is almost as common as "*cheese 'n' crackers*," with deletion before a consonant. Table 11.3 provides the results of the New Zealand English study: preconsonantal tokens are almost six times more likely to be deleted in ordinary words, but only 15 percent more likely in *and.*

Similar exceptional lexical items can be found in many other variable processes, and they regularly show weaker effects of the phonological constraints on the process. Brazilian Portuguese and Caribbean Spanish both have processes of coda -s deletion, and both have prominent lexical exceptions. In Brazilian Portuguese it is the first plural verbal morpheme -*mos* that surfaces as -*mo* at an exceptionally high rate. In Table 11.4 we see the following context effects from a multivariate analysis

Table 11.4. Coda –s deletion in Brazilian Portuguese: following context constraint

Features of following C		Other words		1pl verb forms in ***-mos***
Voice/Manner:	sonorant	.69		.49
	voiced obstruent	.44		.58
	voiceless obstruent	.36		.44
	Range	.33	>	.14
Place:	labial	.32		.58
	coronal	.61		.53
	velar	.44		.39
	Range	.29	>	.19
N:		5880		1225
Goodness of fit (log likelihood)		–704.8		–791.5

for the *-mos* forms versus other words. In the *-mos* forms, the constraints are much weaker, with a smaller effect magnitude (indicated by the smaller range values), and a much poorer model fit.

Similar findings emerge from Hoffman's (2004) study of Salvadoran Spanish, where the three common discourse markers ending in -s behave exceptionally: *entonces*, *digamos*, and *pues*. These are all realized without the final /s/ at exceptionally high rates, and they also show considerably weaker contextual constraints.

Another variable showing exceptional lexical items is the monophthongization of /ay/ in Southern American English. In this case the exceptional words are the pronouns *I* and *my*. The figures in Table 11.5, drawn from the work of Woods 2008, demonstrates that these two words are much more likely to undergo monophongization, and they are completely insensitive to following context (monophthongization is favored in the general vocabulary by a following voiced consonant), and they are also less sensitive to speech rate (typically more monophthongs are produced in faster speech with shorter segment durations). So these words stand out from the rest of the lexicon, in the same way as the previous three cases.

In all of these cases, drawn from three different languages, we find exceptional lexical items that differ systematically from the general vocabulary in two ways: they show exceptionally high rates of occurrence of the relevant variable process, and they appear relatively insensitive to contextual constraints on the process that are prominent for ordinary words. What does this suggest about mental representations?

As we argued previously, individual words, especially high-frequency words, may become associated in the mental representation with an idiosyncratic factor indicating their likelihood of undergoing some general phonetic or phonological operation. But this is not sufficient to capture the exceptional behavior of the cases we have just considered. A random factor in a mixed effects model will leave all the other

Table 11.5. Monophthongization of /ay/ in Southern American English: following context and speech rate constraints

	Other words		*I, my*
% monophthong	34%		53%
Following Context:			
__[+cons, +voice]	.76		(.51)
__[-cons]	.41		(.49)
__[+cons, -voice]	.17		(.48)
Range:	.59	>	.03 (n.s.)
Duration:			
shorter	.89		.68
longer	.49		.45
Range:	.40	>	.23

Source: From Woods (2008).

constraints on the process (the fixed effects) stable, and hence cannot capture the apparent weakening of constraints seen in the data. Rather, these data indicate that the underlying representation of an exceptional lexical item is not exclusively captured by the canonical full form of the word. Rather, each of these exceptional words must have an additional underlying representation that already incorporates the output of the variable process. That is to say, these words have underlying allomorphy. English *and* has an allomorph "*an*" or "*n*." When this allomorph is selected, the surface realization will lack a final /d/ regardless of contextual conditions.[1] The surface corpus includes a mixture of such unconditioned tokens with tokens of the underlying full forms to which deletion has applied, which has the mathematical consequence of appearing to attenuate the contextual constraints.

I suggest that this allomorph of *and* is what we represent orthographically in spellings such as "*rock n roll*." The same argument applies to the other cases we have looked at. The Portuguese first person plural verbal morpheme has an allomorph "*-mo*," lacking the final -s in underlying form. The Salvadoran Spanish discourse markers have underlying forms "*digamo*" and "*entonce*," also lacking final -s. And the words "*I*" and "*my*" in Southern American English have underlying representations with monophthongs.

Priming

The final issue I will consider is that of priming. This is the frequently observed phenomenon, sometimes known as persistence or perseveration, where specific variants tend to occur in clusters. In other words, when speakers make one selection from among the possible alternatives in a variable process, they tend to keep making the same selection, at least over a relatively short time span. This most likely reflects a cognitive property rather than a specifically phonological or linguistic one: the activation of a particular mental pathway or operation is heightened by an initial occurrence, and this heightened activation persists for a period of time, favoring its reuse on subsequent occasions. For present purposes, the utility of priming for diagnosing mental representations is that it involves like priming like. In other words, it provides a test of what mental representation is treated as being "like" another.

One exemplary variable for which priming has been well studied is the *-ing*/*-in* alternation in English. The results we will consider are drawn from the Laturnus et al. study cited earlier. In this study we found, like previous studies such as Houston 1985 and Tamminga 2016, that an occurrence of the velar form *-ing* favors another subsequent *-ing*, while the occurrence of an alveolar *-in* pronunciation favors more *-in* tokens in following words. Thus in Table 11.6 we see that after one token with an /n/, 79 percent of the time the next token also has an /n/, but when the priming word is realized with a velar /ŋ/, the /n/ realization occurs in only 21 percent of tokens. Notably, when there is no priming word—in other words, there hasn't been an *-ing* word in the previous few clauses—the data are split about 50–50 between *-in* and *-ing* realizations. This is an important point about the priming effect: when there is no prior priming event, then the current production gives the plain-vanilla output, the emergence of the unmarked.

Table 11.6. Priming effect for the *-in/-ing* alternation in English

Priming context	N	%[n]	weight
-n	129	79	.64
-ŋ	119	21	.27
null	401	54	.53

The data in Table 11.6 conflate all types of *-ing* words as priming contexts. But as we saw in Table 11.3, this variable is strongly differentiated by the part of speech of the *-ing* word: nouns have more velar realizations, verbs more alveolars. So, a more refined priming question is: do nouns and verbs prime each other, or does a verb have a priming effect only on another verb, a noun on a noun? Here the numbers give a nuanced answer. In Table 11.7, showing the factor weights from a multivariate analysis with Goldvarb (Sankoff et al. 2012), words of the same part of speech prime each other better than words of different parts of speech: /n/ realizations in the target word are strongly favored by an /n/ in the priming word (.70), and disfavored by an /ŋ/ in the priming word (.25). But, cross-priming is still strong and significant: target /n/ is about twice as likely after a prime with an /n/ than after a prime with an /ŋ/ (.52 and .25).

What does this tell us about mental representations? One possible analysis is that nominal and verbal *-ing* are actually two different suffixes: a verbal suffix that prefers the alveolar realization, and a nominal suffix that favors velar *-ing*. This would predict the different priming effects. This analysis is supported, as is well-known, by the historical sources of this suffix: Old English had verbal inflections containing /n/ (infinitival *-an*, participial *-ande/ende*) and a nominal suffix *-ung* or *-yng*. So in this interpretation, the differences between nominal and verbal *-ing* mean that we still have two discrete lexical entries, which are masked by the single standard spelling but revealed in the different priming effects and rates of occurrence of velar versus alveolar realizations.

The problem with this model is that it predicts more divergence between the forms than actually exists. Both nominal and verbal *-ing* words occur with both *-in* and *-ing* variants; the difference between them is probabilistic, not discrete. And their priming effect is also nondiscrete. It's not the case that they can't cross-prime, it's just

Table 11.7. English *-in/-ing*: within and cross-category priming effects

	Probability of /n/ realization in target		
Priming form	prime form /n/	prime form /ŋ/	none
same as target: V to V, N to N	.70	.25	
different from target: V to N, N to V	.52	.25	
no prime			.53

that cross-priming is weaker than same-to-same priming. So the quantitative facts suggest neither identical representations nor discretely different representations, but rather overlapping or partially similar representations. The lexical entry for *-ing* is blurry, not crisply focused on one unitary or two contrasting forms. One possible quantitative model of these data would treat the affix as a single entry with two allomorphs, each with a different probability of insertion into nominal and verbal morphological frames.

The Fuzzy Lexicon

Putting all this evidence together gives us a picture of mental representations that I will call the fuzzy lexicon. Words and morphemes are not stored in memory in crisply focused discrete forms, spelled out by contrastive phonemes, and devoid of any information about usage or past occurrences. Rather, lexical entries can take several forms, and can accrete various additional pieces of information. They may incorporate information derived from their history of usage—such as how frequently they have been used and to what surface realizations they have mapped. Some have allomorphs that are discretely different, like "*and* ~ *an*." They can overlap, be partially similar and partially distinct, or partially merged. Information about their morphological structure is sometimes stored in the lexical representation and sometimes not.

Collectively, these facts require a quantified element in mental representations. I think this is most straightforwardly captured by a probability function. Consider, for example, coronal stop deletion. Its effect is to produce surface forms with and without final stops, so the learner can postulate a phonological form for the word in which the final element is not as stable as the rest of the word; the stable parts of the word have a firm representation with probabilities approaching one, but the final segment is faded, with a probability of less than one. Lexical exceptions emerge when learners postulate that this segment may actually have a probability of zero under certain circumstances.

Frequency information in this model is incorporated by updating the probability function based on experience. I think this is cognitively more plausible than the exemplar model: rather than storing each token one hears, we store only the probability function. Frequency effects operate like an "elsewhere condition," in that high frequency favors lexically specific, marked, and exceptional outcomes over the unmarked general outcomes. In other words, items start with a neutral unmarked probability, and deviate from this only as required by repeated experience. Practice doesn't exactly make them perfect, but it does allow them to become more nuanced.

Morphological information is also at least partially quantified. The resistance of morphological markers to deletion can be restated as a high probability of realization. This was stated in my derivational model of -t,d deletion as a consequence of the stratal structure of the lexicon, but a probabilistic representation of morphemes and morphological boundaries can achieve the same ends.

Priming, as I said, is likely a general cognitive rather than specifically linguistic phenomenon, but it shows us that lexical representations are not necessarily discretely differentiated. The nominal and verbal *-ing* morphemes are partially differentiated, or from a historical perspective, partially merged.

In short, the mental representation of words and morphemes is fuzzy. Items do not have firmly delimited unique identities, but probability functions, with some elements in boldface, and others faded.

Note

1 If the deletion process applies to the full *and* allomorph at the same rate as other words, the probability of selecting the *an'* allomorph can be calculated at about .67.

References

Bybee, Joan. 1985. *Morphology: A Study of the Relationship between Meaning and Form.* Amsterdam: Benjamins.

Bybee, Joan. 2001. *Phonology and Language Use*. Cambridge: Cambridge University Press.

Bybee, Joan. 2002. "Word Frequency and Context of Use in the Lexical Diffusion of Phonetically Conditioned Sound Change." *Language Variation and Change* 14:261–90.

Erker, Daniel. 2008. "Rethinking Coda /s/ Lenition in Spanish: Continuous Descriptions and the Explanatory Value of Lexical Statistics." PhD Qualifying Paper, New York University.

Fruehwald, Josef. 2009. "Summer R Study Group Report: What I Couldn't Have Done Otherwise." Report presented at Spunch. https://jofrhwld.github.io/papers/rstudyhandout.pdf.

Guy, Gregory R. 1980. "Variation in the Group and the Individual: The Case of Final Stop Deletion." In *Locating Language in Time and Space*, edited by William Labov, 1–36. New York: Academic Press.

Guy, Gregory R. 1991. "Explanation in Variable Phonology: An Exponential Model of Morphological Constraints." *Language Variation and Change* 3:1–22.

Guy, Gregory R., and Sally Boyd. 1990. "The Development of a Morphological Class." *Language Variation and Change* 2:1–18.

Guy, Gregory R., Jennifer Hay, and Abby Walker. 2011. "Phonological, Lexical, and Frequency Factors in Coronal Stop Deletion in Early New Zealand English." Paper presented at Laboratory Phonology 11, Wellington, NZ.

Hoffman, Michol. 2004. "Sounding Salvadorean: Phonological Variables in the Spanish of Salvadorean Youth in Toronto." PhD diss., University of Toronto.

Houston, Ann. 1985. "Continuity and Change in English Morphology: The Variable (ING)." PhD diss., University of Pennsylvania.

Labov, William. 1989. "The Child as Linguistic Historian." *Language Variation and Change* 1:85–97.

Laturnus, Rebecca, Natalie de Vilchez, Raquel Chaves, and Gregory R. Guy. 2016. "Dialect, Priming, and Frequency Effects on (-ING) Variation in English." Paper presented at the 45th Annual Conference on New Ways of Analyzing Variation (NWAV-45). Simon Fraser University, Vancouver.

Myers, James, and Gregory R. Guy. 1997. "Frequency Effects in Variable Lexical Phonology." *University of Pennsylvania Working Papers in Linguistics* 4 (1).

Sankoff, David, Sali A. Tagliamonte, and Eric Smith (2012). Goldvarb Lion: A multivariate analysis application for Macintosh. http://individual.utoronto.ca/tagliamonte/goldvarb.html

Tamminga, Meredith. 2014. "Persistence in the Production of Linguistic Variation." PhD diss., University of Pennsylvania.

Tamminga, Meredith. 2016. "Persistence in Phonological and Morphological Variation." *Language Variation and Change* 28:335–56.

Woods, Laurie. 2008. "Whither the Southern Belle?: Language and Identity in the American South." PhD diss., New York University.

Chapter 12

Variation and Competing I-Languages in Creole Genesis: A Synchronic and Diachronic View

MARLYSE BAPTISTA
University of Michigan

LANGUAGE VARIATION CAN BE seen as a pervasive and multifaceted notion that permeates most subfields of linguistics. It is a concept that most linguists must contend with, irrespective of their theoretical orientation and empirical approaches to language study and whether they consider the linguistic or/and extra-linguistic factors conditioning variation. Linguists cast a different light on variation that depends on their theoretical orientation. For instance, historical linguists tend to pair language change and language variation, intimately associating both notions based on their observation that old variants coexist in time and space with new ones before gradually disappearing. Sociolinguists following the Labovian tradition consider extralinguistic factors such as age, gender, social class, educational levels, ethnic backgrounds, and language attitudes as key factors determining speakers' synchronic use of one variant over another (Raumolin-Brunberg 1988). Dialectologists focus on dialectal variation and identify dialects based on a set of distinct lexical, phonological, morphological, and syntactic features.

Generative syntacticians, on the one hand, investigate universal grammar or the language faculty that we are all born with, arguing that as a result of this biological blueprint, all languages are fundamentally alike. On the other hand, they also study "the points of variation," in other words parametric variation (Yang 2006, 28) or the microparameters (Déprez and Martineau 2004) that allow languages to vary from each other along specific dimensions such as word order, or overt and null categories. Contact linguists have had to contend with the (un)stable variation that results from two or more languages coming into contact, as they undergo the pressures of unidirectional or bidirectional influences. Such linguists typically consider both linguistic and extralinguistic factors in order to account for the grammatical features of the new language varieties that emerge from contact between two or more languages. In addition, they try to account for a wide range of linguistic outcomes and contact-induced changes that result from such interactions.

Among contact linguists, creolists in particular have the daunting task of documenting creole languages that, as oral languages, are well-known for the extreme variation they display within a single variety and across varieties of the same creole. Many linguists take such a variation to reflect distinct lects on a creole continuum consisting of an acrolect, basilect, and mesolect. The acrolect is typically viewed as the creole variety closest to the superstrate, the basilect most distant from the superstrate and the mesolect, an intermediate variety between the other two poles. However, I have shown in prior work (Baptista 2015) that creole grammars are not uniformly basilectal or acrolectal. Taking the creole varieties of Cape Verdean Creole spoken on the islands of Santiago and São Vicente, I showed that the variety spoken in Santiago, and which has been traditionally described as basilectal, actually displays acrolectal features in core domains such as gender agreement and Tense, Mood, and Aspect markers. Though a valuable heuristic tool, the serious descriptive limitations of the creole continuum and its lects should invite us to reconsider the angle from which we analyze variation in creoles and other natural languages. This chapter and Baptista (2017) take up this challenge by proposing to analyze variation in terms of competing I-languages.

The main research questions driving this chapter are the following: Is the variation observed in creoles better accounted for in terms of competing I-languages that emerge over time? Would this new lens help us attain a higher level of descriptive and explanatory adequacy than the creole continuum provides?

I explore these questions by examining two grammatical features in the Santiago and São Vicente varieties. I examine both synchronic and diachronic data featuring the distinct Tense, Mood, and Aspect (henceforth TMA) markers used in the two varieties, in addition to negative markers.

This chapter is organized as follows. In the next section, I elaborate on the notion of a creole continuum and explicitly point out its shortcomings. In the third section, I introduce the framework of competing I-languages and argue that it is explanatorily more adequate in accounting for the observed variation. I provide a definition of I-language in light of competing I-languages, drawing from Lightfoot (2006, 2016), Yang (2002), Obata and Epstein (2016), and Epstein (2016), and show how the approach of competing I-languages applies to the study of variation of natural languages like creoles where variation is particularly drastic. In the fourth section, I apply the competing I-languages framework to the analysis of TMA markers and in the fifth section to the study of negation in the two creole varieties under study; I discuss how competing I-languages can play out synchronically and diachronically. In the sixth section, I summarize the key findings of this study.

The Creole Continuum

The next section addresses how the notion of a creole continuum has been used in order to account for variation in creole languages.

Perspectives on the Continuum

The Cape Verde islands represent an ideal site for the study of language variation, in part due to the archipelago setting on which the language developed. The relative isolation of the archipelago, the significant distance between islands, and their different periods of settlement exacerbate such variation, yielding distinct varieties of the same creole language.

The observable variation between speakers has led linguists to postulate a creole continuum that has been traditionally described as composed of varieties going from those farthest from the superstrate (the basilect) to those closest to the superstrate (the acrolect), with mesolectal or intermediate varieties between them (Holm 1988, 9). Each point on the continuum has been viewed as a cluster of linguistic features characterizing speech communities that are said to use these distinct features to index distinct identities and mark solidarity (Tabouret-Keller and Le Page 1985). Bickerton (1973) already sensed that the trilogy of lects (basilect, acrolect, and mesolect) was highly inadequate, for instance in accounting for the pronominal system of Guyanese Creole. In that respect, he noted that the number of variants among the pronominal forms in Guyanese ranges anywhere from one to four between pronominal categories, and did not map onto the continuum's three discrete systems (basilect, mesolect, and acrolect). In some cases, the pronominal variant could be arbitrarily allocated to two lectal systems, and in others, two variants would fit only one (Bickerton 1973, 658). While in that particular study Bickerton tried to show that one can account for variation purely in linguistic terms with no recourse to the social factors that Tabouret-Keller and Le Page put front and center in their view of the continuum, Bickerton was quick at noting that the creole continuum cannot be viewed as static but is instead dynamic and forever changing.

In the next section, I illustrate the limits of the creole continuum as a descriptive tool by showing its descriptive inadequacy when applied to the Santiago and São Vicente varieties of Cape Verdean Creole.

The Creole Continuum and Its Limitations: Lack of Descriptive and Explanatory Adequacy

The Santiago and São Vicente varieties of Cape Verdean Creole have been consistently described as the two extreme poles of the creole continuum. The Santiago variety has been described by linguists and historians alike as being the basilect, given that it was the first island to be settled in 1461 by a majority of slaves. In contrast, São Vicente was settled much later in 1797 (Swolkien 2015) by islanders from neighboring islands and by Europeans and is viewed as representative of the acrolectal variety.

On the topic of TMA markers, I show in Baptista 2015 that some of the TMA forms used in the Santiago variety are closer to Portuguese than their equivalent forms in São Vicente. Example (1b) in Table 12.1 exhibits the progressive form *sta kume* "is eating" in Santiago, which is closer to Portuguese *esta a comer* than in São Vicente *te-te la te keme*, the supposed acrolectal variety. The forms in Table 12.1 express either the present or past progressive or habitual present and range from one marker to the combination of three markers to convey distinct temporal and aspectual readings. Table 12.1 clearly displays that in the Santiago variety, marker combinations as represented in (1a), (1b), (1c), (1e), and (1f) are more similar to Portuguese than their São

Table 12.1. TMA marker combinations

(1)	Santiago Variety	São Vicente Variety	Portuguese	English
	sa ta V	**ti ta V**		
(a)	El sa ta kume	e ti ta kemê	Esta a comer	she is eating
	sta V	**te...te V**		
(b)	El sta kume	e te la te kemê	Esta a comer	she is eating
	sa V	**te V**		
(c)	El sa kume	e te kemê	Esta a comer	she is eating
	sa ta V-ba	**tava ta V**		
(d)	El sa ta kumeba	e tava ta kemê	Estava a comer	she was eating
	staba ta V	**ta V-va**		
(e)	El staba ta kume	e ta kemeva	Estava a comer	she was eating
	sa ta V-du	**jente ti ta V**		
(f)	sa ta kumedu	Jente ti ta kemê	Está-se a comer	One usually eats
	sa ta V-da	**jente tava ta V**		
(g)	sa ta kumeda	jente tava ta kemê	Estava-se a comer	One used to eat

Vicente counterparts. The São Vicente expressions *tava ta* in (1d) and (1g) are the two exceptions to that trend, as they more closely relate to Portuguese *estava*.

These examples taken from Baptista (2015) reflect the inadequacy of the labels basilect and acrolect in describing the grammatical system of individual varieties. In the case of creole languages that oftentimes reveal linguistic traces of the source languages that contributed to their genesis in addition to their own innovations, it is reasonable to assume that some grammatical features may be more influenced by the superstrate and others by the substrates. In the present case, the Portuguese superstrate seems to have passed forms more faithfully on to the Santiago variety (possibly as a founder effect) than to the São Vicente variety of Cape Verdean Creole. Note that it does not mean that the current forms in São Vicente are not derived from Portuguese; what is intended here is just to say that the forms in Santiago have been more faithfully transmitted to the Santiago variety, showing that a core grammatical domain such as TMA markers can be more reflective of the acrolectal system (closer to the superstrate), even in a supposed basilect. Having shown the descriptive inadequacy of the creole continuum in accounting for basilectal and acrolectal grammars, we turn in the next section to the more promising framework of competing I-languages to account for the observed variation. By revisiting TMA markers and negative markers in later sections, using a competing I-language framework, we hope to demonstrate the explanatory power of such framework.

Variation and Competing I-Languages

We now turn to the notion of competing I-languages in order to account for variation in creoles.

I-Language versus E-Language and I-Language versus Multiple I-Languages

In this section, we lay out various perspectives on the nature of variation and its relation with one or multiple I-languages (Lightfoot 2006, 2016; Yang 2002; Obata and Epstein 2016; Epstein 2016).

Lightfoot (2006) provides one of the clearest definitions of I-language while contrasting it with E-language. For Lightfoot, "I" in I-language stands for internal and individual, which corresponds to an individual's mental system and the way his or her linguistic range is reflected in the brain. E-language, in contrast, is language in the external outside world, reflecting the various grammars that the child is exposed to and how people use these grammars. Crucially, these grammars do not represent a single system.

Lightfoot's most recent work (2016) makes the novel proposal that children parse E-language and have recourse to Universal Grammar (UG) when postulating specific I-language elements that are required for certain aspects of the parse itself. In Lightfoot's view, children's entire I-language is merely an aggregation of I-language elements. Lightfoot's model postulates that syntactic variation and change take place when children are exposed to ambient E-language that differs from what they were first exposed to through their caregivers. In sum, language variation and language change result from shifting interactions between E-language and I-language.

Yang (2002) proposes that child language consists of a collection of potential adult languages, arguing that child language acquisition involves a statistical combination of multiple possible grammars that are all allowed by UG but only some of them are retained by the time children acquire their L1. He argues that this finite number of possible human grammars is available to the learner from the very early stages of language acquisition and that the differences among them are based on parametric variation.

Though Yang believes in the biological foundation of language, he proposes that the neural hardware we are all born with must still be plastic in order to accommodate various possibilities resulting in the observed variation among the world languages. To him, language learning involves necessarily both nature and nurture (Yang 2006, 3–4). His learning model is anchored in the notion of multiple competing grammars, and postulates that for any given input datum, a child will select a grammar G with the probability P and upon analyzing the datum will reward grammar G by increasing the probability if the grammar is successful or penalize it by decreasing the probability if the grammar fails (Yang 2002, 26–27). This means that if a child starts out the acquisition process with a set of competing grammars, the successful ones will be rewarded and the failing ones punished by becoming gradually eliminated from the competition. In brief, Yang's learning model involves initial competition of I-languages, ultimately leading to the elimination of failing grammars.

In sum, for both Yang and Lightfoot, language variation can be viewed as the product of the interaction between nature and nurture.

In contrast, scholars like Obata and Epstein (2016) and Epstein (2016) propose that language variation pertains exclusively to the realm of I-language and innatism. For Epstein (2016, 199), language variation is innate and biologically constrained. His premise is that if the original objective of the Principles-and-Parameters model was to capture the possible range of variation across languages allowed by UG, then it would be logical to assume that variation itself is also innate. His position is reflected in the following quote:

> Contrary to the implication of the standard nature vs. nurture dichotomy, "nurture" is then itself definable only in terms of nature, and "human language variation" is a species property or capacity frequently characterized, inaccurately[,] as: "that which is not innate." (Epstein 2016, 201)

In contrast to Yang and Lightfoot, whose idea of variation reconciles nurture and nature, Epstein reduces nurture to nature.

In summary, we have presented a range of views on I-languages: some scholars account for variation by postulating and interaction between E-language and I-language, in addition to competition between I-languages (à la Yang and Lightfoot) leading to the gradual elimination of failing grammars. These same scholars also assume interaction between nature and nurture, whereas others argue that variation is essentially innate and, as a result, there is no need to postulate a distinction between nature and nurture, as nurture can be boiled down to nature (à la Epstein).

In the next two sections, I show that it is possible for I-languages to compete and coexist over a long period of time. Hence, the observable variation would result from diachronic cumulation of forms over successive generations of children acquiring the language.

Variation in the Auxiliary Domain, Pronominal System, and Negative Domain of Cape Verdean Creole

In this section, I start by discussing variation and competing I-languages through the lens of the auxiliary system of Cape Verdean Creole.

The Cape Verdean Progressive Aspect Variable and Its Variants

The Santiago variety of Cape Verdean Creole expresses the progressive variants *sa*, *sa ta*, *sta ta*, *sta* for the present tense, and the single variant *staba ta* for the past tense. The present progressive variants are illustrated in examples (1) through (5):

(1) E **sa** papia ku se fidju.
he be speak with his son
"He is speaking with his son."

(2) E **sa** so **ta** durmi.
he be always ASP sleep
"He is always sleeping."

(3) Gosi go e **sa ta** bebe vinhu.
now now he be ASP drink wine
"Now, he is drinking wine."

(4) E **sta ta** kunpra ropa.
he be ASP buy clothes
"He is buying clothes."

(5) E **sta** kunpra ropa.
he be buy clothes
"He is buying clothes."

On the surface, the variants *sa, sa ta, sta ta, sta* appear to occur in free variation given that they are semantically interchangeable in the present progressive. One could be tempted to assume that they are mere morphophonological variants of each other, but the situation is not that simple: First, the examples in (6) through (9) that follow show that the variants that behave similarly in the present tense act differently when combined with an anterior marker. If they were simple morphophonological variants of each other, the expectation would be that they would all be compatible with the anterior marker; but this is contrary to fact, as shown by the ungrammaticality of the (b) examples in (6) through (8). Second, I present diachronic evidence that some of the forms appeared much earlier than others, suggesting that they have competed and coexisted with each other over a long period of time.

Examples (6) through (8) show that *sa, sa . . . ta, sa ta* are unable to combine with the anterior marker *-ba*, as illustrated by the ungrammaticality of the (b) examples:

(6) a. E **sa** papia ku se fidju.
he be speak with his son
"He is speaking with his son."

b. *E **saba** papia ku se fidju
he be+ANT speak with his son

(7) a. E **sa** so **ta** papia ku se fidju.
he be always ASP speak with his son
"He is always speaking with his son."

b. *E **saba** so **ta** papia ku se fidju
he be+ANT always ASP speak with his son

(8) a. Gosi go e **sa ta** papia ku se fidju.
now now he be ASP speak with his son
"Now, he is speaking with his son."

b. *Gosi go e **saba** **ta** papia ku se fidju.
now now he be+ANT ASP speak with his son
"Now, he is speaking with his son."

The only one of the semantically equivalent forms that can combine with the anterior marker is *sta ta*, as shown in (9b):

(9) a. E **sta** **ta** papia ku se fidju.
he be ASP talk with his son
"He is speaking with his son."

b. **E** **staba** **ta** papia ku se fidju
he be+ANT ASP talk with his son
"He was speaking with his son."

Though they are semantically equivalent, the forms *sa*, *sa . . . ta*, *sa ta* reflect competing I-languages that developed over successive generations of speakers, which accounts for some old forms coexisting with recent ones. I discuss this proposal in Baptista (2017), where I show that similar competing I-languages can be found in diachrony. I show that the form **saba** that is today ungrammatical in the Santiago variety—see ungrammaticality of (6b), (7b), and (8b)—was found in *Língua de Preto*, the speech spoken by Black slaves and described in Teyssier (1959). This Black speech was spoken by slaves shipped to Portugal from the Western coast of Africa and believed to be connected with the Upper-Guinea Creoles of Guinea-Bissau and Cape Verde. The diachronic competing variants found in the *Língua de Preto* include for the progressive the markers *star*, *saa*, *sá*, and *sa* (Teyssier 1959). All of these markers are translated by forms of *estar* "to be" (stage-level copula) in Portuguese. The forms of the verb *ser* "to be" (individual-level copula) are *sou*, *ssar*, *sser*, *soo*, *saa*, *sae*, and *sa* (Teyssier 1959). Table 12.2 shows the competing variants in diachrony.

The forms *sta(r)* and *sa* are reminiscent of the two markers *sta* and *sa* found in the Santiago variety today with the difference that the marker *sa* combined with the anterior marker *-ba* is ungrammatical today, whereas it is found in the *Língua de Preto*, as shown in example (10). This shows that the forms *sta* and *sa* in Santiago are old forms that are now coexisting with the new form *ta* (see Table 12.1) whereas the form *saba*, in contrast, has now become extinct.

(10) . . . como mi **saba** primeyro (Language of the Blacks) (Teyssier 1959, 235)
how I was first
"How I was the first one."

This shows that a form that is unattested synchronically, as evidenced by the ungrammaticality of (6b), (7b), and (8b), was early on a legitimate form, as shown in the diachronic data in (10). We are proposing that this may be due to language change and speakers' reanalysis of the markers over time.

Table 12.2. Forms of *ser* and *estar* in Língua de Preto

Portuguese	Língua de Preto
Estar	estar, star, saa, sá, sa
Ser	sou, ssar, sser, soo, saa, sae

A possible scenario is that in the early stages of the creole, speakers may have analyzed *sa* as a clear derivate of its Portuguese counterpart *estar* and, as such, *sa* may have been viewed as a legitimate carrier of the anterior marker *-ba*, producing *saba*, maybe akin to Portuguese *estava*. As new variants emerged, the simplex forms *sa* and *sta* may have become reanalyzed by new generations of speakers as root infinitives, allowing a new generation of markers—the more recent nonsimplex forms *sta ta*—to become targeted as the new carriers of the anterior marker *-ba*. The nonsimplex forms *sta ta* could have been subsequently parsed by new generations of speakers as two distinct markers and, as such, each would be allowed to head its own finite clause. This in turn would lead to the emergence of a biclausal structure, where both the marker *sta* and the main lexical verb can carry their own individual anterior marker, as illustrated in (11) for the sentence in (12):

(11) João sta**ba** ta kume**ba** katxupa
João be+ANT ASP eat+ANT katxupa
"João was eating katxupa."

(12)

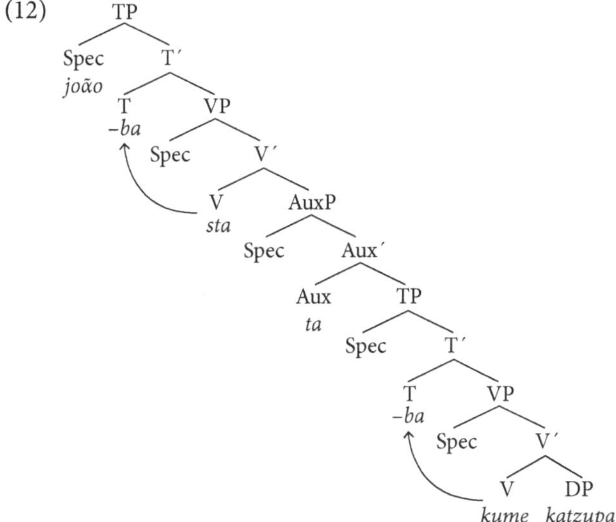

To summarize, the synchronic variants *sa, sa . . . ta, sa ta, sta* appear to be on the surface equivalent when in the present tense but they behave differently in the past, as some can be modified by the anterior marker *-ba* whereas others cannot. They combine old and new forms that have competed and coexisted for a long time.

Variation seen through the lens of competing I-languages that have emerged over time allows us to observe more clearly the distinct properties that variants have acquired over time, fulfilling different roles in the grammar of the language. For instance, *sta*+V involves a monoclausal structure whereas *staba ta V-ba* is biclausal, as seen in (12). Such a perspective reaches a much higher degree of descriptive and explanatory adequacy than the notions of basilect, mesolect, and acrolect to account for the observed variation.

We now turn to negation in Cape Verdean Creole, another domain also illustrative of competing I-languages.

Negation and Competing I-Languages

There are in Cape Verdean Creole two negators that are assumed to characterize distinct varieties of the Cape Verdean language: *ka* is found in most varieties of the language and *ne* in the two leeward islands of Santo Antão and São Vicente (*ka* is also used in these islands). Etymologically, *ka* has been assumed to have a dual etymology and to be derived from the Portuguese negative adverbial *nun**ka*** "never" and substratal negative auxiliaries like Mandinka ***ka** ban* (Kihm 1994). However, *ne* has been assumed to be uncontroversially derived from the Portuguese negator *não* "not." Given their assumed origins, one would predict that *ka* is the basilectal form of the negator and *ne* the acrolectal form. As we will note, such predictions are only partially borne out, if one relies on the creole continuum. Next, we first compare the syntactic behavior of *ka* and *ne* with respect to both lexical verbs and to the individual-level copula *e*, as the two negators behave differently with copular predicates.

The Behavior of ka

When combined with a lexical verb, *ka* must obligatorily appear preverbally (13a), resulting otherwise in ungrammaticality (13b). However, when modifying a copula, *ka* can appear before (14a) or after (14b) the copula, depending on the variety:

(13) a. *N **ka** bai merkadu.*
I NEG go market
"I didn't go to the market."

b. * *N bai **ka** merkadu*
I go NEG market

(14) a. *João **e** **ka** nha pai.*
João COP NEG my father
"João is not my father."

b. *João **ka** **e** nha pai.*
João NEG COP my father
"João is not my father."

The Behavior of ne

Like *ka*, *ne* must precede a lexical verb (15a) or TMA marker (16a); otherwise the sentence would be ungrammatical (15b and 16b):

(15) a. *N **ne** bai.*
I NEG go
"I didn't go."

b. **N bai **ne**.*
I go NEG

(16) a. *N* ***ne*** *tava bai.*
I NEG TMA go
"I hadn't gone."

b. **N tava bai* ***ne***.
I TMA go NEG

However, in copular predicates, negation can follow (17a) or precede (17b) the copula, in contrast to how it behaves with lexical verbs.

(17) a. Xef e ne nha ermãu.
Chief COP NEG my brother
"The chief is not my brother."

b. Xef n' e nha ermãu.
Chief NEG COP my brother
"The chief is not my brother."

Note that the sentence in (17b) can be considered as ungrammatical (Emanuel de Pina, p.c.) or grammatical (Swolkien 2015).

A possible explanation for the alternation observed in (14) and (17) with respect to the copula may lie in the dual identity of *e* as functioning in the Cape Verdean grammar as a pronoun or copula. One could therefore propose that the copula *e*, which is homophonous with the third person singular pronoun *e* "he/she/it," might have been reanalyzed in some I-languages as a subject pronominal. For the generation of speakers who analyzed *e* as a subject pronominal, a pre-Neg position would naturally emerge, as shown in (18), where the subject always precedes Negation (18a), otherwise yielding ungrammaticality (18b):

(18) a. ***e*** ***ka*** *bai.*
he/she/it NEG go
"He didn't go."

b. ****ka*** ***e*** *bai.*
NEG he/she/it go

For the generation of speakers who analyzed *e* as a genuine copula, derived from its Portuguese counterpart *e* (as in 19), NEG will precede the pronoun (19a), not follow it (19b).

(19) a. João **não** **e** alto. (Portuguese)
João NEG COP tall
"João is not tall."

b. *João **e** **não** alto.
João COP NEG tall
"João is not tall."

In sum, speakers' reanalysis could be triggered by the homophony between *e* as a copula and *e* as a pronominal subject. From an I-language perspective, a reanalysis scenario would allow us to understand the variation between pre-Neg and post-Neg positions with respect to the copula if one assumes that speakers who analyze the morpheme *e* as a pronominal subject would position it pre-Neg, given that all subjects precede Neg. In contrast, speakers who analyze it as a copula would position it post-Neg, as is the case with all other verbs in the language; see (13a) and (15a). A good methodology to test such a hypothesis in future work is to collect speakers' profiles with information on their birthplace, degree of education, proficiency in Portuguese, and exposure to the superstrate. An I-language perspective on this variation achieves both descriptive and explanatory adequacy if one assumes the speaker's reanalysis of *e* following either the copula or the pronoun distributional patterns.

Again, a creole continuum account would fall short of explaining why the basilectal negator *ka* is also used in São Vicente (in addition to *ne*) and why negation behaves differently with respect to lexical verbs and with copulas. Competing I-languages once again provide a more satisfying explanation of this state of affairs.

Conclusion

To summarize, we showed that in the domain of TMA markers, variants like *sa*, *sa . . . ta*, *sa ta*, *sta*, which seem semantically equivalent on the surface, actually displayed distinct behaviors when in the past, compatible with monoclausal or biclausal structures. We also showed that TMA markers in this language combine old and new forms that have competed and coexisted for a long time.

In the domain of Negation, we have shown that homophony of the copula and subject pronoun may have triggered reanalysis and competing I-languages leading to the observed alternation of Neg with respect to *e*.

Variation seen through the lens of competing I-languages that have emerged over time allows us to observe more clearly the distinct properties that variants have acquired over time, fulfilling different roles in the grammar of the language. Such a perspective, in my view, reaches a much higher degree of descriptive and explanatory adequacy than the creole continuum.

Note

The paper presented at GURT focused on TMA markers exclusively and was expanded into a longer version that was since published as a column in the *Journal of Pidgin and Creole Languages* (Baptista 2017). This chapter reports on TMA markers and further explores variation in the negative domain of the two varieties under study.

References

Baptista, Marlyse. 2015. "Continuum and Variation in Creole Languages: Out of Many Voices, One Language." *Journal of Pidgin and Creole Languages* 30 (2): 225–64.

Baptista, Marlyse. 2017. "Competing I-Grammars in Creole Genesis: A Synchronic and Diachronic View." *Journal of Pidgin and Creole Languages* 32 (2): 398–415.

Bickerton, Derek. 1973. "The Nature of a Creole Continuum." *Language* 49 (3): 640–69.

Déprez, Viviane, and France Martineau. 2004. "Micro-Parametric Variation and Negative Concord." In *Contemporary Approaches to Romance Linguistics*, edited by Julie Auger, J. Clancy Clements, and Barbara Vance, 139–58. Amsterdam: Benjamins.

Epstein, Samuel. 2016. "Why Nurture Is Natural Too." *Biolinguistics* 10:197–201.

Holm, John. 1988. *Pidgins and Creoles*. Vol. 1. Cambridge: Cambridge University Press.

Kihm, Alain. 1994. *Kriyol Syntax: The Portuguese-Based Creole Language of Guinea-Bissau*. Philadelphia: Benjamins.

Lightfoot, David W. 2006. *How New Languages Emerge*. Cambridge: Cambridge University Press.

Lightfoot, David W. 2016. "Rethinking Catastrophes." Unpublished manuscript.

Obata, Miki, and Samuel Epstein. 2016. "Eliminating Parameters from the Narrow Syntax: Rule Ordering Variation by 3rd Factor Underspecification." In *Advances in Biolinguistics: The Human Language Faculty and Its Biological Basis*, edited by Koji Fujita and Cedric A. Boeckx, 128–38. New York: Routledge.

Raumolin-Brunberg, Helena. 1988. "Variation and Historical Linguistics: A Survey of Methods and Concepts." *Neuphilologische Mitteilungen* 89 (2): 136–54.

Swolkien, Dominika. 2015. "The Cape Verdean Creole of São Vicente: Its Genesis and Structure." PhD diss., University of Coimbra.

Tabouret-Keller, Andrée, and Robert B. Le Page. 1985. *Acts of Identity: Creole-Based Approaches to Language and Ethnicity*. Cambridge: Cambridge University Press.

Teyssier, Paul. 1959. *La Langue de Gil Vicente*. Paris: Klincksieck.

Yang, Charles. 2002. *Knowledge and Learning in Natural Language*. Oxford: Oxford University Press.

Yang, Charles. 2006. *The Infinite Gift: How Children Learn and Unlearn the Languages of the World*. New York: Scribner.

Chapter 13

Transmission Revisited

GILLIAN SANKOFF
University of Pennsylvania

THE PROCESS OF TRANSMISSION is crucial to understanding how language is passed on from one person, one generation, one community to the next. Moreover, a focus on transmission, necessarily involving a temporal dimension, links the fields of sociolinguistics and language acquisition. The implicational relationship between language change and variation, established by Weinreich, Labov, and Herzog (1968), has become a cornerstone of sociolinguistic research. Not for nothing is our flagship journal entitled *Language Variation and Change*.

Transmission, defined as "the unbroken sequence of native-language acquisition by children" (Labov 2007, 346), is at the heart of the relationship between variation and acquisition. However, insofar as speakers alter their language beyond early childhood, does the mechanism of transmission become problematic? Considering research on language change both in historical terms and across individual life spans, this chapter focuses on processes of transmission in acquisition, whether in childhood or beyond.

The Temporal Dimension in Language Acquisition: Early Childhood and Beyond

The temporal dimension in language acquisition is fixed by the human life span and constrained by its maturational states. Thus, it makes perfect sense for L1 acquisition research to be concentrated on early childhood, where most of the action is.

In contrast, studies of acquisition in later life have focused on second languages or dialects. In the case of second languages (henceforth L2), a topic that is beyond the scope of this chapter, the process is usually phrased as one of language LEARNING. In the case of second dialects, however, we hear less about learning than about ACCOMMODATION, a term that nicely encompasses the idea that the changes to be made may be only partial. The two situations also tend to differ in their social consequences.

Accommodating to a second dialect seems to imply tinkering with one's "native language," and involves issues of loyalty that do not arise in the "natural" acquisition of one's first ("native") dialect. In 2017, Welsh politician Leanne Wood was castigated in a constituent's email complaining that her "broad Welsh accent . . . leaves Welsh people open to ridicule." Declaring her Welsh loyalty, Ms. Wood replied via Facebook: "I'm not prepared to pretend to be something I'm not . . . if people don't like it, they can stick it" (BBC 2017). Loyalty issues are framed differently in the L2 case. Partial success in L2 acquisition may lead someone with "a foreign accent" to receive the (often unwelcome) response: "Where do you come from?" Partial success in accommodating to a second dialect may instead evoke the response: "Who does she think she is!" (for trying "to pretend to be something she is not," a strategy Ms. Wood deliberately avoided by embracing her Welsh English).

As with L2 acquisition, interspeaker differences occur in the second dialect case (Payne 1976; Chambers 1992; Starks and Bayard 2002). In "tinkering with" one's original grammar, however, elements of an originally acquired dialect may be replaced, resulting in difficulty in keeping the two apart (Trudgill 1986, 32). Tagliamonte and Molfenter note that, for three Canadian children who returned to Canada after six years in the United Kingdom, "even at the furthest reaches of second dialect success, these children, like most transplanted individuals, will always retain 'flavors' of their mixed repertoires" (2007, 673).

Though the research on second dialect acquisition focuses largely on geographically mobile speakers, the processes involved closely resemble those of dialect diffusion. Labov characterized diffusion as contrasting with transmission, regarding diffusion as "a secondary process:"

> [The] limitations on diffusion are the result of the fact that most language contact is largely between and among adults. . . . Structural patterns are not as likely to be diffused because adults do not learn and reproduce linguistic forms, rules, and constraints with the accuracy and speed [of] children (Labov 2007, 349).

In contrast, sound changes that are TRANSMITTED, incrementing via successive cohorts of children, are those that can "operate at a higher degree of abstraction than low-level phonetic shifts, involving grammatical conditioning, word boundaries, and the systemic relations that drive chain shifting" (Labov 2007, 348).

How similar is the second dialect case to the path of speakers aging in place, where language change has affected speakers younger than themselves, thereby altering the ambient language of their native communities? This question is addressed in the remainder of the chapter.

The first two sections outline three trajectory types that older speakers have been found to take under conditions of language change in their own communities, and discuss the issues these patterns raise for acquisition. The following section addresses the most vexing question: how to explain retrograde change among older speakers "swimming against the historical current," thus contributing to a long tail in the S-shaped curve of language change. "Long tail" issues are then exemplified by data from the acquisition of negation in Canadian French. In conclusion, I suggest directions for future research.

Three Trajectory Types among Older Speakers

Speakers experiencing language change in their communities may follow one of three trajectories in later life (Sankoff 2019):

1. Staying with what they learned in primary language acquisition
2. Altering their speech in accommodation to, or learning from, the ever-increasing number of speakers coming up behind them who exhibit later stages of the change
3. Reverting to a more conservative pattern, associated with reaching a "mature" or "senior" age grade.

Grounded in a longitudinal corpus of sociolinguistic interviews recorded in Montreal in 1971, 1984, and 1995 (Sankoff 2019), three case studies are reviewed, one illustrating each type. This research provides a window on how two kinds of time—historical time and the time of the life course—relate to each other.

Stability in Earlier-Acquired Patterns

As people age, they may retain the grammars they acquired as children, including the constraints on variability, despite being increasingly surrounded by younger people. In Montreal French, one such case concerns auxiliary selection between *avoir* "have" and *être* "be" with a small set of verbs of motion, state, and change of state. For example, interviews where people recounted moving from one location to another featured variable use with *partir* "to leave": *on a/est parti* "we left." In the 120-speaker sample of 1971, people of higher social status and education were more likely to prefer the standard *être* (Sankoff and Thibault 1977). Data from 1984 and 1995 indicated that the community as a whole was undergoing change toward increased use of *être*. However, a panel of the same sixty people between 1971 and 1984 was characterized by stability (Sankoff, Thibault, and Wagner 2004). Though speakers as they aged retained their earlier-acquired pattern, people born later, as educational opportunities increased, exhibited an increased preference for standard *être*.

Older Speakers Participating in Community Change

The phonological change from apical [r] to posterior [ʁ] in Montreal French occurred in the second half of the twentieth century, beginning after World War II (Vinay 1950). Based on a sample of thirty-two speakers from 1971, matched by age, sex, and social class with thirty-two different speakers from 1984, Sankoff and Blondeau (2007) documented rapid change in the community, led by younger speakers. In this case, we discovered many aging speakers who were far from stable. Tracing life span trajectories for thirty-two people recorded in both years, we found that almost all speakers who had been under age 20 in 1971 (i.e., born after 1951) were using posterior [ʁ] virtually categorically by 1984. For those born earlier (older than age 20 in 1971), trajectories were split about equally between stability and participation in the change.

Older Speakers Swimming against the Community Current

Variation between the periphrastic and the inflected future, characteristic of contemporary spoken French, is illustrated in (1) from the 1971 Montreal corpus.

(1) Elle **va** peut-être **arriver** bien vite — on lui **demandera**.
PERIPHRASTIC INFLECTED
"Maybe **she'll arrive** pretty soon—**we'll ask** her."

Serge M. 074, age 16, 1971, 185[1]

In Canadian French, use of the inflected future in affirmative clauses declined from 36 percent in the late 1800s to 20 percent by the end of the twentieth century (Poplack and Dion 2009, 572). Wagner and Sankoff (2011) found that in the Montreal 1971 data, use of the inflected future was less common for younger speakers than for their elders. This seemed to reflect a continuation of the historical trend toward its eventual disappearance. However, the trend for a panel of fifty-nine speakers as they aged over the next thirteen years was in the opposite direction. Mean percentage use was 10 percent in 1971, rising to 15.5 percent in 1984—an increase of more than 50 percent that was most characteristic of highly educated upper-class and upper-middle-class speakers (Wagner and Sankoff 2011, 300). Whereas nineteen of the fifty-nine speakers used no inflected futures at all in the affirmative in their 1971 interviews, only four of them retained this pattern by 1984.

Retrograde life span change was a general trend in the case of Montreal French inflected futures. Elsewhere, this phenomenon has been observed for at least some speakers. Comparing data from the 1970s and 1990s, Zilles (2005) established that the historical first-person pronoun *nos* is giving way to *a gente* (literally, "people") in Brazilian Portuguese. Yet among the same twelve people she followed across the two decades, two elderly women significantly increased their rates of using *nos*, the traditional variant. During community change in which *nos* continued to retreat for every new cohort of younger people, the other ten speakers in the panel study remained stable as they aged over the twenty-year period.

The questions raised in exploring retrograde life span change point to more general issues about the relationship between aging and language change that are addressed in the remainder of this chapter.

Questions about Acquisition

The first trajectory type—stability—prompts no questions, since by definition, stability in later life yields nothing "acquisitional" to be accounted for in that life stage. For the other two trajectory types, however, one set of issues involves individual differences: who is likely to change, and who is not? Age differences are surely important, with decreasing plasticity across the life span. In the cases exemplifying Type 2 and Type 3 trajectories, speakers in their teens and twenties were much more likely than their elders to change. Differences in gender identity, social class, education, opportunity and social pressure, and even personality and motivation may play a role. Other questions relate to the linguistic processes entering into language change in later life. How is later acquisition integrated into previously acquired grammars? Does new learning supplant what was previously learned? Are linguistic, stylistic, and other constraints differentially weighted at different life stages? Are different modules of the grammar (phonetics, phonology, morphology, syntax) equally susceptible to modification?

Most guesses about change in an early-acquired language in later life are based on assessing outcomes, not on studies of the processes themselves. Longitudinal studies linking life span to community language change are still too few in number to assess how typical are the processes outlined in the three attested cases just discussed. The next section reviews several studies of the acquisition of competing variants in childhood and early adolescence, examples of Type 2 trajectories early in the life span.

Acquisition in a Stable Bidialectal Community

Children in Buckie, a small town in northern Scotland, are immersed from birth in both the local dialect and standard Scottish English (Smith, Durham, and Fortune 2007). For the phonological "hoose" variable (including words like *house*, *down*, etc.), the vowel nucleus in the local dialect is monophthongal, in contrast with the Scottish English diphthong. The alternation is conditioned stylistically. In contexts of play and routine, twelve girls and twelve boys ages 2–4 replicated their caregivers' high rates of the monophthong. In contrast, contexts of discipline and of instruction yielded very low rates of the local variant for both caregivers and children (Smith et al. 2007, 75). Nine years later, the children (by then ages 11–13) had maintained the stylistic constraint, approximating adult-to-adult usage with preponderant use of the monophthong to locals, and higher use of the diphthong to outsiders (Smith 2015).

Speech Community Formation among Children

Peer influence in early childhood is documented in the longitudinal study of eleven kindergarten children in a suburb of Grenoble, France (Nardy, Chevrot, and Barbu 2014), examining three stable variables long present in French. In each case in Table 13.1, omission of the final consonant is frequent in spontaneous vernacular speech, whereas the standard language favors its retention.

Arriving in kindergarten at mean age 4.7, the children's use of standard variants ranged between 10 percent and 57 percent, with individual rates most closely resem-

Table 13.1. Variables in the spoken French of Grenoble kindergartners

Variable	Example	Phonetic alternation
1. Final [t] in est (3rd sg. present of être 'to be')	c'est à moi "it's mine"	[se (t) a mwa]
2. /r/ in word-final cluster	ça va être joli "that'll be pretty"	[sa va ɛt(rə) ʒoli]
3. Final /l/ in subject clitic	ils sont tombés "they fell"	[i(l) sõ to bẽ]

bling those of their most frequent conversational partners. A year later, the distance between children's rates had almost halved, ranging only between 20 percent and 44 percent: five children's rates had decreased; four had increased; and two were stable (Nardy et al. 2014, 282). As with adult French speakers, children exhibited both variants and had clearly influenced one another in their spontaneous speech production.

Another study, including eight- and twelve-year-old children along with a cohort of four-year-olds, was undertaken in Milton Keynes, a "New Town" some forty-five miles northwest of London. As a planned city, the population increased from about fifty thousand in 1961 to more than 170 thousand in the three subsequent decades (Wikipedia 2017), absorbing in-migrants with different dialects from across the United Kingdom. In research between 1990 and 1994, speech of the four-year-olds was influenced mainly by the various dialects of their parents, but the twelve-year-olds were coalescing into new, shared dialect patterns (Kerswill 1996; Kerswill and Williams 2000).

Another research project, this time in the United States, again found older children assimilating to linguistic patterns of their peers. Johnson (2010) showed that the advance of the low back vowel merger (*cot* ~ *caught*) along the Massachusetts/Rhode Island border was due to the influx of in-migrants from the Boston area, whose ("merged") children made up a sufficiently large proportion of the local school population to create a tipping point for the spread of the merger among their local ("unmerged") middle school peers. Younger local children typically followed their unmerged parents.

In these and other studies reviewed in Sankoff 2018, peer group influence after primary acquisition was crucial in the linguistic trajectories of children between the ages of about 4 and 12. These studies, and the results of the second-dialect literature reviewed earlier indicate that despite decreasing malleability in adolescence and adulthood, continued exposure to new patterns can result in their later acquisition.

Questions about Retrograde Change among Older Speakers

Retrograde change among older speakers raises puzzling questions about acquisition. In the 1971 Montreal study, data from sixteen speakers under age 30 featured no inflectional futures at all in the affirmative. By 1984, when they were between the ages of 28 and 43, only two of them still showed this pattern. What was going on? We can immediately rule out any idea that they had only begun to acquire inflectional future morphology after age 27, since all of them used it categorically in the negative.[2] As they aged, the fourteen young people had changed a pattern of total complementary distribution (inflectional future in the negative; periphrastic future in the affirmative) to one in which the inflectional future was now permitted in the affirmative.

Early Acquisition, Later Employment: The Retreat of ne *in French*

Longitudinal research in Tours, France (Ashby 1981, 2001), revealed a steep decline in frequency of the negative particle *ne* between the 1970s and the 1990s. This change has progressed even further in Canada. Of sixty speakers examined in the 1971 data, only fifteen used it even once, with a combined rate of 1.1 percent (N = 4,054 negative clauses). The other forty-five never used it, in a total estimated at more than ten thousand negative clauses of *ne* (Sankoff and Vincent (1977) 1980, 300, table 14.1).

In 1995, Louise first uses *ne* in discussing a family conflict (2a), but omits *ne* in the subsequent relative clause (2b):

(2) a. J'ai un frère qui a marié une Anglaise qui **ne** parle **pas** un mot de français.
"I have a brother who married an English girl who doesn't speak a word of French."

b. puis j'ai un frère qui a marié une Québécoise invétérée qui ∅ veut **pas** parler anglais.
"and I have a brother who married an inveterate Québécoise who doesn't want to speak English."

— Louise C., 008, age 53, 1995, 59

Example (2a), from 1995, is in fact the only instance of *ne* for Louise in 759 negative sentences across the three decades of her recorded interviews.[3] Between age 29 (1971) and age 53 (1995), Louise was not alone in registering a first use of *ne* at a later age. Table 13.2 shows that for forty members of a sixty-speaker panel recorded in both 1971 and 1984, *ne* was categorically absent in 1971. By 1984, only thirty-two panelists used no *ne*. "Frequent users" (seven or more instances of *ne*) numbered five in both years.

As with inflected futures, we find a large group of speakers exhibiting no use of *ne* at age 15 plus, with a reduced number registering the same behavior at age 28 plus.[4] Once again, it would seem preposterous to interpret these facts as representing late—very late—acquisition. Is *ne* actually acquired earlier? If so, why start using it only much later? Fortunately, data from early childhood acquisition helps to illuminate the issue.

In a longitudinal study of the acquisition of negation, Choi (1986) recorded French children ages 1;9–2;6, including Adele, a French Canadian. At this early stage, the children produced very few utterances beyond two words. *Pas* was the only negator used by any child, with *ne* completely absent. In contrast, Adele's mother used *ne* at a rate of 18.4 percent (N = 49) in speaking to her daughter, probably much more frequently than in adult conversation. In her early thirties in 1983, she can be compared with her thirty-three young Montreal age-mates in our sample. Only ten used *ne* at all, none registering a rate of more than 2 percent. Adele's mother is clearly off the chart.

Table 13.2. Use of *ne* by the 60-speaker panel in 1971 and 1984

Number of cases of *ne* per speaker	Number of speakers in 1971	Number of speakers in 1984
Zero *ne*	40 (67%)	32 (53%)
1–4 *ne*	15 (25%)	23 (39%)
7+ *ne*	5 (8%)	5 (8%)
Total speakers	60	60

Transcripts of seven recording sessions between Olivier, another Canadian child, and his father, Bruno, provide a more detailed picture of *ne* in parent-child interaction.[5] At age 1;11, Olivier produced only three two-word negative fragments, *pas* "not" with an adjective (e.g., *pas chaud* "not hot"). The next two sessions yielded four more such fragments along with ten clausal negatives, none containing any use of *ne*. In the fourth session, Oliver (2;9) uttered six more negative sentences, including one avatar with *ne*, given in (3):

(3) moi **n'** a pas des autres autos [wɘ nɘ pɑ dɪz ototo]
me NEG have not some other cars
"I don't have any other cars."

Two sessions over the next year featured 24 negative sentences, with no further use of *ne*, as illustrated in (4), recorded at age three years, six months.

(4) parce que j'∅ aime pas ça
because I ∅ like not that
"because I don't like that"

Example (5) is one of two instances of *ne* among Olivier's twenty negative clauses in the final recorded session at age four years, one month.

(5) oui mais pourquoi je **ne** mets pas mon, mon, mon chapeau d'hiver?
yes but why I NEG put not my my my hat of winter
"Yes, but why don't I wear my, my, my winter hat?"

By age four, Olivier had clearly acquired the productive, grammatical use of *ne* in simple sentential contexts. In the light of Adele's mother's 18.4 percent *ne*, it was not surprising that Oliver had by this time received plenty of relevant input from his father, Bruno.

Across the seven recording sessions, *ne* occurred in seventeen of the eighty-six negative clauses Bruno addressed to Olivier, a rate of 19.8 percent. During Olivier's second and third years, in a pattern reminiscent of Buckie parents, *ne* for Bruno was concentrated in contexts of discipline (sternly) and instruction (patiently), as in (6):

(6) Bruno: *Tu **n'**as pas dit bonjour!* "You didn't say hello!"
[modeling for Olivier] *Bonjour, Eléna.* "Hello, Elena"
Olivier: *Bonjour, Eléna.* "Hello, Elena"
— Olivier, age one year, 11 months

By the time Olivier was four years old, however, his father no longer treated him as a baby. Far from the patient teacher in evidence when Olivier was three, in the last session (Olivier age 4;1) Bruno loses his temper, repeatedly admonishing Olivier: *C'est ∅ p(l)us drole!* "It's not funny anymore."[6] The reduction of *ne* in speech to the four-year-old undoubtedly reflects his vernacular use with adults.

How does the evidence from Adele and Olivier help to clarify the sudden appearance of an old-fashioned variant later in the life span? Adults who are able to trot out *ne* occasionally have been exposed to it as young children. There are of course some children who may not encounter it until they go to school and learn to read.

However, middle- or upper-middle-class children, like Olivier and Adele, have probably internalized the basic grammar of *ne* by about age four. In school, they probably discover that most of their peers don't use it. They stash it away for use in writing proper school compositions, where they do better than the other children, and use it in speech only when reaching an age and a status in life when they find it appropriate.

Nardy et al. reported on some children arriving in kindergarten with a higher than average use of Standard French variants. After a year, these children, like those with a lower than average use, converged somewhere in the middle. As in the situations analyzed by Smith et al. in Scotland, Johnson in New England, and many others, peer influence is crucial. There are, of course, individual differences—more, with increasing age—but the peer group, as local representatives of the wider speech community, makes it clear that there are consequences for outliers.

I do not take a position here as to whether variation in *ne* is best encompassed within a single grammar or whether it results from two grammars in competition, though I think the latter is likely. I do believe that once acquired, the grammar of negation that includes the use of *ne* is available for use. Its association with formal education and the written language continues to be felt across the life span, as its use in speech is restricted almost entirely to formal contexts (Sankoff and Vincent (1977) 1980, 302–3).

Conclusion

If stylistic constraints are an important factor in conditioning variation, it is likely that those speech styles appropriate for using particular (formal) variants simply do not often occur for younger speakers. This brings us back to age grading. If seniors indulge in retrograde change as they get older, linguistic features typical of preceding generations of elders will not die with them. Instructing their children and grandchildren, they use them with a higher frequency than in their usual spontaneous interactions with their own peers, providing input that the children incorporate into their grammars, but wait for an appropriate time to deploy. The tail of language change may then be slowed to a crawl (not, I would argue, to a halt). The case of *ne* makes it clear that stylistic variation is an important component of research on life span change. For those who almost never use it, *ne* appears in co-occurrence with other features of Standard French associated with formality, such as the formal second person plural pronoun (*vous, vos, votre*) used to a singular addressee.

Considering transmission as the starting point for incrementation as children leave the primary influence of their parents, Labov and others have produced models yielding an adolescent peak that has been verified in a number of studies in recent years. We now see that in this plastic, early period, there is also language learning taking place that may not be realized in people's active repertoires until many years later.

This chapter has only scratched the surface in suggesting links between language change, with its concomitant variation, and language acquisition. Very little is actually known about language change at all stages across the life span. Current evidence leads me to believe that the door does not slam on the critical period, but that it does creak shut. If I had any advice to give young researchers about a strategic research site into issues of transmission, I would choose that life stage where lability still gives young people some linguistic maneuverability, just as their social world is opening up.

Notes

Many thanks to Hélène Blondeau, Henrietta Cedergren, Soonja Choi, Eve Clark, Daniel Ezra Johnson, Jordan Kodner, Bill Labov, David Sankoff, Jennifer Smith, Sali Tagliamonte, Pierrette Thibault, Diane Vincent, Suzanne Evans Wagner, and Charles Yang for the contributions that their research, their collegiality, and their friendship have made to this chapter.

1 Citations from the corpus include speaker's pseudonym, identification number, age at time of the recording, date of recording, and line number in the transcription.

2 The near complementary distribution of inflectional futures (categorical in the negative and prohibited for many speakers in the affirmative), first discovered by L. Emirkanian and D. Sankoff (1985), has been observed in every study since.

3 This rate of 0.13 percent (1/759) is based on clauses negated with *pas* "not" (1/683), *jamais* "never" (0/24), and *rien* "nothing" (0/52).

4 The age range of speakers interviewed in both years was 15 to 62 in 1971, thus 28 to 75 in 1984.

5 Transcripts from the GNP (Genesee-Nicolaidis-Paradis) Bilingual Corpus were downloaded from the CHILDES database (http://childes.talkbank.org/access/Biling/GNP.html, accessed September 24, 2017). Speaking French (with his father) and English (with his mother), Olivier's acquisition followed monolingual norms in each. Studying syntactic acquisition, Paradis and Genesee report that for the three bilingual children in their corpus, "no indications were found of transfer, acceleration, or delay in acquisition. The hypothesis that the grammars are acquired autonomously was supported" (Paradis and Genesee 1996, 1).

6 In six repetitions, negative *plus* "no longer" occurs as [py] as distinguished from affirmative *plus* [ply] in Canadian French.

References

Ashby, William J. 1981. "The loss of the negative 'ne' in French: A syntactic change in progress." *Language* 57:674–87.

Ashby, William J. 2001. "Un nouveau regard sur la chute du *ne* en français parlé tourangeau: s'agit-il d'un changement en cours?" *French Language Studies* 11:1–22.

BBC. 2017. "Leanne Wood told to 'Moderate' Rhondda Welsh accent." *BBC News*, February 24. http://www.bbc.com/news/uk-wales-politics-39076393.

Chambers, Jack K. 1992. "Dialect acquisition." *Language* 68:673–706.

Choi, Soonja. 1986. "A cross-linguistic developmental study of negation in English, French and Korean." PhD diss., SUNY Buffalo.

Emirkanian, Louisette, and David Sankoff. 1985. "Le futur simple et le futur périphrastique." In *Les tendances dynamiques du français parlé à Montréal*, edited by Monique Lemieux and Henrietta Cedergren, 189–204. Gouvernement du Québec: Office de la langue française.

Johnson, Daniel Ezra. 2010. "Stability and Change across a Dialect Boundary: The Low Vowels of Southeastern New England." *Publications of the American Dialect Society* 95 (1).

Kerswill, Paul. 1996. "Children, Adolescents, and Language Change." *Language Variation and Change* 8:177–202.

Kerswill, Paul, and Ann Williams. 2000. "Creating a New Town Koine: Children and Language Change in Milton Keynes." *Language in Society* 29:65–116.

Labov, William. 2007. "Transmission and Diffusion." *Language* 83:344–87.

Nardy, Aurélie, Jean-Pierre Chevrot, and Stéphanie Barbu. 2014. "Sociolinguistic Convergence and Social Interactions within a Group of Preschoolers: A Longitudinal Study." *Language Variation and Change* 26:273–301.

Paradis, Johanne, and Fred Genesee. 1996. "Syntactic Acquisition in Bilingual Children: Autonomous or Interdependent?" *Studies in Second Language Acquisition* 18:1–25.

Payne, Arvilla. 1976. "The Acquisition of the Phonological System of a Second Dialect." PhD diss., University of Pennsylvania.

Poplack, Shana, and Nathalie Dion. 2009. "Prescription vs Praxis: The Evolution of Future Temporal Reference in French." *Language* 85:557–87.

Sankoff, Gillian. 2017. "Before There Were Corpora: The Evolution of the Montreal French Project as a Longitudinal Study." In *Panel Studies of Language Variation and Change*, edited by Suzanne Evans Wagner and Isabelle Buchstaller, 21–52. New York: Routledge.

Sankoff, Gillian. 2018. "Language Change across the Lifespan." *Annual Review of Linguistics* 4:297–316.

Sankoff, Gillian. 2019. "Language Change across the Lifespan: Three Trajectory Types." In press, *Language* 95.

Sankoff, Gillian, and Hélène Blondeau. 2007. "Language Change across the Lifespan: /r/ in Montreal French." *Language* 83:560–88.

Sankoff, Gillian, and Pierrette Thibault. 1977. "L'alternance entre les auxiliaires avoir et être en français parlé à Montréal." *Langue Française* 34:81–108.

Sankoff, Gillian, Pierrette Thibault, and Suzanne Wagner. 2004. "An Apparent Time Paradox: Change in Montréal French Auxiliary Selection, 1971–1995." Paper presented at NWAV 33, Ann Arbor, Michigan.

Sankoff, Gillian, and Diane Vincent. (1977) 1980. "L'emploi productif du *ne* dans le français parlé à Montréal." Translated by Gillian Sankoff. Chap. 14 of *The Social Life of Language*. Philadelphia: University of Pennsylvania Press.

Smith, Jennifer. 2015. "Parenting Style: From Preschool to Preadolescence in the Acquisition of Variation." Presented at NWAV 44, Toronto, Canada.

Smith, Jennifer, Mercedes Durham, and Liane Fortune. 2007. "'Mam, My Trousers Is fa'in Doon!' Community, Caregiver and Child in the Acquisition of Variation in a Scottish Dialect." *Language Variation and Change* 19:63–99.

Starks, Donna, and Donn Bayard. 2002. "Individual Variation in the Acquisition of Postvocalic /r/: Day Care and Sibling Order as Potential Variables." *American Speech* 77:184–94.

Tagliamonte, Sali A., and Sonja Molfenter. 2007. "How'd You Get That Accent?: Acquiring a Second Dialect of the Same Language." *Language in Society* 36:649–75.

Trudgill, Peter. 1986. *Dialects in Contact.* Oxford and New York: Blackwell.

Vinay, Jean-Paul. 1950. "Bout de la langue ou fond de la gorge?" *French Review* 23:489–98.

Wagner, Suzanne, and Gillian Sankoff. 2011. "Age Grading in the Montréal French Inflected Future." *Language Variation and Change* 23:275–313.

Weinreich, Uriel, William Labov, and Marvin Herzog. 1968. "Empirical Foundations for a Theory of Language Change." In *Directions for Historical Linguistics*, edited by Winfred Lehmann and Yakov Malkiel, 97–195. Austin: University of Texas Press.

Wikipedia, s.v. 2017. "Milton Keynes," accessed September 24, 2017, https://en.wikipedia.org/wiki/Milton_Keynes.

Zilles, Ana M. S. 2005. "The Development of a New Pronoun: The Linguistic and Social Embedding of *a gente* in Brazilian Portuguese." *Language Variation and Change* 17:19–53.

Chapter 14

The Value of Small Communities in a Big Data World: Investigating Smith Island English in Real and Apparent Time

NATALIE SCHILLING
Georgetown University

IN THIS ERA OF "big data," it is increasingly tempting to base our linguistic and sociolinguistic studies on large corpora, often of internet data, and to focus on big-picture patterns of language and dialect variation and change. For example, researchers might study historic patterns of variation and change as revealed in corpora of written records such as the Corpus of Early English Correspondence (e.g., Nevalainen and Raumolin-Brunberg 2003). Alternatively, sociolinguists might focus on national dialect maps grounded in large-scale telephone surveys, as in Labov, Ash, and Boberg's (2006) *Atlas of North American English*; or they may utilize crowd-sourced data from social media, as for example with Leemann, Kolly, and Britain's (2016) English Dialect App, through which residents of England use smartphones to upload information on dialect variation. While studies grounded in very large data sets amenable to automated analysis certainly increase our linguistic and sociolinguistic knowledge and understandings in ways never before dreamed possible, I here hope to demonstrate that in-depth, in-person sociolinguistic studies of small communities retain immense worth and should not unthinkingly be relinquished in favor of big data.

At the time of this writing, my students and I are engaged in a sociolinguistic study of a very small community, Smith Island, in Maryland's Chesapeake Bay. This is a follow-up to two previous studies, one conducted in 1999–2001 by my former students and me, and another conducted in the mid-1980s by a former student at Georgetown University. In this chapter, I use data from real-time study across these time periods, and apparent-time study across generations, to illustrate three points about the value of small community studies in a big-data world. First, they help fill in gaps left by broad-scale dialect surveys. For example, the current study shows that, as Labov (2016, 590) indicates, the phonological systems of small communities at dialect borders cannot be presumed to be "weaker versions" of the phonological systems of large cities or core dialect areas. Second, in-depth studies of small communities provide detail on the patterning of variation and change *within* dialect regions and communities. The current study demonstrates that linguistically and socially conditioned intracommunity dialect variation is present in even the smallest, seemingly homogeneous communities. In fact, small communities can often sustain *more* intricate patterns of within-community variation than larger ones. Finally, our continuing work with the Smith Island community shows us that sustained interaction between researchers and community members in small communities affords access to intra-individual variation and its social meanings, over time and across situations, illuminating how variation across and within communities and individuals is acquired, sustained, and valued in this increasingly globalizing world.

The Smith Island Community and Its Dialect

Smith Island is located in the Chesapeake Bay, about ten miles from the mainland Delmarva Peninsula, on the mid-Atlantic coast of the United States. It is accessible only by boat. The island is actually a small group of islands, and there are three different towns. The towns of Ewell and Rhodes Point are on one island; Tylerton is on another and can be reached only by boat from the other two island towns. Smith Island has been inhabited by English speakers since the mid-1600s and has existed in relative independence from the mainland since that time. Its economy traditionally has been based on small-scale maritime operations. To this day, the island is a key source of soft-shell crabs, considered a delicacy in many parts of the world (see, e.g., Hierstetter 2015).

During their centuries of comparative independence, islanders developed a distinctive dialect of American English. This language variety is characterized in part by lexical and grammatical retentions from older forms of English. For example, the term *proging* for "collecting arrowheads and other artifacts from the marshlands" dates back to at least the late fifteenth or early sixteenth century, and *kofered* for "bent or warped" derives from the obsolete verb *coffer*. The island dialect is also replete with terms related to crabs and the crabbing industry, for example, the terms *whales*, *jimmies*, *peelers*, and *busters* for different types of crabs and crabs at different stages of their molting cycle.

Grammatical features include older constructions such as *a*-prefixing (e.g., "I was a-fishin'") and genitive temporal constructions (e.g., "We used to go swimming of a night" for "We used to go swimming at night"), as well as other distinctive features like static locative *to* (e.g., "I work to the restaurant" for "I work at the restaurant"), existential *it* (e.g., "It's no money in crabbing anymore" for "There's no money in crabbing anymore") and regularization of past *be* to *weren't* rather than *wasn't*, as in "I weren't home" or "It weren't right."

Smith Island English also has a number of distinguishing phonological features, including a lax HAPPY vowel in words like [mɛnɪ] for "many," intrusive /g/ in productions like [jʌŋg] for *young*, and a number of interesting vowel productions. Of special note are the production of the /ay/ diphthong with a raised nucleus, as in something like [wəɪt] for *white* and the production of /aw/ with a fronted rather than back glide, as in something like "dine" or "dane" for *down*. Glide-fronted /aw/ is something of an icon of Smith Island speech, whereas raised /ay/ is barely noticed. Islanders demonstrate glide-fronted /aw/ for outsiders, and mainlanders talk about it as well.

Another important emblem of the Smith Island dialect is a discourse feature islanders call "backwards talk." Essentially, backwards talk is irony, but on Smith Island it is distinctive in its pervasiveness, its often elaborate formulation, and its iconic status. "Backwards" utterances can be relatively transparent in meaning, as in "Well, there's a pretty time!" to indicate that the weather is bad; or they can be opaque, at least to nonislanders, as in "He ain't headin' it none!" to refer to someone who is driving a boat too fast—that is, making too much headway.

Since the second half of the twentieth century or so, the island community has faced a number of challenges impacting its economy and population. It has become increasingly difficult to make a living through small-scale oystering and crabbing operations, and more and more islanders are traveling or moving to the mainland for work. In addition, the island is contending with ongoing loss of land mass due to erosion and possible submersion. US Census figures show the profound impact of economic and geographic factors on the Smith Island population. When data for the original study were gathered, there were probably more than five hundred people living on the island. At the time of the first restudy, in 2000, the population had declined to 364. By 2010, that figure had further dropped to 276, and the 2014 population estimate made shortly before the current restudy indicated a population of only 176.

Hence, in addition to its many distinguishing lexical, grammatical, and phonological features, Smith Island English is interesting because it is endangered, since it is losing its speaker base, and it is important to consider not only the characteristics of the dialect in its "classic" form but also changes that have taken place over the decades, in real time, as well as apparent change across generations.

Data and Methodology

As noted earlier, there are three sets of data on Smith Island English. The 1985 data set consists of sociolinguistic interviews with forty-one islanders in three generational groups, roughly evenly balanced across females and males, with birth dates ranging from 1899 to 1971. The 2000 data set consists of interviews with islanders in the same age cohorts as the original study but focuses mostly on the then-youngest generation, young adults and teenagers with birth dates ranging from 1973 to 1987. Again, forty-one speakers were interviewed. At the time of this writing, the 2015 data set comprises thirty-four speakers across generational groups, including the new youngest generation, whose birth dates range from 1997 to 2010. The original 1980s data set was divided into three generations based on even age divisions (under age 21, 21–50, and 51+), hereafter referred to Generations I, II, and III. Generation IV is the youngest age group from the first restudy; Generation V consists of today's young adults, teenagers, and children.

An apparent-time analysis based on the earliest data set was conducted in the 1990s and consisted of quantitative variationist study (based on auditory analysis) of the linguistic and social patterning of /ay/ and /aw/ (Schilling-Estes and Wolfram

1999). For the first restudy, usage levels for a subset of key features were compared against those of the three generations in the original study, following Trudgill (1988). To date, the data set for the current restudy has not been subjected to quantitative variation analysis; instead the focus is on the acoustic phonetic analysis of the vowel space of several individuals across the generational groups. The focus of what follows is on /ay/ and /aw/, augmented by holistic observations on general patterns of dialect maintenance and change, including grammar, lexicon, and discourse (i.e., backwards talk) as well as phonology.

Vowel plots were generated by conducting automated acoustic phonetic analysis using the Forced Alignment and Vowel Extraction (FAVE) program suite (Rosenfelder, Fruehwald, Evanini, and Yuan 2011) and the NORM vowel normalization and plotting suite, version 1.1 (Thomas and Kendall 2007). For clarity and relevance, only tokens of /ay/ followed by voiceless and voiced obstruents were included on the vowel plots (e.g., *nice*, *ride*); for /aw/, tokens in prevoiceless obstruent (*house*), prevoiced obstruent (*loud*), prenasal (*down*), and word-final (*cow*) position were included. Measurements were not normalized, since each speaker's vowel space is presented individually; the ellipses are true ellipses indicating the dispersion of each vowel nucleus at 1 standard deviation from the norm. Symbols are in ARPABET; those that may not be clear are AH for /ʌ/, AO for /ɔ/, and AA for /ɑ/.

Between the Dialect Lines

The focus of Labov et al.'s (2006) *Atlas* is on larger urban areas, so Smith Island is not covered. However, its location makes it an ideal site for investigating the nature of the phonological systems of smaller dialects at the periphery of coherent dialect areas. It is situated between the US South, almost certainly the most salient of all North American dialects, and the mid-Atlantic, which comprises cities like Wilmington, Philadelphia, and Baltimore. At the heart of the mid-Atlantic is the Philadelphia dialect, which has been thoroughly studied by Labov and his students for decades, beginning in the 1970s (e.g., Labov, Rosenfelder, and Fruehwald 2013). The core of the US South is the Inland South, encompassing the mountainous areas of North Carolina, Tennessee, northwestern South Carolina, northern Georgia, and much of northwestern Alabama, especially the more rural areas.

The /ay/ vowel makes for a useful point of comparison between Smith Island and the South. The defining feature of the US South is monophthongal or glide-shortened /ay/, often with a fronted nucleus, as in something like [ta:m] for "time." Labov et al. (2006, 242–48) point to /ay/ monophthongization as a key trigger, or first stage, of the Southern Vowel Shift, one of the major vowel shift patterns that has recently taken place in the United States. Stage II of the shift involves the backing and lowering of /ey/, so that "take" sounds something like "tike." Concurrently, /ɛ/ raises toward /e/ and takes on a glide, so that a word like "set" sounds almost like "say it." In essence, then, /e/ and /ɛ/ are somewhat "reversed." Stage III, the reversal of /i/ and /ɪ/, is found only in some parts of the South, most commonly the Inland South.

Labov et al. (2006) also note a second southern shift pattern with a different trigger—the backing and raising of /ay/ rather than monophthongization and fronting. This pattern is found in other world Englishes (e.g., Australian) and in some coastal areas of the US South, for example Ocracoke Island, North Carolina. Here, backed/raised /ay/ is an icon of the distinctive dialect of island residents, known as "hoi toiders" for "high tiders." Sociophonetic study indicates that the "hoi toid" vowel is situated well to the back of vowel space, in /ɑ/ territory, though a bit more raised, with prevoiceless /ay/ typically a bit more backed than prevoiced (Thomas 2001, 127–32).

Vowel plots for Smith Island indicate a different configuration, illustrated in Figure 14.1. In these plots of two islanders from Generation II in their mid-seventies, we see that /ay/ is raised, but mostly in prevoiceless position; in addition, prevoiceless /ay/ is centralized, not backed, near /ʌ/ territory rather than /ɑ/. There is some glide reduction, but only in non-prevoiceless contexts. In other words, Smith Islanders do not quite have either of the two possible triggers for the Southern Vowel Shift—/ay/ monophthongization/fronting or /ay/ backing/raising. At the same time, though, the man, Morris M., has at least some elements of the Sothern Shift. His mid-front vowels have not quite reversed position, but they are essentially overlapping, indicating movement toward reversal. Hence, we see that Smith Island, located at the edge of the Southern US dialect region, is neither completely non-Southern nor a "weaker" version of Southern English. Rather, its vowel system is complex, or perhaps a mix of different systems.

The /ay/ diphthong also makes for interesting comparison of Smith Island with the mid-Atlantic. In his early studies of the core mid-Atlantic city of Philadelphia, in

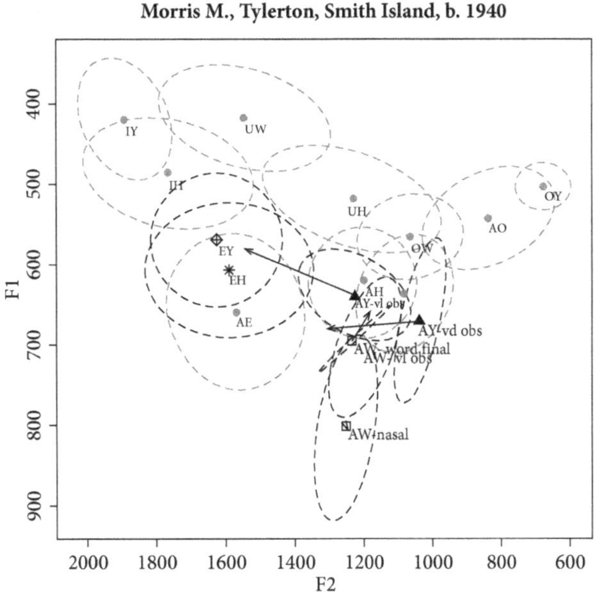

Figure 14.1a: Morris M., Tylerton, Smith Island, b. 1940

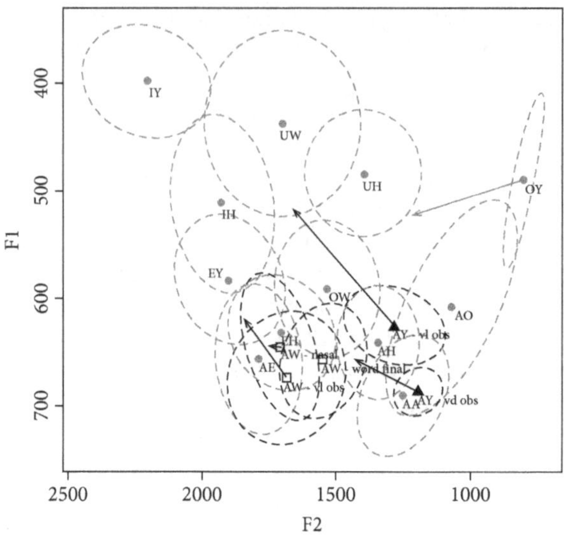

Figure 14.1b: Sharon B., Ewell, Smith Island, b. 1943

the 1970s, Labov noted /ay/ raising in prevoiceless contexts as a change in progress (e.g., Labov 2001). In a 2005 follow-up study, Conn also noted prevoiceless /ay/ raising, as well as a change in progress toward backing, with prevoiceless /ay/ being more backed than the prevoiced variant, not more centralized, as in Smith Island.

In terms of the front of the vowel space, one of the more salient features of the Philadelphia dialect is the production of /aw/ with a very fronted and raised nucleus, so that /aw/ is well into /e/ territory, as in productions like [θeʊsnd] for "thousand." This contrasts with Smith Island, where the /aw/ nucleus is typically relatively low, and where front gliding is prevalent. As we saw in Figure 14.1, Sharon B. clearly illustrates low, front-glided /aw/ in non-word-final position; Morris M. shows some raising in prevoiceless and word-final position, but the raised variants are centralized, not fronted as in Philadelphia. So just as Smith Island English is not a watered-down version of Southern English, it is not watered-down Philadelphia or mid-Atlantic either.

Regarding why there is a mixed system in Smith Island, or a mix of systems, it may be that the near-reversal of /e/ and /ɛ/ in the absence of either trigger of the Southern Vowel Shift is the product of the diffusion of one *element* of the Southern Vowel Shift, originally brought into the community by adults, not part of the transmission of a wholescale vowel shift passed down to children across the generations. In this, the situation is like that described for the St. Louis Corridor by Labov (2007), where we find *elements* of the Northern Cities Vowel Shift, such as the backing and lowering of /ɛ/ and some fronting of /ɑ/, but not its trigger, the generalized fronting and raising of /æ/, and where it can be demonstrated that the initial introduction of the Northern Cities vowel productions into the area was through adults, not children.

It is difficult to determine whether prevoiceless raised/centralized /ay/ in Smith Island represents a transmission or a diffusion. This variant has been noted in the Tidewater Virginia dialect area since the 1920s (Shewmake 1925). However, the split between centralized versus noncentralized /ay/ in prevoiceless versus prevoiced contexts doesn't seem to have been as sharp in the early twentieth century as in later decades. And, as just noted, prevoiceless /ay/ raising is a newer variant in the mid-Atlantic, one that could have been diffused to Smith Island by adults with contacts to the north. The latter possibility is intriguing, given that between the late 1800s and midtwentieth century, many Smith Island watermen would leave the island for months at a time to conduct oystering operations in the far northern Chesapeake Bay, above Baltimore, quite close to Philadelphia.

Intracommunity Variation and Change

The development of glide-fronted /aw/ in Smith Island across generational and gender groups is also intriguing and is illustrative of the surprising amount of regularly patterned dialect variation that can sometimes be found in very small communities. Results of a quantitative study of usage levels for this feature in Generations 1–4 (from the 1985 data set as well as the youngest generation in 2000) indicates sharp cross-generational and cross-gender differences. Usage levels of the now iconic variant were quite low in Generation I (4 percent glide-fronted /aw/ for women; 7 percent for men), then suddenly much higher in Generation II, with the increase led by women (82 percent for women; 21 percent for men). Levels held steady in Gen-

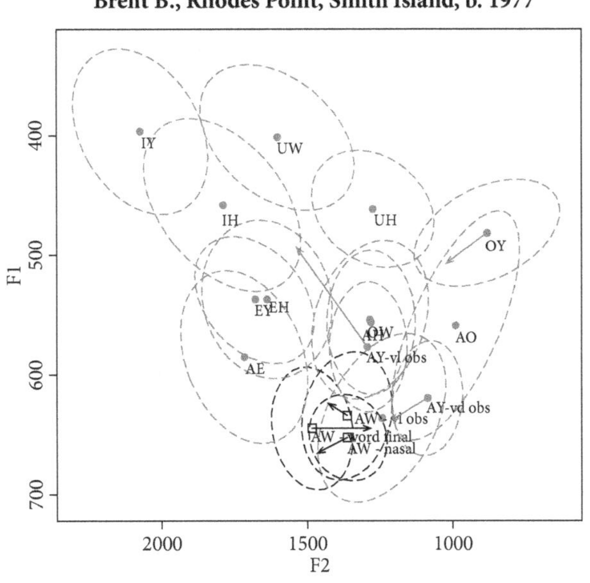

Figure 14.2a: Brent B., Rhodes Point, Smith Island, b. 1977

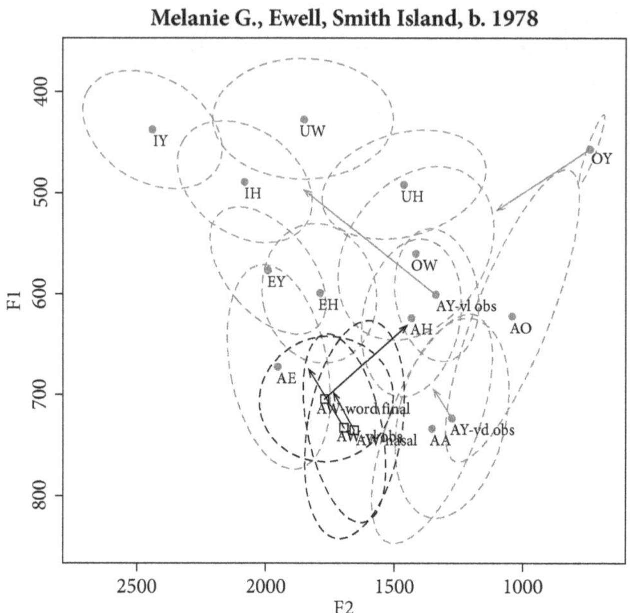

Figure 14.2b: Melanie G., Ewell, Smith Island, b. 1978

erations III and IV, with men catching up to women by the turn of the twenty-first century (67 percent glide-fronted /aw/ for women in Generation IV; 64 percent for men). These patterns are borne out in vowel plots of current speakers across the generations. As we saw in Figure 14.1, Sharon B., in Generation 2, has clear glide fronting, while her generational peer, Morris M., has a shorter, more centralized glide. By the time we get to Generation IV, men too have adopted the fronted variant, as shown in the two vowel plots in Figure 14.2. The vowel plots also support the finding from earlier quantitative analysis that /aw/ is never fronted in word-final position.

The quantitative analysis of /aw/ in the first two data sets indicates not only drastic change but change in a quite unexpected direction—toward increasing rather than decreasing dialectal distinctiveness. This pattern of "dialect concentration" was found in previous studies of Smith Island to hold not only for glide-fronted /aw/ but also a number of other features, including raised /ay/, regularization of past *be* to *weren't*, and existential *it* (Parrott 2002; Schilling-Estes 2005; Schilling-Estes and Wolfram 1999). For example, regularization to *weren't* increased from 22 percent in Generation I to 100 percent in Generation III, with a slight though insignificant dip to 96 percent in Generation IV.

One of the main reasons for launching the 2015 restudy was to investigate whether dialect concentration is sustained among today's youngest generation. Figure 14.3 shows a vowel plot for Kathleen B., eighteen years old at the time of our interview with her in 2016. In contrast to the women in the three older generations,

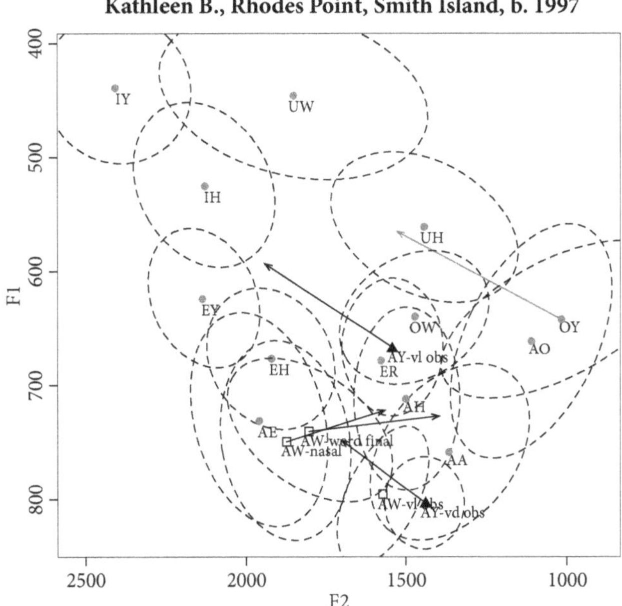

Figure 14.3: Kathleen B., Rhodes Point, Smith Island, b. 1997

Kathleen's /aw/s are clearly back-glided, in all positions. We have not yet managed to interview any of the few young adult men remaining on the island. However, auditory analysis of data from two young boys we interviewed (both age 7) indicates that they still use the glide-fronted variant. Hence, it is not yet clear whether glide-fronted /aw/ is being relinquished or not, though it is likely that young adult women are more representative of community change in progress than young boys who haven't yet fully acquired their dialect.

In addition to cross-generational and cross-gender differences in /aw/, there may be a third type of inter-community difference—between Tylerton, accessible only by boat from Ewell and Rhodes Points, and the other two island towns. Islanders have told us that there are dialect differences among the island's three towns, and they sometimes even demonstrate different variants of /aw/. Preliminary quantitative analysis using auditory coding bears out their beliefs. Figure 14.4 shows usage levels for two variants of /aw/ in the speech of three young islanders from the 1980s data set—glide-fronted /aw/ and raised/centralized /aw/, the variant seen in Morris M.'s vowel plot above. DM and JE grew up on Tylerton, while RD grew up in Ewell. Interestingly, the most prominent variant in Tylerton in the 1980s doesn't seem to have been the iconic glide-fronted variant but rather the raised/centralized variant, often referred to as Canadian raising (e.g., Chambers 1973). The occurrence of this variant in at least parts of Smith Island is not surprising, since it often goes hand-in-hand with raised/centralized /ay/, as seen for example in Labov's

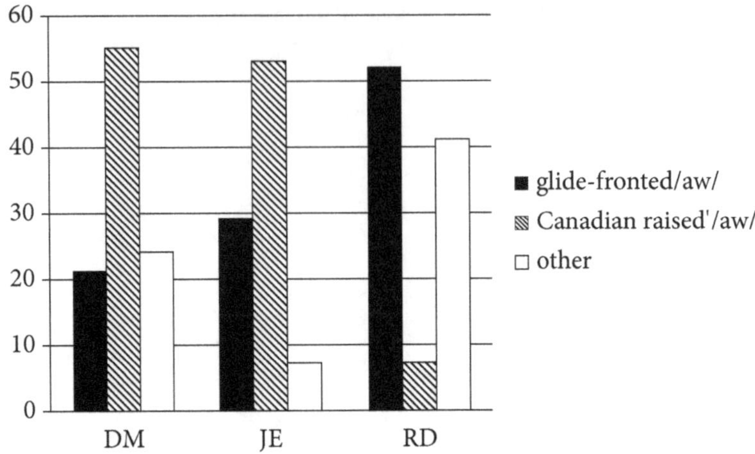

Figure 14.4: /aw/ in Tylerton versus Ewell, 1980s (DM = age 17, Tylerton; JE = age 26, Tylerton; RD = age 12, Ewell)

(1963) foundational study of Martha's Vineyard. We have not yet conducted comprehensive analysis of Tylerton versus the other island towns, in either the 1980s or later data sets; in fact, we have not yet interviewed any young adults from Tylerton. However, we again recorded some young children, and auditory analysis indicates a back-glided variant in Tylerton that contrasts with the front-glided production we observed in the speech of the two seven-year-olds mentioned above, from Ewell and Rhodes Point.

Intra-community dialectal heterogeneity may seem unexpected in a small, rural community, but as Trudgill (2002) and others have pointed out, the close-knit, stable social networks that often characterize smaller communities can allow for the inter-generational transmission of subtle patterns of variation that are typically leveled out in larger, more diffuse networks. In addition, as Eckert (2000) demonstrates, close-knit groups that are focused on local ties are important sites for the creation and proliferation of locally important social meanings, including intragroup distinctions like resident of Tylerton versus native of Ewell. And social meanings are of course often marked by linguistic distinctions. However, further study is needed to determine whether intra-island differences across towns will prove to have been robust in past generations or are still being sustained today.

It also remains to be seen exactly what will happen to *inter*-community differences in /aw/, between Smith Island and more mainstream dialects. What is clear, though, is that islanders still remain quite conscious of the uniqueness of the "classic" Smith Island dialect, and even young women who no longer use glide-fronted /aw/ in everyday conversation still use the iconic island variant in performances and demonstrations of dialect features. The excerpts in (1) and (2), from Kathleen B. and her generational peer Rebekah K., illustrate.

(1) FW: What do usually people pick up on?
KB: Mmm. Definitely like "house" [heis], "mouse" [meis], like all that like that's like big Smith Island like words and that. Definitely the "house" [heis].

(2) FW: Some of the older generation said it used to be like a big difference in terms of accents between like Tylerton and Rhodes Point and here, in terms of like how people would say the word "house" [haus] and stuff like that.
RK: Oh, like "house" [heis]?
KB: Yeah. Is that still like pretty common do you think for young people like, or are they starting to talk more
RK: I think we talk more normally, like "house" [haus] instead of "house" [heis].

Intra-Individual Variation and Performance Style in Dialect Endangerment

The preceding excerpts illustrate that in addition to providing insight into inter- and intracommunity variation, studying small communities like Smith Island enables researchers to enhance our understanding of intra-individual variation. We can maintain sustained interactions with such communities, which can afford access to individuals across time periods, in different types of social situations and speech events. Hence, Kathleen B. and Rebekah K. have quite different styles depending on whether they are using their dialect as a vehicle for communication or for display. And performance styles can be especially prominent in endangered language and dialect communities, as the variety recedes from everyday use and becomes more of an object of display or so-called "object language" (Schilling-Estes 1998; Tsitsipis 1989). Smith Islanders of all ages still perform their iconic /aw/. In addition, the other dialect icon mentioned above, "backwards talk," is often demonstrated for researchers as well, even though islanders maintain that backwards talk is typically for use only with other islanders. Islanders are also quick to tell us how central to their way of speaking they consider backwards talk to be. The excerpts in (3) and (4) illustrate:

(3) So what do you want to know about how we talk around here? Well, we talk backwards. (forty-three-year-old man, 2000s)

(4) FW: What's, what's some other words like you guys say here?
CE: Um. We ain't got really many words, we just say 'em backwards. (teenage boy, 2000s)

And even when backwards talk is used in everyday conversation rather than demonstration or discussion of dialect, it is always inherently performative. It is irony, and so it is figurative, not literal. In addition, while it can be quite creative, it is also often formulaic. It is often indicated with special syntactic, lexical and prosodic markers. The examples above, "Well, there's a pretty time!" and "He ain't headin' it none!," illustrate two common syntactic markers: phrase-initial *well* and phrase-final *none*. Phrase-initial *god, gollee, gah* or similar are also frequent, as are the lexical items *pretty, ugly, fair, poor*, and, with expressions evaluating weather or events, *time* (e.g., "Here's a hot time!"). In addition, although positive irony, the use of overtly negative utterances to indicate positive meaning, is typically considered to be more rare than negative irony (e.g., Attardo 2013, 44–45), the former is quite common among Smith Islanders. Positive irony is more "dangerous" than negative, since the consequences are graver if one fails to "get" the irony. Islanders are close-knit, and they maintain that they rarely if ever fail to understand when talk is "backwards." However, they do have to be careful with outsiders. The excerpt in (5), from an interview with a teenage girl in 2000, illustrates.

(5) I was scared to death 'cause sometimes I'll go over to the mainland and I'll be like, look at a baby, we'll be "Gollee he's ugly!" And then I'm scared that that's just gonna, somebody is just gonna punch me one of these days!

This excerpt also illustrates that, just as with Smith Island /aw/, backwards talk serves as a point of contrast between the island dialect and mainland ways of talking. And as it turns out, retaining a sense of dialectal—and cultural—distinctiveness is quite important to Smith Islanders, despite, or perhaps because of, the challenges facing the longstanding community.

Dialect Retention, Extension, and Social Meaning

Although the iconic glide-fronted /aw/ seems to be fading from conversational speech in Smith Island, this does not mean that all of the dialect's distinguishing features are receding or being relegated to performance objects. Young islanders are still using a distinctive variant for /ay/. In fact, they may even be increasing the distance between prevoiced and prevoiceless productions, as seen in Kathleen B.'s vowel plot in Figure 14.3, where prevoiceless /ay/ is realized well above /ʌ/ and prevoiced /ay/ is below /ɑ/. Young islanders are also holding onto other "classic" pronunciation features such as intrusive /g/ and a lax HAPPY vowel. In addition, they are still using grammatical features like regularization to *weren't* and existential *it*, as illustrated in (6) through (8), from Kathleen B.'s interview. Interestingly, these occur during discussions of university and changing career plans, topics where she might be expected to use more mainstream grammatical features.

(6) This past semester **it was** one class that **it** weren't even 10 people in there.
(7) **I weren't** able to go [to class] because the boat didn't run that morning.
(8) **I weren't** fully into it, and I felt that **it weren't** right, so that's what I done.

Further, our sustained observations of the island community indicate that backwards talk is still going strong, in everyday conversational speech as well as in dialect demonstration. In addition, it has spread to new contexts, including social media.

For example, under a Facebook posting from 2014, of an island culinary icon, Smith Island (multilayered) cake, two commenters used positive irony to indicate how delicious the cake appeared: "That was poor, nothing like it!" and "Good Lord! That don't look too good!" Another posting, a baby picture of a much-loved islander, was followed by two comments indicating that the traditional markers of backwards talk have also moved into social media: "**Well**, you don't look like your dad!" and "**Ga**, you ain't sweet!" Finally, a third posting provides evidence for the continuing creativity of backwards talk. Under a photo of a cute island couple posted in 2013, a commenter posted "W[h]ere is that damn dislike button!"—well before Facebook actually did have a "damn dislike" button, or at least an "angry" one.

In sum, Smith Island English is retaining its dialectal distinctiveness in many ways—and even enhancing it in some. At the same time, today's young Smith Islanders use quite a few features found in the English of young people in general, for example discourse marker *like*, as well as features characteristic of Southern American dialects such as the use of *whenever* for "when" (see example 10).

We have learned over the course of our studies that Smith Islanders maintain a persistent sense of cultural distinctiveness, as well as awareness of dialect as a key part of their community identity. Recently, there has even been an upsurge in community cohesiveness. A group called Smith Island United was founded in 2014, and islanders and others work through this organization to invigorate a small but growing tourism industry, to lobby for government support for engineering projects to protect their shorelines, and to preserve their cultural—and linguistic—heritage. This strong sense of community extends to the youngest islanders. So far, every young adult we talked to has acknowledged that they probably will not be able to stay on the island and earn a living; at the same time, they adamantly insist that Smith Island will always be their home. The excerpts in (9) and (10), again from Kathleen B., illustrate.

(9) Like I do love it over here, but unfortunately I don't see like a future here for me.

(10) Probably a big worry of mine now is uh like whenever I'm gonna be moving over, like making the jump to the mainland. And unfortunately now, it's kinda just not a "if," it's a "when," am I. So . . .

And mixed emotions can lead to mixed dialects—relinquishing some features that may be too local for wider audiences (e.g., glide-fronted /aw/), retaining other localized features (e.g., raised /ay/), and adopting some features in wider usage (e.g., discourse marker *like*). Smith Island English is an important symbol of islander identity, and it does not have to be preserved in static form to preserve its distinctiveness or its cultural value.

Summary and Final Conclusions

It remains to be seen whether further study will bear out the initial analyses of today's young islanders presented here. It is also unclear if the island community will continue to survive and if the pattern of population loss can be reversed. However, I hope I have made clear in this chapter that even though linguists can now easily obtain extremely large quantities of real language data, often without leaving the comfort of their armchairs and laptop computers, there is still a lot of value to the up-close and sustained study of small communities like Smith Island. Small communities lend insight into the characteristics of phonological systems far removed from urban centers and other dialect hubs. They also can contain a surprising degree of regularly patterned within-community variation, patterns that lend insight into the conditions under which children acquire and sustain subtle patterns of variation versus when they level things out. In addition, small communities are rich in intra-individual variation, including performative styles that can highlight pride in dialectal and community distinctiveness even if, and perhaps especially when, cultural uniqueness falls under threat. Finally, working in small communities is not only linguistically valuable but personally rewarding. In our continuing work on Smith Island, my students and I have learned a lot, we have had exciting (mis)adventures, and we have made great friends.

References

Attardo, Salvatore. 2013. "Intentionality and Irony." In *The Pragmatics of Irony and Humor*, edited by Leonor Ruiz Gurillo and M. Belen Alvarado Ortega, 39–57. Amsterdam: Benjamins.

Chambers, J. K. 1973. "Canadian Raising." *Canadian Journal of Linguistics* 18:113–35.

Conn, Jeff. 2005. *Of Moice and Men: The Evolution of a Male-Led Sound Change*. PhD diss., University of Pennsylvania.

Eckert, Penelope. 2000. *Linguistic Variation as Social Practice: The Linguistic Construction of Identity in Belten High*. Malden/Oxford: Blackwell.

Hierstetter, Brad S. 2015. *Still, the Faithful Sing: A Glimpse of Life on Maryland's Smith Island*. N.p.: Hierstetter.

Labov, William. 1963. "The Social Motivation of a Sound Change." *Word* 19:273–307.

Labov, William. 2001. *Principles of Linguistic Change*. Vol. 2: *Social Factors*. Malden/Oxford: Blackwell.

Labov, William. 2007. "Transmission and Diffusion." *Language* 83 (2): 344–87.

Labov, William. 2016. "Afterword: Where Are We Now?," in "Labov and Sociolinguistics: Fifty Years of Language in Social Context," edited by Allan Bell, David Britain, and Devyani Sharma. Special issue, *Journal of Sociolinguistics* 20 (4): 581–602.

Labov, William, Sharon Ash, and Charles Boberg. 2006. *The Atlas of North American English: Phonetics, Phonology, and Sound Change*. Berlin/New York: Mouton de Gruyter.

Labov, William, Ingrid Rosenfelder, and Josef Fruehwald. 2013. "One Hundred Years of Sound Change in Philadelphia: Linear Incrementation, Reversal, and Reanalysis." *Language* 89 (1): 30–65.

Leemann, Adrian, Marie-José Kolly, and David Britain. 2016. "English Dialects: An English Dialect Application for the Smartphone" (smartphone application). https://itunes.apple.com/us/app/english-dialects/id882340404?l=de&mt=8&ign-mpt=uo%3D8.

Nevalainen, Terttu, and Helena Raumolin-Brunberg. 2003. *Historical Sociolinguistics: Language Change in Tudor and Stuart England*. Amsterdam: Benjamins.

Parrott, Jeffrey K. 2002. "Dialect Death and Morpho-syntactic Change: Smith Island Weak Expletive *It*." *University of Pennsylvania Working Papers in Linguistics* 8 (3): 175–89.

Rosenfelder, Ingrid, Josef Fruehwald, Keelan Evanini, and Jiahong Yuan. 2011. "FAVE (Forced Alignment and Vowel Extraction) Program Suite." http://fave.ling.upenn.edu.

Schilling-Estes, Natalie. 1998. "Investigating 'Self-Conscious' Speech: The Performance Register in Ocracoke English." *Language in Society* 27:53–83.

Schilling-Estes, Natalie. 2005. "Language Change in Apparent and Real Time, the Community and the Individual." *University of Pennsylvania Working Papers in Linguistics* 10 (2): Selected Papers from New Ways of Analyzing Variation (NWAV) 32:219–32.

Schilling-Estes, Natalie, and Walt Wolfram. 1999. "Alternative Models of Dialect Death: Dissipation vs. Concentration." *Language* 75 (3): 486–521.

Shewmake, Edwin F. 1925. "Laws of Pronunciation in Eastern Virginia." *Modern Language Notes* 40:489–92.

Thomas, Erik R. 2001. *An Acoustic Analysis of Vowel Variation in New World English*. Publication of the American Dialect Society 85. Durham: Duke University Press.

Thomas, Erik R., and Tyler Kendall. 2007. "NORM: The Vowel Normalization and Plotting Suite" (web interface). Version 1.1. http://lingtools.uoregon.edu/norm/index.php.

Trudgill, Peter. 1988. "Norwich Revisited: Recent Linguistic Change in an Urban Dialect." *English World-Wide* 9 (1): 33–49.

Trudgill, Peter. 2002. "Linguistic and Social Typology." In *The Handbook of Language Variation and Change*, edited by J. K. Chambers and Natalie Schilling-Estes, 707–28. Malden/Oxford: Blackwell.

Tsitsipis, Lukas D. 1989. "Skewed Performance and Full Performance in Language Obsolescence: The Case of an Albanian Variety." In *Investigating Language Obsolescence: Studies in Language Contraction and Death*, edited by Nancy C. Dorian, 139–48. Cambridge: Cambridge University Press.

Chapter 15

All Zeros Are Not Equal in African American English

LISA GREEN
University of Massachusetts–Amherst

ONE OF THE CENTRAL issues in the study of African American English (AAE) that has remained in the forefront is variable morphosyntactic marking, especially in the contexts of [Tense] and [Agreement], as in *She grab the bowl and open the bag of flour*, which is ambiguous between "She grabs the bowl and opens the bag of flour" and "She grabbed the bowl and opened the bag of flour." Research addressing morphological marking in AAE spans a period of almost fifty years (e.g., Labov, Cohen, Robins, and Lewis 1968; Wolfram 1969; Wolfram and Fasold 1974; van Hofwegan and Wolfram 2010; Terry, Hendrick, Evangelou, and Smith 2010), but questions about this topic remain unanswered, such as: what is the status of nonovert (or zero (∅)) morphological marking? Considerable emphasis has been placed on determining the rates at which adult AAE speakers produce overt and zero morphological marking, and the same methodological approach has been extended to research on morphological marking in child AAE. The approach has led to quantitative descriptions of the presence and absence of tense and agreement morphemes in child AAE, but it has not provided much insight into the acquisition path of variable marking and development of AAE and the representation of [Tense] and [Agreement] categories.

One of the challenges of research on child AAE is determining to what extent zero morphological marking and variation are a result of input on the one hand and developmental factors on the other. If zero marking and variation in production of morphosyntactic forms in child AAE are results of input-related factors, such as influence by their caregivers or adult AAE speakers in the speech communities, then it is necessary to raise questions about whether patterns of acquisition in child AAE are solely determined by variation in the input. On the other hand, because variation and zero marking are also characteristics of development (Anderssen, Bentzen, and Westergaard 2010), questions about the possibility of developmental zero morphological marking should also be investigated in child AAE. Although there is no assumption here that children already have the adult AAE grammar at early ages, it is clear that as they are growing up in AAE-speaking communities, their target grammar is that of the adults in those communities, so the path to it is of interest.

In this chapter, I investigate past and nonpast contexts in data from developing three- to six-year-old AAE-speaking children to test the claim that not all nonovert or zero morphological marking (e.g., third person singular ***She go***$_{\emptyset\text{-}s}$ *to the chickens* "She goes to the chickens"; past tense *He* ***open***$_{\emptyset\text{-}ed}$ *the icebox and got some food* "He opened the refrigerator and got some food") is equal. The data reveal patterns in zero marking associated with third person singular *-s* and past tense morphology that are related to the difference in their status in the AAE grammar. Furthermore, the data also reveal that although developing AAE might resemble adult AAE in zero morphological marking, such marking in some stages in child AAE grammar may not be equivalent to zero marking in adult AAE.

Characterizing AAE

African American English, one of the most studied varieties of American English, has been the topic of many discussions, sometimes controversial and heated debates, especially when claims about its historical origin are made. In heated debates, it is hypothesized by some that the variety originated as a creole, by others that it is a dialect that has maintained old forms of English, and by still other groups that it is underlyingly similar to grammars of West African languages and only superficially like English. Nonmonolithic hypotheses, which appeal to elements of creole and dialectal views to account for the historical origin of AAE, have also been proposed (Winford 1998).

Different definitions of AAE are assumed, ranging from those in which the variety is characterized according to the people who speak it and the types of features that are used by its speakers. For example, it might be defined as a variety spoken by working class African Americans, a characterization that does not give much information about the system itself, but that does satisfy some of the questions about social factors and AAE. One of the most common ways to characterize the variety is to take a features approach by delineating a list of differences that distinguish AAE from mainstream American English or by underscoring the non-standard forms in AAE that correspond to the standard English forms. Another characterization of AAE is what is referred to as the dual components approach, which tags AAE as being composed of two components, a general English (GE) component, which is a complete grammar, and an African American (AA) component, which is not a complete grammar but is argued to give the variety its unique features that distinguish it from general American English and other varieties of English (Labov 1998). Through the dual components window, the two constituents making up AAE are separable, but it is clear that the AAE system is not so easily sectioned into two parts, with a discrete line dividing the GE component and the AA component. When children learn AAE, they learn a system that cannot so easily be segmented into two. The dual components approach leads us to raise probing questions about the extent to which such a view of AAE is one that is compatible with some notion of code-shifting. That is, does the presence of these two components facilitate code-shifting between AAE and mainstream English? I cannot pursue the questions here, but they are important and, when answered, will shed important light on issues such as code-shifting and variation. The characterization of AAE that I am assuming in this chapter is the patterns and systems approach, in which AAE is taken to be an inherently variable linguistic variety with set syntactic/morpho-syntactic, phonological, semantic, pragmatic, and lexical patterns that are intertwined with structures of general American English (Green 2011).

Third Person Singular -s

Research on child AAE started in the 1970s, relatively late compared to developmental focus on other groups of children. In a brief summary, research on third singular *-s* can be divided into three categories: emergence of third singular *-s*, comprehension of third singular *-s*, and comparison of properties of *-s* in child AAE to properties of adult AAE.

Brief Overview of Research on Third Person Singular -s in Child AAE

Steffensen (1974) and Reveron (1979) are early studies on child AAE that directly addressed the production of third singular *-s* and other morphosyntactic markers, such as plural *-s* and possessive *-s*. After reviewing recordings from two developing AAE-speaking children ages 17 months to 26 months and 20 months to 26 months, Steffensen concluded that in the early developmental stages, the two children did not differ in their production of third singular *-s* from children developing general American English. Basing her conclusion, in part, on Torrey's (1972) finding that children and adults in Standard English-speaking communities understand third singular *-s* "less than perfectly," Steffensen predicted that *-s* would emerge in AAE-speaking children's language at a stage later than 26 months. In other words, Steffensen argued that at 26 months, the children did not seem to be displaying any dialectal properties by using verbs in their "neutral" (or unmarked) forms. The view was that the unmarked forms were not a reflection of any pattern of zero third singular marking in adult AAE.

The study in Reveron (1979) was conducted with 40 AAE-speaking children, ranging in age from 2;6 years to 6;3 years, who were from low socioeconomic status and forty children of the same age who were from middle socioeconomic status. The participants were presented with novel words in phrases such as: *This man likes to nack. What does he like to do? ___ Nack. He does it every day. What does he do every day? Every day he ____.* According to her findings, both groups produced third person singular *-s* less frequently than any of the other morphemes. In addition, Reveron also noted that production of the morpheme increased at each age, but there was no difference in production at any age level. Finally, Reveron concluded that the AAE-speaking children developed AAE ∅ third singular *-s* by age 4 and did not produce the standard English pattern of overt *-s* by age 6.

Most of the research on the development of third person singular marking has focused on production, that is, whether the marker is overt or covert, so there is limited research on comprehension of the marker. In one study, de Villiers and Johnson

(2007) concluded that AAE-speaking children lack comprehension of third person singular *-s*. In a study of older children, Terry et al. (2010) also addressed comprehension of third singular *-s*. They found that second grade AAE-speaking children performed worse on mathematical word problems on the Woodcock Johnson standardized test if the descriptions included verbs marked with *-s*. They took the result as an indication that in encountering third person singular *-s*, children were faced with a processing difficulty owing to their uncertainty about the marker.

Third Person Singular -s Data: The Louisiana-Mississippi Study

Previous research on third person singular *-s*, though limited, has shown that the marker is not produced in early stages of development and that $\varnothing_s$ is acquired later (around age 4). The third person singular data collected from three- to six-year-old developing AAE-speaking children in Louisiana and Mississippi are from Newkirk-Turner and Green (2016). Twenty-six three- to six-year-old children from AAE-speaking communities participated in the study. Seventeen were from Mississippi, and nine were from Southwest Louisiana, as shown in Table 15.1.

The five- and six-year-olds were combined owing to the small number of participants in those age groups. Data from a repetition task and story retell task were collected and analyzed to answer questions about the morphological marker *-s* on verbs in third singular contexts. The elicitation task was based on the pictures in the picture book *Pancakes for Breakfast* by Tomie de Paola. A narrative based on the pictures in the book was developed from descriptions of the pictures on each page in the book. The narrative was written in nonpast, so all of the verbs were inflected to agree with a third person singular subject. The average number of words per sentence was seven. Two examples from the scripted narrative are given in (1) and (2):

(1) The dog stretches and the lady wakes up.
(2) She goes to the washbowl to wash her face.

For the repetition task, the children were instructed to play a game of copycat by saying exactly what the investigator said. The investigator read a sentence to the child and waited for the response. If the child had trouble remembering or repeating the words, the investigator read the sentence again or repeated words or phrases. After the child completed the repetition task, she was asked to retell the story while looking at the pictures in the book.

Table 15.1. Participants in third singular -s tasks

Age	N	State
3	9	Mississippi
4	5	Mississippi
	5	Louisiana
5	3	Mississippi
	2	Louisiana
6	2	Louisiana

The verbs produced by the children were analyzed for overt -*s* and zero marked forms. The verbs were classified as state, activity, achievement, accomplishment, or habitual. The verbs that were classified as state were zero marked least often, and those that were classified as habitual were zero marked most often. In dividing the verbs according to allophonic variation, we found that there was no significant difference in overt morphological marking between verbs ending in a voiceless consonant and taking the [s] allophone (e.g., *walk*/*walks*) and those ending in voiced consonants (e.g., *pour*/*pours*) and taking the [z] allophone. The rates of $\varnothing_s$ marking for the repetition task and the retell task were comparable across all age groups. For the repetition task, the rate of $\varnothing_s$ marking for the three-year-olds was 77 percent, and the rate for the four-year-olds was 72 percent. The rate for the five- and six-year-olds was 54 percent. The overall mean rate was 69 percent. For the retell task, the rate of $\varnothing_s$ marking for the three-year-olds was 80 percent, and 71 percent for the four-year-olds. The rate of marking for the five- and six-year-olds was 53 percent. The significant difference in rates was between the youngest group and the oldest group. The overall mean rate for the retell task was 69 percent. Also, the results indicated that the older children had lower rates of zero marking in both tasks.

The results led Newkirk-Turner and Green (2016) to make the following observations:

i. Third singular -*s* is not part of the AAE grammar.
ii. $\varnothing_s$ marking should not automatically be assumed to be a reflection of $\varnothing_s$ in adult AAE, which is part of the grammar.
iii. The difference between the production of -*s* in the youngest and oldest groups is a result of a combination of factors, such as the older children's exposure to the marker in non-AAE speaking environments.

In the case of the three- and four-year-olds, there is more zero marking than overt -*s* production, and although the overt -*s* morphological marking increases with age, the five- and six-year-old participants are just over 50 percent overt marking. Such results, especially from the five- and six-year-olds, can be taken as evidence that the marker is not part of the AAE grammar. As reported in Newkirk-Turner and Green (2016), children's actual production of -*s*, especially in the repetition task, suggests that they clearly heard -*s* when it was produced by the investigator (in both Louisiana and Mississippi) and although they did not model the investigators' production with any sense of accuracy and put an -*s* on verbs, they sometimes produced -*s* on nouns. In (3) *cat* is pluralized; the -*s* ends up on *cats*, not on *walk*, and in (4), the child produces plural *messes.*

(3) The cats walk with her. (three years; MS)
(4) They make the messes (four years; LA)

If the children's -*s* production on nouns in (3) and (4) is induced by the -*s* on the third singular verbs produced by the investigator in the repetition task, then there is some merit to claims about the absence of third singular -*s* from the grammar of AAE or at least limited -*s* competence in the early stages.

If we consider the results in work such as de Villiers and Johnson (2007), we find that although young children in communities speaking Mainstream American English (MAE) do not know the meaning of third singular *-s*, they produce it at 90 percent by about thirty-six months. That is, even without full comprehension of the marker, developing MAE-speaking children produce the marker consistently. AAE-speaking children, in contrast, are only at about 50 percent at five to six years old. Careful analysis of third person singular contexts helps to begin to answer the question about the extent to which zero marking in adult AAE and zero marking in child AAE are the same phenomenon. It is clear that children develop the adult AAE grammar; however, they might start at a point at which they too are producing zero marking as part of development long before they acquire the zero marking of the adult grammar. One factor that is likely to contribute to the increased production of third singular *-s* by five- and six-year-olds is their greater interaction in settings, such as school, where their networks will begin to include speakers of varieties in which third singular *-s* is part of the grammars. Appealing only to a production task limits the information about the extent to which there is a correlation between production and meaning of the morpheme, so it is not clear what type of meaning and/or function, if any at all, the children actually assign to *-s*.

Third person singular *-s* production data in developing AAE-speaking children helps to bring to the forefront questions about development and variation and the development of variation. Owing to the flavor of AAE variation, which is often reflected in overt versus covert (zero) forms (e.g., variable copula as in: *He nice/He IS nice*), it is easy to overlook what might be developmental patterns and take all zeros in child AAE as a reflection of features of the target language. The data and observations in Newkirk-Turner and Green (2016) call for a reanalysis of zero morphological forms in child AAE. Further analysis is needed to determine ways to distinguish zero forms that are reflected in the developing stages from those that occur alongside overt forms in older AAE. More specifically, young children might produce "bare" verb forms initially as a way of indicating events without marking tense, agreement, or aspect. Consider the verb forms in (5), from one of the story retells:

(5) She *pop* out the house and she *buy* some more butter
She *go* back home
The cat <u>spilled</u> the milk and the dog *make* a mess on the floor
She unhappy and she *smell* some food. (four years, LA)

All of the verbs are unmarked except *spilled*, which is overtly marked for past tense. With the unmarked verbs, it might be that what children are actually capturing is the event, as in a pop out of the house, buy some more butter, or smell some food event, and they may not be marking information about time (e.g., past or nonpast), number (singular or plural), or aspect (imperfective or perfective). Such data might lead us to the conclusion that there is a developmental stage in which children use zero marking, not as a variable form of overt morphological marking, but as a way to mark events. Later as children begin to acquire morphological marking, they might variably mark tense. It is at this stage that variable marking will emerge more productively. Variable marking might look different for different forms. That is, we might expect third singular variable marking to look different from variable marking of an inflectional form (e.g., past) that is part of the AAE grammar. This point can be illustrated with comparison of third singular marking and past tense marking. Data from past tense contexts will be explored in the next section, which will provide a good basis of comparison for production of third singular *-s* marking.

Past Tense Marking

A number of studies have reported on morphological marking in language of children from the four- to six-year-old age group, but there is insignificant information on the early development (i.e., before four years) of production and comprehension of morphological marking in child AAE.

Brief Overview of Past Morphological Marking in Child AAE

Studies consistently report that children in the four- to six-year-old age group produce overt past marking at a much higher rate than they produce zero past marking. Seymour, Bland-Stewart, and Green (1998) reported that the five- to eight-year-old AAE-speaking children in the study use zero past marking for only 9 percent of the verbs, and similarly Pruitt and Oetting (2009) reported that the AAE-speaking kindergartners in their study produced zero past marking for 11 percent of their verbs. Craig and Washington (2004) analyzed data from four hundred AAE-speaking children and reported that although 40 percent of kindergartners in the study zero marked past tense verbs, none of the first graders did. Lee and Oetting (2015) provided data from sixty-three AAE-speaking five-year-old kindergartners, showing that they produced 3,984 simple past verb forms in data samples. They produced 413 verbs with zero-marked past, and the remaining 3,171 verbs were overtly marked for past. They used mainstream American English marking for 3,151 verbs, and they used nonmainstream (on nonstandard) past tense marking for 420 verbs. Lee and Oetting took the results from their study as well as from previous research on morphological marking of past tense verbs in child AAE as evidence that by age 6 child AAE speakers use overt morphological marking and infrequently use zero past marking.

Variable Past Marking in Child AAE: The Louisiana Study

Twenty-five 4;2- to 5;11-year-old developing AAE-speaking children from AAE-speaking communities in southwest Louisiana participated in a past tense production study. These children, shown in Table 15.2, all attended the same child development center.

Table 15.2. Participants in past tense task

Age	N
4;2–4;10	13
5;2–5;11	12

Data from a story retell task were collected and analyzed to answer questions about the morphological marking of *-ed* on verbs in past contexts. The retell task was based on the pictures in the picture book *Good Dog, Carl* by Alexandra Day. For the task, a narrative was developed from descriptions of the pictures on each page, and regular verbs inflected for past were used to depict the actions conveyed in the pictures. Sample descriptions from the narrative are given in (6):

(6) a. The mom went for a walk.
    b. Carl danced to the music. The baby watched as he danced and danced.
    c. The baby climbed out of his crib onto Carl's back.

The participants were instructed to look at the pictures and listen carefully as the story was being read because they would get to tell the story right after they heard it. This process was followed for each child. If a child was hesitant to talk about a picture, she was prompted with a question such as "What happened here?" or "What did he do?" Two sample passages from two children's story retells are in (7) and (8). The unmarked verbs are italicized, and the marked ones are underlined. Auxiliary *be* + progressive and *had* + verb sequences were analyzed separately, so they will not be discussed here. Forms of main verb *be* were also analyzed separately and are not discussed in this overview.

(7) Then they *play* dress up.
Then, then the baby went down the slide. Then Carl went down the stairs.
Then the baby went into the laundry thing. Then the baby *say*, "Weee this fun."
Then the dog went back up the stairs.
The baby runned up back again.
Then, them went to the fish bowl.
And they saw the fishes.
And then they went in the fish bowl. Then, then the dog turned the music on. And the dog
was dancing and the baby
Then dog went to the . . . the the the dog and the baby went to the ice box and the dog *open*
the ice box. And a ate some bread and and then the baby . . . (*whispers to LG*) (4;7)

(8) This is the mama; this is the baby; and this is the dog.
The dog was lookin out the window then the baby had woke up.
And then the baby had got on the bed and *climb* on the dog.
The baby went in the bed a bedroom.
And then it *bounce, bounce, bounce.* (5;5)

The verbs produced by the children were analyzed and categorized according to the following: regular/irregular; marked/unmarked. The results for the four-year-olds and the five-year-olds were combined after it was determined that the mean percentages for the two groups were similar. The overall rate of marked verbs was 75 percent (standard deviation 16 percent), and the overall rate of unmarked verbs was 32 percent (standard deviation 13 percent). The irregular verbs were morphologically marked at a higher rate than the regular verbs: 73 percent versus 27 percent. When we consider the unmarked verbs, we find that the regular verbs were unmarked at a higher rate than the irregular verbs: 68 percent versus 32 percent. This is summarized in Figure 15.1.

The results lead to a number of observations:

i. Past tense marking appears to be part of the AAE grammar, or, at least, children are producing it at rates that suggest that it is.
ii. Data from some children suggest that they are in a stage at which past marking is variable.
iii. At least superficially, some of the results are similar to those of adults.
iv. There was no difference between the production rates for the youngest four-year-olds and the oldest five-year-olds.

The data clearly show that developing AAE-speaking children mark past tense on irregular as well as regular verbs although they mark past tense on irregular verbs at higher rates than they mark past on regular verbs. In producing irregular verbs in past, the children use mainstream English irregular forms (e.g., *went*, *saw*), and they also use *-ed* past marking for irregular verbs (e.g., *runned*). The use of forms such as *runned* is likely to be overgeneralization that has been reported for children in other American English-speaking communities. However, because some of these nonstandard forms are also part of the AAE grammar, they might also be produced by their caregivers and other adult speakers in their close networks, so it would be useful to consider data from older and younger children to gather more information about overgeneralization and nonstandard forms that are part of the AAE grammar. Reviewing the data in aggregate, we find consistent variable marking, such that children sometimes mark past and do not at other times. Evidence in support of an argument for development of variable past tense marking at the four- to five-year-old stage can be found in the children's production of irregular verb forms. That is to say that although they are marking past at a high rate, there are still instances of unmarked

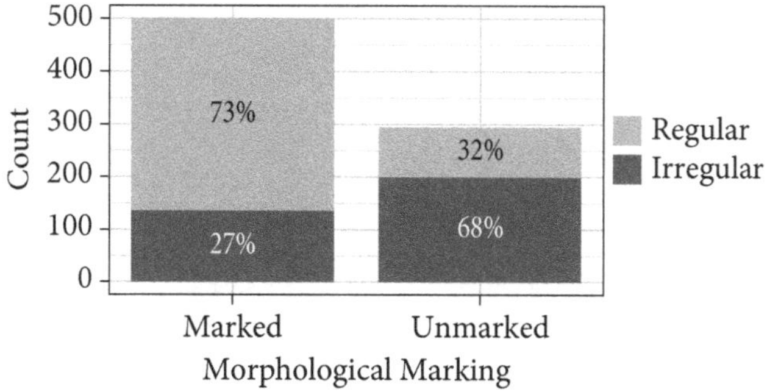

Figure 15.1. Rate of Past Tense Marking for Regular and Irregular Verbs

forms. Here again data from younger children would be useful in determining what early development of past marking looks like, especially from the angle of zero forms. Although we can be confident about children's production of past marking, we still need more production data from children younger than four years. In addition, comprehension data would be useful in determining how children understand past marking in early stages of development.

Conclusion

The results from the studies on third person singular and past tense morphological marking presented in this chapter cannot be directly compared because the studies were not designed with the goal of comparison in mind. It is possible, however, to make some observations that can be pursued in future research. The results from research on children's productions of verb forms in third person singular and past contexts help to shine light on the complexity of variation in AAE in general and in child AAE in particular. Although more extensive studies must be devised to draw solid conclusions about the ways in which the development of variable third person singular marking and variable past tense differs, some properties have already been revealed that strongly suggest that the status of the morphological marking of the two forms in the AAE grammar is different. The dissimilar rates of production of third person singular and past tense seem to point to the different status of the markers in the grammar. Along similar lines, children's treatment of the morphological markers provides some insight into further questions that could shed more light on how children actually comprehend the markers. For instance, we find cases of displaced third singular *-s* markers, but we do not find evidence of floating *-ed*/past markers. It is clear that data from comprehension tasks are needed to formulate more precise questions about how children actually understand third person singular *-s* and past morphology; however, some of the data point in the direction of early progress on past tense marking but not on third singular *-s*. AAE is generally understood as a variety that employs zero inflectional morphology, but not all zeros are equal. At least in early stages, some zeros may stem from development, and at later stages, they may be the result of variable production. Still others may be explained by the absence of a marker from the grammar.

References

Anderssen, Merete, Kristine Bentzen, and Marit Westergaard, eds. 2010. *Variation in the Input: Studies in the Acquisition of Word Order*. Berlin: Springer.

Craig, Holly K., and Julie A. Washington. 2004. "Grade-Related Changes in the Production of African American English." *Journal of Speech, Language, and Hearing Research* 47:450–63.

de Villiers, Jill G., and Valerie E. Johnson. 2007. "The Information in Third Person /s/: Acquisition across Dialects of American English." *Journal of Child Language* 34:133–58.

Green, Lisa J. 2011. *Language and the African American Child.* Cambridge: Cambridge University Press.

Labov, William. 1998. "Co-existent Systems in African-American Vernacular English." In *African-American English: Structure, History and Use*, edited by Salikoko S. Mufwene, John R. Rickford, Guy Bailey, and John Baugh, 110–53. New York: Routledge.

Labov, William, Paul Cohen, Clarence Robins, and John Lewis. 1968. *A Study of Non-Standard English of Negro and Puerto Rican Speakers in New York City*. Philadelphia: US Regional Survey.

Lee, Ryan, and Janna B. Oetting. 2015. "Zero Marking of Past Tense in Child African American English." *SIG 1 Perspectives on Language Learning and Education* 21:173–81.

Newkirk-Turner, Brandi L., and Lisa Green. 2016. "Third Person Singular *-s* and Event Marking in Child African American English." *Linguistic Variation* 16 (1): 103–30.

Pruitt, Sonja, and Janna Oetting. 2009. "Past Tense Marking by African American English–Speaking Children Reared in Poverty." *Journal of Speech, Language, and Hearing Research* 52 (1): 2–15.

Reveron, Wilhelmina Wright. 1979. *The Acquisition of Four Black English Morphological Rules by Black Preschool Children*. PhD diss., Ohio State University.

Seymour, Harry N., Linda Bland-Stewart, and Lisa Green. 1998. "Difference versus Deficit in Child African American English." *Language, Speech, and Hearing Services in Schools* 29 (2): 227–38.

Steffensen, Margaret Siebrecht. 1974. *The Acquisition of Black English*. PhD diss., University of Illinois at Urbana–Champaign.

Terry, J. M., R. Hendrick, E. Evangelou, and R. L. Smith. 2010. "Variable Dialect Switching among African American Children: Inferences about Working Memory." *Lingua* 120:2463–75.

Torrey, Jane W. 1972. *The Language of Black Children in the Early Grades: Studies on Developing Competence in Standard English*. New London: Connecticut College.

van Hofwegan, Janneke, and Walt Wolfram. 2010. "Coming of Age in African American English: A Longitudinal Study." *Journal of Sociolinguistics* 14 (4): 427–55.

Winford, Donald. 1998. "On the Origins of African American English—A Creolist Perspective, Part II: Linguistic Features." *Diachronica* 15 (1): 99–154.

Wolfram, Walt. 1969. *A Linguistic Description of Detroit Negro Speech*. Washington, DC: Center for Applied Linguistics.

Wolfram, Walt, and Ralph Fasold. 1974. *Social Dialects in American English*. Englewood Cliffs, NJ: Prentice-Hall.

Contributors

Alicia Avellana received her PhD in linguistics from Universidad de Buenos Aires in 2012. She is an associate researcher at CONICET and a head lecturer at Universidad de Buenos Aires. Her work focuses on grammars in contact, having worked on the contact between Spanish and Guarani, Toba, and Quechua from a generative perspective. Her dissertation examines the acquisition of Spanish by speakers of Toba, Guarani, and Quechua. Her work has appeared in journals and edited volumes including *Revista Española de Lingüística* and *Verba*. She is also a co-principal investigator on an NSF grant examining the acquisition of Spanish by Paraguayan immigrant children in Buenos Aires.

Marlyse Baptista is a professor of linguistics in the Linguistics Department with an affiliation with the Department of Afroamerican and African studies at the University of Michigan. She specializes in the morpho-syntax of creole languages and in theories of creole genesis. In addition to conducting generative and descriptive analyses on a variety of creoles, she has used in her research experimental methods and agent-based modeling to examine cognitive processes involved in language emergence.

Lucía Brandani received her PhD in linguistics from the Universidad de Buenos Aires in 2013. She is a head lecturer at Universidad de Buenos Aires and Universidad Nacional de General Sarmiento. Her work focuses on the acquisition of morphology and syntax with a special focus on dialects of Spanish. Her dissertation provides a distributed morphology account of the acquisition of gender, number, and person agreement by Rioplatense children. Her work has been published in *Lengua y Migración*, RASAL, and other journals and volumes. She is a co-principal investigator on an NSF grant examining grammar acquisition by Paraguayans living in Buenos Aires.

Norbert Corver is a professor of Dutch linguistics at Utrecht University. His research interests lie in theoretical and comparative syntax, Dutch syntax, with special focus on the nature of functional categories, displacement and locality, NP-ellipsis phenomena, and the interface between language and emotion. He is currently working on the morpho-syntactic encoding of affect by means of functional categories, the inner structure of adverbial expressions, locality phenomena, and ellipsis patterns. Recent publications include *Diagnosing Syntax* (editor, with Lisa Lai-Shen Cheng, 2013, OUP) and *The Syntax of Dutch: Verbs and Verb Phrases*, Vols. 1–3 (with Hans Broekhuis, Riet Vos, 2015–17, AUP).

Elizabeth Cowper is a professor emeritus of linguistics at the University of Toronto. Her current research deals, both synchronically and diachronically, with the grammatical features of nominals (definiteness, person, number, and gender) and clauses (finiteness, tense, mood, and aspect), and what they reveal about the human language faculty. She has published on the features of tense and aspect in Spanish (Language 1995), number in Hopi and Zuni (*Linguistic Inquiry* 1995), and the rise of contrastive modality in English (*Linguistic Variation* 2017). She is the author of *A Concise Introduction to Syntactic Theory: The Government-Binding Approach* (University of Chicago Press).

B. Elan Dresher is a professor emeritus of linguistics at the University of Toronto. He has published on phonological theory, learnability, historical linguistics, contrastive feature hierarchies, West Germanic and Biblical Hebrew phonology and prosody, and the history of phonology. His books include *Old English and the Theory of Phonology* (1985) and *The Contrastive Hierarchy in Phonology* (2009). He is the author of "The Phoneme" in *The Blackwell Companion to Phonology* (2011), "Rule-Based Generative Historical Phonology" in *The Oxford Handbook of Historical Phonology* (2015), and recent articles in *Linguistic Variation*, the *Annual Review of Linguistics*, and *Transactions of the Philological Society*.

Hannah Forsythe is currently working at the University of California–Irvine as a fellow in the National Science Foundation's SBE Postdoctoral Research Fellowship Program. She received her PhD in linguistics from Michigan State University in 2018. Her dissertation examines the interpretation of pronouns by Spanish-speaking children and how different types of information (morphological, syntactic, and discourse factors) are used by children from 3 to 6. Some of her work on acquisition and semantics has appeared in the Proceedings of BUCLD and WCCFL, respectively.

Heidi Getz is a postdoctoral research fellow at the Center for Brain Plasticity and Recovery at Georgetown University. She received her PhD in linguistics and cognitive science from Georgetown in 2018. Her research examines the learning mechanisms involved in morphosyntax acquisition. She has also studied the brain bases of language acquisition and language processing.

Lisa Green is a professor of linguistics at the University of Massachusetts–Amherst. Her research and teaching interests include syntax, syntactic variation, child language acquisition, and development of African American English, and linguistics and education. She is the author of two Cambridge University Press books, *African American English: A Linguistic Introduction*, 2002, and *Language and the African American Child*, 2011, and journal articles and book chapters on the syntax and semantics of African American English (e.g., tense and aspect, negation, left periphery phenomena). Her work also addresses the practical applications of linguistic descriptions of African American English in educational contexts. Green is the founding director of the Center for the Study of African American Language at the University of Massachusetts Amherst. Its goal is to foster and integrate research on language in the

African American community and applications of that research in educational, social, and cultural realms.

Gregory R. Guy is a professor of linguistics at New York University. His research interests focus on the study of social and geographic diversity in language and the use of quantitative analysis in the construction of linguistic theory. He has done original research on variation and change in varieties of English, Spanish, and Portuguese. He has held faculty positions at Sydney, Stanford, Cornell, York (Canada), and Pontifícia Universidade Católica – Rio de Janeiro. His publications include *Towards a Social Science of Language* (Benjamins, 1995, 1996) and *Sociolingüística Quantitativa: Instrumental de Análise* (Parábola, 2007). He gave his first professional presentation at Georgetown in 1973.

Daniel Currie Hall is an associate professor of linguistics at Saint Mary's University in Halifax, Nova Scotia. Before taking up his current position, he completed his PhD at the University of Toronto in 2007 and worked as a postdoctoral researcher at the Meertens Instituut in Amsterdam. His research deals with features and contrasts in both phonology and morphosyntax, and has appeared in journals such as *Linguistic Variation*, *Glossa*, *Nordlyd*, *Lingue e linguaggio*, and *Phonology*.

Jonathan Havenhill is an assistant professor in the Department of Linguistics at the University of Hong Kong. His research focuses on articulatory variation, sound change, and speech perception. He received his PhD in linguistics from Georgetown University in 2018; his dissertation investigates the role of audiovisual perception in constraining patterns of articulatory variation and, as a result, the ways in which language changes over time.

David Lightfoot has published eleven books and written over a hundred articles, book chapters, and reviews, dealing with syntactic theory, language acquisition and change. He is general editor for the Generative Syntax series published by Wiley-Blackwell, and serves on linguistics editorial boards at Cambridge and Oxford University Presses. In 2004, he was elected a fellow of the American Association for the Advancement of Science and, in 2006, as a first-cohort fellow of the Linguistic Society of America. He was also elected president of the LSA, serving 2010–2011. At Georgetown, he is a professor of linguistics, codirector of the Interdisciplinary PhD Concentration in Cognitive Science, and director of the Communication, Culture & Technology masters program.

A graduate of the University of Maryland (2012), **Terje Lohndal** is a professor of English linguistics at the Norwegian University of Science and Technology in Trondheim and Adjunct Professor at UiT The Arctic University of Norway in Tromsø. Together with Marit Westergaard, he is the leader of the AcqVA (Acquisition, Variation & Attrition) research group. His work focuses on formal grammar and language variation, including various aspects of multilingualism. *Formal grammar: Theory and variation across English and Norwegian* recently appeared in the Routledge Leading

Linguists series. In addition, Lohndal often writes in Norwegian media on linguistics and the humanities.

Daniel Milway is a doctoral candidate in the Department of Linguistics at the University of Toronto. His research is in syntactic theory. In particular, he focuses on the logical problem of language acquisition and how it can be fruitfully addressed within the Minimalist Program in a principled manner.

Marjorie Pak is a senior lecturer in the Program in Linguistics at Emory University. Her main research interests are in morphology, syntax, and the syntax-phonology interface; her 2008 UPenn dissertation *The Postsyntactic Derivation and Its Phonological Reflexes* proposes a model for phrasal phonological domains based on data from Luganda, Huave, and other languages. More recently she has been working on the development of allomorphy and allomorphy-like alternations in child English. See her 2016 *Glossa* paper "How allomorphic is English article allomorphy?" for more background information related to her paper in this volume.

Gillian Sankoff (professor emerita of linguistics, University of Pennsylvania) conducted research in Papua New Guinea in the 1960s and 1970s on language contact and the creolization of Tok Pisin. More recently, she has focused on the differentiation of the three southwestern Pacific English-based creoles: Bislama, Solomon Islands Pijin, and Tok Pisin. Her current research relating change across individual life spans to real-time language change is based on data from her 1971 sociolinguistic study of Montreal French (jointly with David Sankoff and Henrietta Cedergren), and continued in the 1980s and 1990s by former students in Québec. Her paper "Language Change Across the Lifespan: Three Trajectory Types" will appear in *Language* 95, 2019.

Natalie Schilling is a professor of linguistics at Georgetown University. She specializes in the study of language variation and change in American English dialects, including regional, ethnic, and gender-based varieties. Her main expertise is stylistic variation—how individuals vary their speech styles to shape personal, interpersonal, and group identities. She does forensic linguistic consulting on cases involving language evidence and provides training sessions for law enforcement and security professionals. She is the author of *Sociolinguistic Fieldwork* (Cambridge University Press, 2013), coauthor of *American English: Dialects and Variation* (Wiley-Blackwell, 2016), and coeditor of *The Handbook of Language Variation and Change* (Wiley-Blackwell, 2013).

Cristina Schmitt received her PhD in linguistics from the University of Maryland at College Park in 1996. She is an associate professor of linguistics at Michigan State University. Her work focuses on the syntax-semantics interface of noun phrases from a comparative point of view. In acquisition, her work has examined properties of noun phrases and the role of sociolinguistic variation in the acquisition of grammar. She has published in *Natural Language and Linguistic Theory*, *Journal of Language*

Acquisition, and *Language Learning and Development*. Her work has been funded by NSF and MSU internal grants.

Betsy Sneller received her PhD in linguistics from the University of Pennsylvania in 2018. She is a postdoctoral research fellow in the Learning and Development Lab at Georgetown University. Her work provides a variationist approach to phonological change, both on a macrosocial and a microsocial perspective. Her dissertation examines how the production of individual speakers drives a community-wide phonological change. She is currently working on an artificial language experiment aimed at investigating how children acquire social and grammatical conditioning on phonological variation.

Marit Westergaard is a professor of English linguistics at UiT The Arctic University of Norway (Tromsø) and an adjunct professor at the Norwegian University of Science and Technology (Trondheim). Together with Terje Lohndal, she is the leader of the AcqVA (Acquisition, Variation and Attrition) research group. Her research interests include language acquisition (L1, 2L1, L2/L3), linguistic variation, heritage languages and language attrition, as well as diachronic language change. She has published widely in these fields, focusing mainly on word order and grammatical gender. She has also proposed the micro-cue model of language acquisition, arguing that young children do not start out by making major generalizations but are sensitive to fine syntactic distinctions from early on.

Index

CPSIA information can be obtained
at www.ICGtesting.com
Printed in the USA
LVHW090027050719
623186LV00007B/34/P